W9-CHC-868

WITHDRAWN

To My Mother and Father

The Nightmare of History

The Fictions of Virginia Woolf and D. H. Lawrence

Helen Wussow

Lehigh
University
Press

Bethlehem: Lehigh University Press
London: Associated University Presses

Associated University Presses
440 Forsgate Drive
Cranbury, NJ 08512

Associated University Presses
16 Barter Street
London WC1A 2AH, England

Associated University Presses
P.O. Box 338, Port Credit
Mississauga, Ontario
Canada L5G 4L8

The paper used in this publication meets the requirements
of the American National Standard for Permanence of Paper
for Printed Library Materials Z39.48-1984.

Library of Congress Cataloging-in-Publication Data

Wussow, Helen.
    The nightmare of history : the fictions of Virginia Woolf and D.H. Lawrence / Helen Wussow.
        p.   cm.
    Includes bibliographical references (p.   ) and index.
    ISBN 0-934223-46-7 (alk. paper)
    1. English fiction—20th century—History and criticism. 2. World War, 1914–1918—Great Britain—Literature and the war. 3. Woolf, Virginia, 1882–1941—Knowledge—History. 4. Lawrence, D. H. (David Herbert), 1885–1930—Knowledge—History. 5. Historical fiction, English—History and criticism. 6. War stories, English—History and criticism. 7. War in literature. I. Title.
PR888.W65W87   1998
823'.91209358—dc21   98-16573
                                                                         CIP

PRINTED IN THE UNITED STATES OF AMERICA

The Nightmare
of History

Contents

Acknowledgments

I WOULD LIKE TO ACKNOWLEDGE THE SOCIETY OF AUTHORS AS THE literary representative of the Estate of Virginia Woolf for granting permission to reprint material from *Orlando: A Biography*. For permission to quote from *The Diary of Virginia Woolf*, volume 1, I wish to thank the Executors of the Virginia Woolf Estate and Hogarth Press as publisher. I would like also to thank Harcourt Brace & Company for granting permission to reprint excerpts from the above mentioned volumes. Acknowledgements are also made to Laurence Pollinger Limited and the Estate of Frieda Lawrence Ravagli for granting permission to use material from *The Letters of D.H. Lawrence*, volume 2.

I would like to thank Dr. Bernard Richards for his suggestions and insights as this book was taking formation. Dr. Stephen Gill helped inspire the original concept. The staff of the Bodleian Library provided immeasurable assistance.

I have been blessed with many friends, without whom my work would be, if not impossible, then distinctly less pleasurable. As I acknowledged in a previous volume, Ann, Jack, and John Maidman, Margaret Morth, and Chris Rude are unstinting in their generosity. Maria Croghan deserves thanks for her hospitality and kindness during a particularly stressful period of composition. Angela Fost, Gary Hancock, Maria and Peter Taylor, and Penny Walker were always patient and encouraging listeners, even when the argument was flat and repetitive. I would particularly like to thank Zoë, who gave up her favorite spot to make way for my impromptu desk.

It is, as always, my mother and father to whom I owe the most. Without their supporting presence I may have never had the courage to make the journeys. It is to them that this essay is dedicated.

List of Abbreviations

Works by D. H. Lawrence

AR	*Aaron's Rod*
A	*Apocalypse and the Writings on Revelation*
CP	*The Complete Poems of D.H. Lawrence*
C	*"The Crown"*
EME	*England, My England and Other Stories*
F	*The Fox, The Captain's Doll, The Ladybird*
K	*Kangaroo*
LCL	*Lady Chatterley's Lover*
LL	*The Letters of D.H. Lawrence*
LAH	*Love among the Haystacks and Other Stories*
MEH	*Movements in European History*
PO	*The Prussian Officer and Other Stories*
R	*The Rainbow*
SL	*Sons and Lovers*
STH	*The Study of Thomas Hardy and Other Essays*
T	*The Trespasser*
TI	*Twilight in Italy*
WP	*The White Peacock*
WL	*Women in Love*

Works by Virginia Woolf

BA	*Between the Acts*
CE	*Collected Essays*
D	*The Diary of Virginia Woolf*
JR	*Jacob's Room*
VWL	*The Letters of Virginia Woolf*
MD	*Mrs. Dalloway*
ND	*Night and Day*
O	*Orlando: A Biography*
RF	*Roger Fry: A Biography*
AROO	*A Room of One's Own*

TG	*Three Guineas*
TL	*To the Lighthouse*
VO	*The Voyage Out*
W	*The Waves*
Y	*The Years*

The Nightmare
of History

Introduction

> I believe one's point of reference should not be to the great
> model of language (*langue*) and signs, but to that of war and
> battle. The history which bears and determines us has the
> form of a war rather than that of a language: relations of
> power, not relations of meaning.[1]
> —Michel Foucault, "Truth and Power"

FOUCAULT'S ASSERTION THAT WAR IS THE BASIC STRUCTURE OF HU-
man existence is exemplified throughout the writings of Virginia Woolf and D. H. Lawrence. Both authors portray the
dynamics of war as informing all human activity, whether linguistic, domestic, recreational, or emotional. For these two authors, the battles of the First World War differ only in scope
from the daily struggles between individuals. It may seem unusual at first to link the names of Woolf and Lawrence. They
are often regarded as diametrically opposed because of their
differing attitudes toward gender and class. Yet their opinions
on organized conflict and violence in general complement and
reveal one another. They both adopted the perspective of the
marginalized other while viewing the events of the Great War.
Woolf observed the war from her position as woman, pacifist,
and reluctant participant in the events of a patriarchal society.
Lawrence, declared medically unfit for service, ill, penniless,
an author whose work was censored and condemned, simultaneously regarded the war as the death throes of a society in
which he was caught as well as the apocalyptic beginnings of
a new, promising world order. Both writers saw the war as
possessing a dialectical structure similar to the Hegelian
struggle for self-definition between the subject, "I," and the
other. They perceived themselves as the other to society's self,
outsiders excluded from the language of the subject. Like Foucault, they considered patterns of war or battle as informing
the actions and language of daily life. This study focuses on
Woolf and Lawrence because their opinions and experiences

15

serve as excellent foils to one another; through the comparison of the "self" of one to the "other" author, their differing attitudes to war, language, and conflict are revealed. This exploration will provide a basis or angle of approach for similar studies of their contemporaries.

Even before the advent of the Great War, Woolf and Lawrence were writing conflict into their fictions. The sexual violence depicted in novels written before the war, such as *The Voyage Out* (1915), *The White Peacock* (1911), and *The Trespasser* (1912), foreshadows the authors' own sense of asphyxiating enclosure, harassment, and persecution during the war itself. In writing war into their novels, Woolf and Lawrence were concerned with the battles fought on the front of language, the problems of communication, and the intimate relationship between linguistic misunderstanding and physical violence. They recognized the essential connection between the self and the enemy, the "I" and the necessary "other" that defines the boundaries of the "I."

In writing this essay, I have taken into account Mikhail Bakhtin's assertion that social situation determines the structure of utterance.[2] The events in a writer's life inform the method of his or her writing. Interminable political upheavals, a distrust of authority, and confusion as to where the future will lead are matters that interest me and are, therefore, to be found in my discussion of Woolf and Lawrence. Their own works reflect the military violence and human cruelty that characterized the years of the Great War. Indeed, I would argue that the writing of fictions and histories does more than merely reflect a situation. In keeping with Bakhtin's theory of the interdependence between social milieu and discourse, I suggest that "discourse does not reflect a situation, it *is* a situation."[3] In the very act of writing fictional representations of violence, Woolf and Lawrence create discourse situations that not only reflect the violence in the world around them but that also provide new sites of conflict and aggression.

Of course, in reconstructing "the social world" in which texts have their being, we must have recourse to other texts, other imperfect, fictional constructs. The Chinese boxes of self-conscious critical theory are infinite. We perceive texts only through other texts; indeed, we regard all writings from within our own ideological compositions, the texts of our selves. Despite the endless regression of textual distortion, I believe it fruitful to attempt to rediscover the social background of

Woolf's and Lawrence's fictions. In so doing we may come to know how they perceived their world and expressed their observations in their work. A close examination of their writings reveals their continual interest in the dynamics of conflict and war, a subject articulated through their use of military imagery and the more general themes of linguistic conflict and the struggle for self-definition.

In researching the historical backdrop to their work I follow a precedent set by the authors themselves. Woolf read Elizabethan writers in order to acquire a sense of their time and place.[4] She perceived the past as part of her present. In her works she frequently depicts the contemporaneity of time. For her, the simultaneity of history could take on physical qualities. Sitting by Hadrian's Wall on 16 June 1938, she reasoned "why the hills are still Roman—the landscape immortal . . . what they saw I see."[5] A few days later, in a letter to Ethel Smyth, she mused, "dear me, were I a writer, how I could describe that: the immensity and tragedy and the sense of the Romans, and time, and eternity."[6] Despite her reservations about historical methods, Woolf neither regarded the past as impenetrable nor considered the reading of history a futile occupation.

Lawrence similarly attempted to enter the spirit of the past. In *Apocalypse* (1931), he advises his reader to dispel the nineteenth-century view of linear time in order to see the world as the ancients saw it:

> To appreciate the pagan manner of thought we have to drop our own manner of on-and-on-and-on, from a start to a finish, and allow the mind to move in cycles, or to flit here and there over a cluster of images.[7]

The synchronicity of time, the capacity to "flit" from cycle to cycle of history's spiral structure, is displayed throughout his work. During the cataclysmic events of the First World War Lawrence advocated a vision of historical continuity. In a letter to Lady Ottoline Morrell of 27 January 1915, he exclaims, "It is an Absolute we are all after, a statement of the whole scheme—the issue, the progress through Time—and the return—making unchangeable eternity."[8] From out of the furnace of the war, Lawrence perceived a new era taking shape; time was not destroyed but rather re-created from war's fire.

Both Woolf and Lawrence turned to the chronicles of history to develop a sense of identity. Woolf was a devoted reader of diaries and letters. She read with interest the private writings of Samuel Pepys, the Reverend James Woolforde, and Fanny Burney. Woolf wrote several biographies, both serious and satirical in nature—consider *Orlando* (1928), *Flush* (1933), and *Roger Fry* (1940). Similarly, Lawrence frequently read historical and anthropological works. He enjoyed Burnet's *Early Greek Philosophers* (1892) and Leo Frobenius's *The Voice of Africa* (1913). Lawrence himself wrote a history text. *Movements in European History* (1921) recaptures the past through vivid portraits of history's most famous actors.

If Woolf and Lawrence were content to regain the past through verbal artifacts, is it not possible for us to read their fictions to rediscover the tensions and crises of their period? In exploring the significance of war and conflict in the writings of Woolf and Lawrence we may gain insight into the works and lives of these two authors as well as an understanding of the essential part played by violence in the modern world.

Writing *In Bluebeard's Castle*, George Steiner argues that the crises of our time—the questioning of values, disbelief in the validity of language, a search for direction—grow not from the cataclysmic events of the two world wars but from a previous era. Steiner suggests that the basis for what he terms "the great 'ennui'" rests in Napoleonic France, the France that produced the oppressive violence of Sade's *Justine* (1791) and Flaubert's *Salammbô* (1862).[9] Steiner perceives the brutality of these two works as personifying the extremity of society's boredom and lassitude, conditions that stretch into the present. The self-mutilation evident in Sade's and Flaubert's novels correlates directly with the impetus to self-destruction revealed in Nazism.[10]

Steiner's tracing of the metamorphosis of the creative impulse to military aggression suggests that all human experience can be transformed into conflict. In Lawrence's *Aaron's Rod* (1922), Rawdon Lilly argues that hate is the "recoil" of love:

The anarchist, the criminal, the murderer, he is only the extreme lover acting on the recoil. But it is love: only in recoil. It flies back, the love-urge, and becomes a horror.[11]

For Lawrence, conflict is as basic to human relations as love. The historian Jean Bethke Elshtain proffers a similar opinion: "War is a structure of experience, a form of conflict; a pervasive presence."[12] War is a means of constructing identity. In attacking the other, the boundaries of the self and nation are defined.

The politics of the world are the politics of war. Such is the opinion Virginia Woolf voices in her writings. Woolf considered the First World War as an event that completely altered the modern world. In "The Leaning Tower" (1940), she marks a change in contemporary literature that begins with the outbreak of war in 1914. She sees the representatives of the postwar "leaning-tower group"—C. Day Lewis, W. H. Auden, Stephen Spender, Christopher Isherwood, and Louis MacNeice— as condemning the world that gave them their education and upbringing. She argues that this attitude could not have occurred without the war: "The nineteenth century ended; but the same conditions went on. They lasted, roughly speaking, till the year 1914. . . . Then suddenly, like a chasm in a smooth road, the war came" (CE 2:167). Woolf compares the First World War to a chasm in a road in order to illustrate the specific changes she perceives between prewar and postwar English literature. She repeats this simile to depict the distressing abyss she sees as running beneath her own life:

> Why is life so tragic; so like a little strip of pavement over an abyss. I look down; I feel giddy; I wonder how I am ever to walk to the end. . . . its life itself, I think sometimes for us in our generation so tragic—no newspaper placard without its shriek of agony. . . . Unhappiness is everywhere; just beyond the door; or stupidity which is worse. . . . And with it all how happy I am—if it weren't for my feeling that its a strip of pavement over an abyss. (D 2:72–73)

This abyss or emptiness is present in many of her writings. In *Orlando*, a work that many regard as her most light-hearted achievement, hollowness rests at the novel's center. Orlando feels "something strange in the shadow that the flicker of her eyes cast . . . without substance or quality of its own, yet has the power to change whatever it adds itself to."[13] The vacuum at the center of life is further illustrated in *The Waves* (1931). Percival participates in a great military game. He dies not from a battle wound, but from a fall from his horse during a polo game while stationed with the British army in India. The voice of Neville comments, "'Now I say there is a grinning, there is a subterfuge. There is something sneering behind our backs.'"[14] The characters of *The Waves* struggle against the "blank and brutal face" of death (*W*, 166), as indeed do all of her characters.

Woolf often offers an apparently optimistic alternative to the violence of war, one that can only work in tension with the forces of annihilation. She proposes a vision of unity, a unity consisting of various forms, such as the continuity of past and present, the breaking down of chronological and spatial distinctions. This sense of wholeness is described by Woolf as a silver globe, a precious world held in shape by conflicting pressures. For example, in the last chapter of *Night and Day* (1919) Katharine Hilbery achieves a sense of oneness through her relationship with Ralph Denham: "It seemed to her that the immense riddle was answered; the problem had been solved; she held in her hands for one brief moment the globe which we spend our lives in trying to shape, round, whole, and entire from the confusion of chaos."[15] In *Night and Day*, harmony is achieved through love. Yet Woolf suggests that love is not an unfailing cure for the world's ailments. Throughout her novels, love is a two-edged blade. It brings people together, but it also destroys the integrity of the individual and may result in a relationship based upon domination of the one at the expense of the other. The dual nature of love is the subject of *Night and Day*. The reader is asked to laugh at Mrs. Hilbery's extravagant claims for the power of love. In mocking Mrs. Hilbery, Woolf satirizes her own vision of unity. Woolf's reliance upon concord in life was so great that she constructed a concept of historical integrity in which the past always influences and gives continuity to the changing present. This insistence upon the concurrence of past and present appears to serve as an antidote to the cruelty and horror of existence. However, this remedy is not absolute. In arguing that the past invades the present, Woolf makes all war and bloodshed simultaneous and thereby underscores the tragedies of history.

Lawrence, too, was sensitive to the pervasiveness of conflict in his world. In a letter to Edward Marsh of 25 August 1914, he complained,

> I can't get away from [the war] for a minute: live in a sort of coma, like one of those nightmares when you can't move. I hate it— everything. (*LL* 2:211)

Throughout his work Lawrence portrays the ubiquitous battle between individuals, an animosity manifested through physical violence and linguistic conflict. In the prewar *The White Peacock* and *The Trespasser*, violence is rife. He represents the inescapable cruelty of human relationships through images of strangulation and the nexus between hunter and prey. In *The Trespasser*, Siegmund and Helena's mutual desire is exemplified by their fascination with one another's throats. For Lawrence, the throat is the focal point of human attractiveness and frailty. In order to define their relationship and themselves, Helena and Siegmund go for one another's throat quite literally.

Lawrence connects individual human cruelty and the international conflict of war. In a letter of 27 July 1917 to the American novelist Waldo Frank, he explains the correlation between the characters in *The Rainbow* (1915) and the catastrophe of the First World War. Although it "was all written before the war," Lawrence "knew [he] was writing a destructive work. . . . What [he] did through individuals, the world has done through the war" (*LL* 3:142–43). In *The Rainbow*, he foreshadows the war's destructive force through his characters' relationships. The cloying dependence of Will Brangwen upon his wife, Anna, contains within it the desire to control and consume. Will's love for Anna is self-centered; in embracing Anna, Will seeks to embrace himself. His craving for murder, for blood, is metamorphosed into a hawk's frenzy for prey. Anna seems a willing target. Yet the roles of pursuer and victim are reversed:

> She too was a hawk. . . . she harassed him from his unperturbed pride, till he was mad with rage . . . and recognised her as the enemy.[16]

The mutually destructive relationship between the parents has its parallel in the later generation of Ursula Brangwen and Anton Skrebensky. In their meetings, Anton and Ursula act out, on a small scale, the international differences that result in war. Son of a Polish refugee and a soldier who has served in the Boer War, Skrebensky is an attractive enemy for Ursula, a threatening other whom she must conquer and make her own. Like her mother, Ursula is stronger than the male who seeks to overcome her. The struggle for domination ends in a mechanical grapple to the death. Like George and Lettie in

The White Peacock, the dynamics of the contest between Anton and Ursula are those of hunter and prey:

> he must weave himself round her, enclose her, enclose her in a net of shadow, of darkness, so she would be like a bright creature gleaming in a net of shadows, caught. Then he would have her, he would enjoy her. (*R* 297)

As in Lawrence's early novels, the exchange between hunter and prey is reversed. Skrebensky's mechanical force is turned against him, and Ursula develops a cold "corrosive" power of her own (*R* 299).

Similarly, the reversed relationship between slave and master is depicted by Lawrence in "The Prussian Officer" (1914). Like Anna and Ursula, Schöner is the captive who suddenly turns murderer. Unlike the two women, however, he has waited too long to assert himself over his captain. Through conflict with the other, Schöner loses his sense of identity. His speech, too, is conquered. He dies silent, strangled by his thirst for elusive freedom.

Lawrence perceives Schöner's final paroxysm of desire as synonymous to that of Europe. On 5 September 1915, he writes to Lady Cynthia Asquith, "I am writing a book of sketches, or preparing a book of sketches, about the nations, Italian German and English, full of philosophising and struggling to show things real" (*LL* 2:386). He worked on revising these sketches from July 1915 to February 1916, bringing them together to form *Twilight in Italy* (1916). As the title suggests, the book communicates Lawrence's pessimistic view of Italy's future. He perceives Italy's old, free culture as disintegrating into northern self-repression. He describes a renaissance of the Italian spirit in the sensual revelry of "The Dance," in the Panic beauty of "Il Doro." Yet he is careful to convey the essential hollowness of these vigorous, non-mechanistic Italians. For instance, the crippled woodcutter in "The Dance" is "like some violent natural phenomenon rather than a person." He is "not a human being." His dance is "perfect, too perfect."[17]

In "The Return Journey," Lawrence portrays "the sun-dried, ancient, southern slopes of the world," the home of the god Pan as seen from the cold blandness of Switzerland (*TI* 222). However, he finds a "sordidness," "a quality that has entered Italian life now, if it was not there before" (*TI* 223). The disintegration of Italy is the result of the slow encroachment of the mechanical north upon the south, the advance of cold industrialism that finds its consummation in the war. The flow of the mountain chill into the life of the Mediterranean south represents Italy's rejection of its pagan past in favor of the mechanisms of modern society. The mechanical voluptuousness that Lawrence perceives as instigating Italy's twilight is also the source of the First World War.

Whereas Woolf focused on male aggressiveness, by 1915 Lawrence blamed women for the continuation of the war.[18] He forges a connection between industrialism and the insincere, flirtatious, modern woman. The best known example of such a woman in Lawrence's work is Pussum in *Women in Love* (1920). Her "beautiful eyes, dark, fully-opened" are covered with "a film of disintegration, a sort of misery and sullenness, like oil on water."[19] Frail and childlike, Pussum is nevertheless capable of wielding a weapon and inflicting injury.

Pussum is not the only dangerous female in Lawrence's wartime writings. In the poem "Frost Flowers" (1917), the war's destruction is personified by a certain kind of feminine beauty.[20] In *England, My England* (1922), the independent female tram conductors of "Tickets, Please" are portrayed as bloodthirsty and vindictive. The competent Miss Stokes in "Monkey Nuts" is sexually voracious. The female figures in his wartime fictions personify a desire for "completeness in horror and death."[21] They possess a "craving" for power and destruction (*L* 2:342). "Clytemnestras" eager to murder their soldier-husbands, they work to destroy society (*LL* 3:79).

Throughout Lawrence's fictions, female aggressiveness is frequently associated with linguistic conflict. He theorized that the ongoing differences between Frieda and Lady Ottoline Morrell were due to clashes of language. In a letter of 27 January 1916, he advised Ottoline, "Let the trouble between you and F[rieda] be forgotten now. Your natures are different and opposite. . . . You will always speak different languages" (*LL* 2:517). He is consistently interested in the difficulties inherent in speech. The stories that comprise *England, My England* portray the problem of wartime communication. Arguments, lies, and verbal abuse add to the pugnacious atmosphere of the stories. Postwar poverty of language is particularly evident in "The Captain's Doll" (1923). Like Marta Hohenest in "The Mortal Coil" (1916), Johanna zu Rassentlow seeks self-identity from her signature. However, neither the written word nor the act of speech carries any significance in Lawrence's story. Johanna's conversation with Alexander circles around the subject of nothingness and "meaning-lessness."[22] The hollowness of Johanna's and Alexander's relationship is reflected in their empty conversation. In an odd authorial comment Lawrence notes that between them "there was a long and pregnant silence: we should not like to say pregnant with what" (*F*, 94). Inexpressible in its very absence, meaning in Johanna's and Alexander's discourse is non-existent. Silent as puppets, they can speak only through gestures. Their actions convey denial and displacement of their unexpressed emotions.

The spiritual weakness of Alexander Hepburn is a quality that Lawrence allocates to all his soldier figures. Whatever his own attitude to the war, he consistently questions the nature of those who serve authority. The captain's "irritable tension" and Schöner's confusion exemplify the essential inadequacy Lawrence finds in the soldier.[23] In "England, My England," Egbert seeks "the great forgetting of death."[24] Although Maurice Pervin, in "The Blind Man," has come to an "incomprehensible peace" through the war, he nevertheless has had to lose his vision in order to gain spiritual insight (*EME*, 46). The Hepburns, in "The Thimble," learn to communicate only after the husband has had his jaw smashed by a bomb.

Like Woolf, Lawrence suggests that war is a dangerous game in which nothing is gained except knowledge of death and the extremities of human brutality:

> we go to war to show that we can throw our lives away. Indeed, they have become of so little value to us. We cannot live, we cannot *be*. Then let us tip-cat with death, let us rush throwing our lives away. Then at any rate we shall have a sensation—and "perhaps" after all, the value of life is in death.[25]

He equates war with a violent children's game in which missiles are hurled into the face of the opponent. In comparing war to a pointlessly dangerous sport, he illustrates "how little we value ourselves at bottom" (*STH*, 16).

Throughout the war Lawrence fluctuates between despair and exuberant hope. In a letter of 28 November 1915 to Lady Cynthia Asquith, he expresses both emotions. The war is at once the Passion and the Resurrection:

> I want to begin all all again. All these Gethsemane Calvary and Sepulchre stages must be over now: there must be a resurrection. (*LL* 2:454)

In the midst of a gloom that lasted throughout November and well into December 1915, he was able to write to Ottoline Morrell, "Oh, life is not ended yet: these are the splendid days ahead: we will forget these past days of destruction and misery" (*LL* 2:449–50).

Lawrence perceived a new beginning in the midst of destruction. He believed that from the war would come "the dawn of a new historical epoch" (*LL* 2:426). The theme of an apocalyptic resurrection finds expression throughout much of his postwar work, such as *St. Mawr* (1925), *The Plumed Serpent* (1926), and *The Man Who Died* (1928). Although Lawrence first regarded the Great War as the inevitable outcome of a decomposing society, he came to see it as an apocalyptic event heralding a new cycle of history. He observed the seeds of hope among the ashes of destruction. His confidence in a personal and social resurrection is expressed throughout letters, fiction, and poetry of the war years. Yet the reader often wonders if the destruction that leads to "The Great Day" may not in turn destroy this promised utopia.

Samuel Hynes has called the First World War the "great *imaginative* event" of the twentieth century.[26] For Woolf and Lawrence, the war and conflict in general provide the structures around which the worlds of their fictions are organized. Both writers regard strife in sexual relationships as similar to armed conflict. For them the war is also a gender war in which women battle against misused patriarchal power. Claire Tylee argues that the Great War is often portrayed as a battle between human beings, male versus female, in the literature of the period.[27] For Woolf and Lawrence, war is a constant; it is a part of the conflict between men and women acted out upon the sites of sexual relations and verbal communications.

It is impossible to ascertain which came first, whether it was a word or physical violence directed against the original other. I would argue, however, that the war of words created by these two writers presages and sustains the memory of the most significant international conflict of their lives. In writing war into their fictions, they helped immortalize the battles of the world. Elaine Scarry has argued that the reality of war and its fictionalized presentations are not as separate as we might think. There is, Scarry suggests, a distinct connection between making up and making real.[28] The balanced tip between imagination and reality in Woolf and Lawrence's works is a fine one;

all too often, imagined acts of violence and conflict turn into action, just as their prewar fictions antedate but also antici- pate the war to come.

Both authors sought to escape life's inevitable battles by con- structing a concept of cyclical history. The First World War becomes an Armageddon, "a chasm in a smooth road" after which a new era will occur (*CE*, 2:167). However, within their vision of a holistic history in which past and present become one resides the tension between war as both creative and de- structive impulse. Ultimately, the problem of whether time is concurrent and simultaneous or divisive and linear is never solved within their fictions.

The cyclical form of history set forth by Woolf and Lawrence is their attempt to escape what James Joyce describes as "the nightmare of history."[29] Their blueprints for a possible utopia afford the authors a release from the ongoing battles of exis- tence. For Woolf, "a room of one's own" is a workplace where sexual distinctions are abolished. More extensive than the sin- gle "room of one's own" were Woolf's plans for a "Society of Outsiders" that would pledge "to maintain an attitude of com- plete indifference" in the face of war.[30] Comprised of "educated men's daughters," the society "would refuse in the event of war to make munitions or nurse the wounded" (*TG*, 193–94). Woolf does not advocate a pacifist stance for her society; instead, she requests that all efforts at persuasion against the carrying of arms be abandoned. She argues that "fighting . . . is a sex char- acteristic in which [woman] cannot share" (*TG*, 194). The best attitude, Woolf asserts, is one of abstinence. Women must ab- sent themselves from nationalistic politics. She argues that women are compelled to be "outside" the boundaries of the nation which claims to speak for them. Consequently, their country must be the world, a society of sisterhood. In *To the Lighthouse*, Cam dreams of a world free of conflict and despot- ism. Forced to endure the fights between her father and her brother and to serve as peacekeeper, she looks wistfully back at the shore and imagines a land beyond hostility and domination:

> she said nothing, but looked doggedly and sadly at the shore, wrapped in its mantle of peace; as if the people had fallen asleep, she thought; were free like smoke, were free to come and go like ghosts. They have no suffering there, she thought.[31]

Although peaceful, Cam's oasis is a land of "ghosts," a continent of the dead. Ironically, she looks back to the shore that has provided the setting for so many of Mr. Ramsay's tirades. Caught in the boat with two struggling men, like a hapless mackerel on a hook, she cannot escape the battle indulged in by Mr. Ramsay and James. Unhappily, her hopes for the future are never to be realized. Already she has taken up the role of peacemaker held previously by her mother. Cam's utopia exists far across an untraversable sea.

Lawrence also hoped for a place beyond the realm of an embattled history. He formed his concept of "Rananim" within the first year of the Great War. Rananim is first mentioned by Lawrence in a letter to S. S. Koteliansky of 3 January 1915: "What about Rananim? Oh, but, we are going. We are going to found an Order of the Knights of Rananim" (*LL* 2:252). The word *Rananim* apparently comes from a Hebrew musical version of the first verse of Psalm 33.[32] The concept provided Lawrence an imaginary release from the difficulties he experienced during the war. Rananim is a country without "war and squalor" (*LL* 2:259). The setting for Rananim changed throughout the war. At first, Lawrence envisages it on an island. It would be a self-contained society, both physically and spiritually; it is Lawrence's response to the war's fragmentation of life. However, as with all things during the war, his attitude toward his dream changes. On 25 February 1916, he writes to Lady Ottoline Morrell and describes Cornwall as his Promised Land, the site of his new society:

> When we came over the shoulder of the wild hill, above the sea, to Zennor, I felt we were coming into the Promised Land. I know there will a new heaven and a new earth take place now: we have triumphed. I feel like a Columbus who can see a shadowy America before him: only this isn't merely territory, it is a new continent of the soul. (*LL* 2:556)

Lawrence's jubilation over his new land of the self is not constant. Only a few weeks before the letter quoted above, his enthusiasm is nonexistent. In a letter to John Middleton Murry of 9 January 1916, he sourly discards all hope to establish Rananim in England or America: "There is no Florida, there's only this, this England, which nauseates my soul, nauseates my spirit and my body—this England" (*LL* 2:500). His lack of belief in the possibilities of Rananim are combined with his conviction that he is a hunted man, condemned and betrayed by those around him. As the war years progress, Lawrence moves the site for Rananim to more improbable places, as if he were anxious to position himself beyond the physical reach of others. In the early months of 1915, Rananim is situated in Cornwall, but by May 1917 Russia becomes "the only country where I can plant my hopes" (*LL* 3:124). In October 1917, Rananim moves to an entirely different hemisphere. Lawrence's plans become more outlandish. As the unfeasibility of his plans becomes more apparent, the more incredible his suggestions become. He dreams of the possibilities of South America. He urges Catherine Carswell to accompany him on his journey despite the difficulties afforded by her pregnancy (*LL* 3:173). By 21 February 1918, he is willing to go to Palestine, an interesting proposal given his lifelong suspicions of Judaism (*LL* 3:214).

Although Woolf's construct of the Society of Outsiders and Lawrence's Rananim appear utopian, neither are strictly a blessed unification of diverse peoples. Within the very concepts of these two societies rests the essence of battle and conflict. Woolf's Society of Outsiders will combat fascism through difference. In drawing up a list of those who would join him in Florida, Lawrence was eager to bring together Frieda, John Middleton Murry, Katherine Mansfield, and Lady Ottoline Morrell, a group of people who, as time later proved, would hardly have lived peacefully together. Just as Woolf's and Lawrence's fictions revolve around the matrices of war and conflict, so their visionary societies center around the idea of uncompromising difference. Both societies are attempts to fight against the mores of the larger society. The Society of Outsiders and Rananim were devised as strategies to engage, albeit from a distance, in life's battles.

These visions of Woolf and Lawrence are concurrent with their picture of themselves as political and spiritual outsiders. In a letter of 15 February 1916 to Lady Ottoline Morrell, only ten days before his letter in which he describes his "Promised Land," Lawrence characterizes himself as "anti-social . . . a pirate or a highwayman" (*LL* 2:540). Determined to reside beyond the reaches of authority, Lawrence sees himself as "out" of the "law" (*LL* 2:540). Woolf also saw herself as an outlaw. On 20 May 1938, while awaiting the publication of *Three Guineas*, Woolf proudly proclaims in her diary, "I am an outsider" (*D* 5:141). Her position as outcast recalls Bernard in *The Waves*.

As a writer and observer, he stands aloof from the other characters in the novel. He perceives the flimsiness of all human
constructs, particularly those that delimit history and time.
Throughout her diary, Woolf records the success of her efforts
to command "Time" to "stand still here" (D 2:212). The very
act of writing is Woolf's weapon against the fleetingness of
time: "I feel time racing like a film at the Cinema. I try to stop
it. I prod it with my pen. I try to pin it down" (D, 2: 158).
Writing against time, she becomes a true outsider, one who
exists beyond temporal distinctions. Through her writing, she
battles the destructiveness of time. She lectures governments
on the temporality of their tyranny. Richard Aldington, in
D. H. Lawrence: An Indiscretion, makes a similar point about
Lawrence. Aldington sees Lawrence as "a true Anarchist, living
outside human society, rejecting all its values," working to establish his code of being through the printed word.[33] For both
Woolf and Lawrence, the word affords an immense power for
change.

The actions conceived by Woolf and Lawrence within their
fictions subvert the established order of political authority and
traditional, linear time. Woolf, in The Years (1937), destroys the
concept of narrative placement and character identification.
Like the brown-clad "Macintosh" of Joyce's Ulysses (1922),[34]
the "poor-looking shabby woman prowling on the outskirts" is
never allowed into the construct of the novel. She is neither
named nor identified; she is the perfect outsider looking in.
She judges and evaluates the human rituals in which she does
not or cannot take part.

Virginia Woolf once mourned, "Lord—how tired I am of being caged with Aldous, Joyce & Lawrence!" (L 4:402). Yet in
comparing the lives and fictions of the two writers we may
come to understand better how prevalent was the urge to and
fear of conflict before, during, and after World War I. They
read and emphatically disliked the jingoism of the prowar
press. They were discomfited by the herd-consciousness of
British citizens who thoughtlessly accepted the bombast of
Horatio Bottomley and Lord Northcliffe. Both writers recorded their responses to the war while the conflict was in
progress. In his letters, Lawrence examines the war's effect
upon civilization and history along with his own sense of persecution at the hands of authority. Woolf, in her diary and
letters, shows her interest in the state of a world at war and
her concern over the plight of friends and relatives. In their

fictions, they consistently explore the dynamics of war and its gendered dimensions. For both writers the war was the pivotal event in modern history.

Makiko Minow-Pinkney has argued that Woolf's eventual search to achieve permanence amid conflict through language fails:

> Woolf's fiction is driven forwards by this desire for a meaning that would at last halt the frustrating play of signs. The quest takes as its starting-point the signs which fill the world, but the endeavour to read them correctly and grasp truth only fabricates more signifiers.[35]

I disagree with Minow-Pinkney; I would argue that through the very act of writing both Woolf and Lawrence assert that linguistic meaning, the stability of verbal signifiers, can be attained. Granted, Woolf and Lawrence were uncertain about the nature of language. Their indecision over whether utterance is a benign or aggressive act points to the dual role language assumes in their fictions. For both authors, linguistic acts can be efforts toward unification as well as deadly offensives. Although they questioned the nature of language, they continued to write. Their fictions reveal a belief in meaning, a surety that language does, for better or worse, communicate the ideas of those who use it, and that it immortalizes the conflicts of their, and our, times.

1

Our Sad Eventful History: Woolf, Lawrence, and the Great War

In times of storm and darkness it is the part of artists and philosophers to tend the lamp. This duty they perform unconsciously by simply minding their own business.[1]
—Clive Bell, "Art and War," October 1914

CLIVE BELL COULD HARDLY BE ACCUSED OF FOLLOWING HIS OWN counsel. Instead of striving for artistic aloofness in the face of war, he wrote and published a vehement antiwar pamphlet entitled *Peace at Once* (1915), which was subsequently burned by order of the Lord Mayor of London in the autumn of 1915 after its appearance in the spring of that year. In a letter dated 30 September 1915, Virginia Woolf reported the uproar the work caused at Seend, Bell's family home in Wiltshire: "I hear from Vanessa that old father Bell threatens complete rupture with Clive if he writes more in the style of the pamphlet" (*VWL* 2:65).

Bell's advice to artists in wartime parallels what is frequently assumed to be Bloomsbury's indifference to the war.[2] For example, in *Pacifism in Britain, 1914–1945*, the historian Martin Ceadel argues that most of the famous conscientious objectors associated with Bloomsbury—such as James Strachey, David Garnett, and Duncan Grant—were not what he terms "true pacifists"; they did not subscribe to the belief that "war is *always wrong* and should never be resorted to, whatever the consequences of abstaining from fighting."[3] Rather, Ceadel groups them under the heading of "elitist quasi-pacifists" and he suggests that their "entitlement to be recognized as C.O.s depended on their higher personal obligation, as creative artists, to Beauty and Truth."[4] Samuel Hynes expands Ceadel's thesis and states that Bloomsbury was against the

31

war for *pleasure*'s sake.[5] What Ceadel and Hynes do not realize is that the refusal of these men to participate in the war effort was not based upon an aesthete's sense of superiority but was a rejection of the bearing of arms on behalf of a cause in which they did not believe. David Garnett records that Duncan Grant was unable to justify violence of any kind:

> Duncan took the line that he belonged to a tiny minority and that his views differed *in toto* from the majority on almost every subject. His opinions would never be attended to, and he would never fight for those of the majority, particularly as he believed it was always morally wrong to employ violence.[6]

Bloomsbury's pacifism was based upon a refusal to exchange blow for blow, or to fight against the mass opinion that excluded their own perspectives. Such a position kept figures such as Roger Fry from engaging in public insults and accusations, a stance made evident even before the war. In October 1913, Wyndham Lewis, along with other artists associated with the Omega Workshops, accused Fry of stealing a commission for a Postimpressionist room at the Ideal Home Exhibition held in London during that month. Fry made no effort to respond to Lewis's allegations, and they later proved unfounded. Another example of this extreme rejection of conflict occurred prior to the Omega incident and involved Duncan Grant. Grant took part in the famous *"Dreadnought* hoax" organized by Horace Cole, friend of Adrian Stephen. Grant and Virginia Stephen masqueraded as Abyssinian princes. In the guise of the Abyssinian emperor and his retinue, the group boarded and inspected the pride of the British fleet, the *Dreadnought.* Some days after the event, when naval authorities realized what had happened, several officers burst into the London home of Grant's parents, bundled him into a cab, and drove him to a field in Hendon. They were dismayed when he refused to put up a fight. The disgruntled officers ended up giving Grant two perfunctory taps to satisfy their honor and offered him a lift home, which he refused.[7]

Despite these early examples of Bloomsbury's antipathy toward violence, Michael Holroyd has argued that at the beginning of the Great War, Bloomsbury was less resolutely pacifist than is popularly supposed:

> That September [1914] Clive Bell . . . wrote to James Strachey asking for information as to how to join the Army Service Corps

or some other non-fighting unit, since his health prevented him from going into the fully combative forces. Duncan Grant immediately entered the National Reserve.[8]

Lytton Strachey thought that intellectuals should fight to protect their country—that is, if any physically fit intellectuals could be found. Nevertheless, Strachey's attitude wavered during the first years of the war; by the early months of 1916 he was an enthusiastic campaigner and pamphleteer against conscription. Other individuals who are frequently regarded as members of the Bloomsbury fringe group, namely Bertrand Russell and Philip Morrell, were opposed to the war from its very beginning. If all of Bloomsbury was not entirely pacifist during the early stages of the war, it became so by the time the Military Service Act was passed in January 1916. From this point onward, Bloomsbury was actively pacifist and worked to establish a negotiated peace settlement.

Bertrand Russell was the most vociferous pacifist associated with Bloomsbury. On 15 August 1914, the Union of Democratic Control (UDC) was formed. It was one of the first groups to agitate for a negotiated peace and can be seen as a precursor to the League of Nations, since its aims were international in scope. Russell quickly became involved in the union's activities, as did Leonard Woolf, who in the early months of 1915 was working hard on what was to become the influential *International Government: Two Reports* (1916). Another UDC member of note was Ramsay MacDonald, well-known pacifist and cofounder, with Leonard Woolf, of the politically oriented 1917 Club.[9]

The UDC's active canvassing for a negotiated peace was complemented by articles published by Bertrand Russell in the *Atlantic Monthly*, some of which were subsequently reprinted in *Justice in War Time* (1916). Propacifist in nature, these articles argue that war stems from excessive national pride. Russell works hard to dispel the notion that pacifism is equivalent to cowardice: "To oppose force by passive non-obedience would require more courage, and would be far more likely to preserve the best elements of the national life."[10] This argument appealed to Bloomsbury figures such as Duncan Grant, who stood up against majority opinion and asserted his absolute pacifism. On the other hand, Russell did not wholeheartedly applaud the activities of his pacifist friends, considering it more practical to work toward a postwar international peace alliance. He regarded pacifist meetings as futile. He was once persuaded, however, to speak at a meeting on the "pacifist philosophy of life," held on 8–9 July 1915. Other speakers at the conference included Goldsworthy Lowes Dickinson, J. A. Hobson, and Vernon Lee—all acquaintances of the Woolfs.[11]

Perhaps the most interesting moments during Russell's long and vigorous stop-the-war campaign were his conversations with D. H. Lawrence during the summer of 1915. Russell and Lawrence hoped to give a joint series of lectures in the autumn of 1915. However, the famous falling-out between the two men occurred before the lectures took place. Lawrence felt that Russell's essays were too traditionally democratic and lacked the impetus for "an immediate destructive and reconstructive revolution in actual life" (*LL* 2:381).

Despite Lawrence's abandonment of the project, Russell continued to work on his lectures and eventually delivered them on Tuesday evenings from 18 January to 17 March 1916 in Caxton Hall, London. He later gathered the papers together and published them as *Principles of Social Reconstruction* (1916). Although the lectures were extremely popular, Lawrence claimed that a friend regarded them as "unimportant, nothing vital" (*L* 2:528). Virginia Woolf voiced her doubt as to the real value of Russell's lectures in a letter to her friend Margaret Llewelyn Davies, who was also interested in the social problems created by the war (*L* 2:133). Woolf may have questioned the significance of Russell's speeches, but in fact she was interested in the topics that Russell emphasized. In keeping with the tenets of Moore's *Principia Ethica* (1903), he argues that people must substitute a conformity inspired by fear with active, intelligent consideration of the problems at hand. Woolf, too, disliked the herd consciousness of wartime England. "Perhaps the horrible sense of community which the war produces, as if we all sat in a third class railway carriage together, draws one's attention to the animal human being more closely" (*D* 1:153).

Lawrence also deplored the mob mentality evident during the war. In a cautionary letter to Russell of 2 June 1915, Lawrence warns,

> *Never* expose yourself to the pack. Be careful of them. Be rather their secret enemy . . . working to split up and dismember the pack from the inside, not from outside. (*LL* 2:352)

Earlier, in a letter of 1 February 1915, Lawrence outlines to Lady Ottoline Morrell his role as saboteur: "We will deal cunningly with the mob, the greedy soul, we will gradually bring it to subjection" (*LL* 2 : 273). Lawrence, however, did not always attack the pack "hydra" with silent cunning (*LL* 2 : 352). In "The Reality of Peace," he vociferously condemns "the obscene herd."[12] In an attempt to bring about the social revolution he so desired, he sets the verbal "bombs" of his novels (*LL* 2 : 547) into society at large.

Russell's efforts for a negotiated peace on behalf of the UDC were augmented by the work of the No Conscription Fellowship (NCF). Founded in November 1914 the NCF was comprised of young men pledged to resist compulsory military service. The fellowship's purpose was to oppose the Military Service Act, campaign for pacifism, encourage conscientious objectors, and work for their total exemption from participation in the war. Several affiliates of Bloomsbury belonged to the NCF; Adrian Stephen, Duncan Grant, David Garnett, and James Strachey were members. In May 1915, Vanessa Bell signed up when the fellowship created associate memberships for those who, though not liable for conscription, shared the NCF's belief in the sanctity of human life. Lytton Strachey joined the NCF immediately after the introduction of the Military Service Bill in January 1916. Strachey even went to the effort to write anticonscription leaflets for the fellowship. Pamphlet 3 argues that the government had actually engaged in the war in order to crush labor demands. Half a million copies were distributed before the leaflet was withdrawn as seditious.

Despite his strident propagandizing, Strachey disagreed with Russell's vehement antigovernment articles published in the *Nation* during the early months of the war. Strachey argued for a Stop the War Party to be instituted in the cabinet, although given popular opinion during this period of the war, it is highly doubtful whether this scheme was in any way practical. Eventually, Strachey, joined later by Russell, decided to "wait and work for a constructive post-war peace."[13] A negotiated and constructive peace was exactly what Leonard Woolf had been struggling to attain throughout the war.

Although the Military Service Act provided much of Bloomsbury—such as the unmarried Duncan Grant, David Garnett, James and Lytton Strachey—with something to worry about and struggle against, with the General Conscription Act of 24

June 1916 even the married males of Bloomsbury were liable
for conscription. Leonard Woolf received his first medical exemption in June 1916, due to a permanent nervous tremor. In
the general comb-out of 1917 Woolf was again called in for
examination and Virginia Woolf's diary entry for 9 October
1917 registers their mutual concern:

> We had a horrible shock. L. came in so unreasonably cheerful
> that I guessed a disaster. He has been called up. . . . It was piteous
> to see him shivering, physically shivering, so that we lit the gas
> fire, & only by degrees became more or less where we were in
> spirits; & still, if one could wake to find it untrue, it would be a
> mercy. (*D* 1:56)

Like Lawrence, who had his own examinations during this
period, Leonard Woolf was none too pleased with the treatment he received at the hands of the army doctors, as Virginia
Woolf describes:

> I waited in a great square, surrounded by barrack buildings, & was
> reminded of a Cambridge college. . . . A disagreeable impression of
> control & senseless determination. A great boarhound, emblem of
> military dignity I suppose, strolled across by himself. L. was a
> good deal insulted: the drs. referred to him as "the chap with senile
> tremor", through a curtain. (*D* 1:59)

The reprieve was only temporary; Leonard was again exam-
ined in November of that same year. This time, however, his
exemption paper read "'permanently & totally disabled'" and
Virginia Woolf speculated that "this might fetch £500 if sold"
(*D* 1:72).

In addition to worrying about Leonard's medical exemption,
Virginia Woolf actively worked to secure an exemption from
combat service for David Garnett and Duncan Grant. She may
have feared that, as conscientious objectors, they would suffer
ill treatment at the hands of the army. In order to deal with
the problem of total disobedience by COs who refused to perform the noncombatant duties assigned them, the army sent
thirty-four men to France to be shot in the early summer of
1916. The sentences were repealed at the last moment, but
word of these events found their way to Virginia Woolf at Ashe-
ham. In a letter to Vanessa Bell of 12 April 1916 she remarked,
"London seems miles away, except for these damned news-
papers—[Charles] Sanger [a barrister friend of Woolf] has

awful stories about conscientious objectors shipped to France and there shot" (*VWL* 2:90–91). In order to spare Garnett and Grant a similar fate, Woolf wrote several letters during June 1916 to her old friend, Lady Cecil. Although Lady Cecil failed to influence the government, Woolf hoped that she could induce her brother-in-law, James Cecil, fourth Marquis of Salisbury and chairman of the Central Tribunal, to help Grant and Garnett.

Woolf was not alone in attempting to impress authority with its own power. In his autobiography, David Garnett recalls his joint appearance with Duncan Grant before the Local Tribunal in Blything, Suffolk. Garnett had already served quite some time in France with the Friends' War Victims' Relief Fund. Now he and Grant were applying for exemption from conscription as necessary agricultural laborers on Vanessa Bell's farm. Although Adrian Stephen, who had studied law, stated their case, the hearing was a fiasco. Stephen's defense was muddled and the tribunal became so confused that when he tried to make the point that Garnett's mother had once visited Tolstoy in Russia—thereby providing Garnett with a long pacifist tradition—one tribunal member dismissed the evidence as irrelevant, saying that he was uninterested in what villages Mrs. Constance Garnett had toured.

This failure prompted Garnett and Grant to pull out all stops and bring J. M. Keynes to their Appeal Tribunal hearing at Ipswich. Keynes impressed the tribunal by announcing he had little time to spare while he opened a dispatch case stamped with the royal cipher. Philip Morrell, at that time M.P. for Burnley, was counsel for the two men. Not surprisingly, their appeal was successful and Grant and Garnett were ordered to essential noncombat work for the war's duration.

It is this glibness in the face of authority that is frequently condemned as Bloomsbury's most unattractive feature. As the *Dreadnought* hoax illustrated, Bloomsbury was fully capable of manipulating authority in order to denigrate it. Yet, except for Virginia Woolf, no figure in the Bloomsbury circle questioned the double standard that both criticizes authority while manipulating it for personal ends.

Unlike the rest of Bloomsbury, Woolf considered the Great War a completely masculine occupation. On 23 January 1916, she clearly stated her position in a letter to Margaret Llewelyn Davies:

> I become steadily more feminist, owing to the Times, which I read at breakfast and wonder how this preposterous masculine fiction

keeps going a day longer—without some vigorous young woman pulling us together and marching through it—Do you see any sense in it? I feel as if I were reading about some curious tribe in Central Africa—and now they'll give us votes. (*VWL* 2:76)

Woolf insists throughout her wartime writings that only men indulge in war. She constantly argues that women have neither the time nor the inclination to engage in armed conflict.

Given her belief that war is antithetical to female nature, Woolf was greatly distressed to find women who were willing to participate in the war effort. Although Woolf found the versifying of "an insinuating, elderly lady" amusing (*VWL* 2:77), the poem "Kitchener's the Man" is a fine example of the irrational patriotism that she vehemently rejected:

> Kitchener's the man we all will trust
> To see us through this conflict first
> Kitchener's the man we British adore
> Give him his sway and he'll do more.
>
> (*VWL* 2:77 n. 1)

Less humorous was Mrs. Humphry Ward's vociferous militarism. Her attack upon Strachey's *Eminent Victorians* (1918) denounced the work as brutal and pro-German (*D* 1:166). Woolf disliked Mrs. Ward not only for her virulent antisuffragism but also for such propagandizing novels as *The War and Elizabeth* (1918). "How I dislike writing directly after reading Mrs. H. Ward!—she is as great a menace to health of mind as influenza to the body" (*D* 1:211).

Woolf was particularly dismayed to find that women were capable of physically engaging in war. In a diary entry for 7 June 1918, she notes that

> L. was told the other day that the raids are carried out by women. Women's bodies were found in the wrecked aeroplanes. They are smaller & lighter, & thus leave more room for bombs. Perhaps its sentimental, but the thought seems to me to add a particular touch of horror. (*D* 1:153)

This rumor must have struck Woolf as especially depressing, considering her conviction that war is a completely male activity.

Part of the male-dominated world at war were the numerous laws that controlled all aspects of home life. The most wide-reaching of these was the Defence of the Realm Act (DORA), originally passed on 18 August 1914. The DORA provided the police with power to search premises at any time, and to seize documents or any item naval or military authorities considered suspicious. Suspects could be arrested without warrant and detained without charge. Although the DORAs of 1914–16 curtailed civil liberties more than any other acts passed during the war, they were not the only such restrictions. At the beginning of the war, on 5 August 1914, the Aliens Restriction Act was created. On 13 May 1915 orders were given to arrest all aliens of military age. These prisoners were transported to an internment camp on the Isle of Man.

Women had cause to fear government policy during the war. For example, although married to a native Englishman and a naturalized British subject, Frieda Lawrence, along with other German-born female citizens, was threatened with deportation and internment. Frieda Lawrence's fears of expulsion give proof to Woolf's later comment that Englishwomen did not have the same political status as their brothers and that all women are aliens in their native land. Citizenship and the privilege to vote can be revoked. Given this perspective, it is not surprising that Woolf sneered at the decision of the House of Lords to give women suffrage (D 1:104).

In addition to the vote, the government also presented the wives of soldiers a separation allowance of fifteen shillings a week. This favor, too, was not irrevocable. In a remarkable memorandum entitled "Cessation of Separation Allowances and Allotments to the Unworthy," the Home Office issued instructions to chief constables to place all women in receipt of the allowance under police surveillance. Policemen were given the power to decide whether or not these women were "worthy" enough to continue receiving their allowance. The suffragette and feminist E. Sylvia Pankhurst indignantly records that

Reports of alleged unworthiness, received from the relief committees, the soldiers or their commanding officers, or any other source, were to be investigated by the police, and if in their opinion proved, the separation allowance and the husband's allotment were to be discontinued, for unchastity, drunkenness, neglect of children or conviction on a criminal charge.[14]

Pankhurst goes on to give examples of how this communiqué was enforced:

> It was not merely an affair of official communications; the police in some districts began entering and inspecting the homes of soldiers' wives and mothers, inquiring of them, and also of their neighbours, whether they were in the habit of getting drunk and catechising them on the disposal of their bedrooms, and what visitors they admitted.[15]

Pankhurst's statements provide an interesting precursor to Woolf's later opinion that for centuries the concept of chastity has been used by men to control women (*TG*, 169).

In addition to the powers of search and seizure authorized by the DORA, the military authorities were given power to direct

> that persons who contravened or were suspected of contravening the regulations would be precluded from living in any specified area, when thus driven from home, should be compelled to report the address to which they might afterwards go.[16]

Sylvia Pankhurst, in *The Home Front* (1932), does not indicate what these specified areas were. She reports, however, that when Bertrand Russell was denied a passport to travel to America and decided instead to lecture throughout Great Britain on the part of pacifism, the government served him with a notice forbidding him to enter any prohibited area without written permission. Subsequently, Russell was not given leave to enter Glasgow to deliver a course of lectures there on the ground that his pacifist arguments would prove prejudicial to the manning of the army.[17] D. H. Lawrence also experienced the far-reaching power of the DORA. In March 1916, Lawrence and Frieda moved to Higher Tregerthen, Cornwall. During his stay there, Lawrence, like Russell, applied for a passport to America but was rejected. More irritating was the incident in the summer of 1917 when the Lawrences were stopped by the police on their way home from market. Their rucksack was searched in hopes that a camera, supposedly used to photograph the Cornish coastline for German submarines, would be found. The Lawrences were indignant, and their anger was not lessened by the search of their cottage on 12 October 1917. A few days later they were ordered to leave the area under section 14B of the DORA, which denied access to any coastal region or major port.

In *Society at War, 1914–1916* (1931), C. E. Playne claims that spy alarms were particularly frequent in the west of England. One instance she recounts is similar to the experiences of the Lawrences:

> An artist and his wife living in a cottage were said to be German spies. Both were entirely English. This artist was born in the Midlands, and since the war has made a considerable name for himself. People came after dark and rattled the door of the cottage shouting out threats. Once bricks were thrown at them. The only ground for this persecution appeared to be that he wore a soft, flat, wide-brimmed hat, and her cloak was also of an unusual shape.[18]

All around the country spy alarms were rife. Mrs. C. S. Peel, in *How We Lived Then, 1914–1918* (1929), records: "respectable persons of British nationality were reported to the authorities merely because they were heard 'whispering,' because they had 'voices like Germans.'"[19] During the first winter of the war, the Lawrences suffered the suspicions of their neighbors and the local police. The early months of the war set the pattern for the months to come. Even after the Lawrences left Cornwall under military orders, they were watched by the official eye. On 11 December 1917, Lawrence was questioned by a man from the Criminal Investigation Department a few days after Cecil Gray had encountered a CID agent eavesdropping outside the Lawrences' door in Earls Court. Lawrence suspected that letters to the police had been sent by patriotic busybodies in Cornwall:

> It is quite evident that somebody from Cornwall—somebody we don't know, probably—is writing letters to these various departments—and we are followed everywhere by the persecution. (*LL* 3:188)

Lawrence's feelings of victimization at the hands of the authorities were hardly alleviated by the outspoken xenophobia of his fellow Englishmen. Effectively silenced by the censorship of *The Rainbow* and unable to find a publisher for *Women in Love*, Lawrence nevertheless had to withstand the verbal denunciations of others:

> People write letters of accusation, because one has a beard and looks not quite the usual thing. . . . I want to be in a quiet retreat

in my own place in Cornwall—but they haul me out and then follow me round: really, it is too maddening. One would think they did it to amuse themselves. (*LL* 3:190)

This ongoing game of cat and mouse lasted well after the war. Even by April 1919 Lawrence's mail was still being inspected by the censors.

Although Woolf did not suffer the extreme financial exigencies experienced by Lawrence, her own wartime observations were not unlike his own. Both authors could not decide how to make sense of the war, and often their remarks reveal inner tensions and frustrations. For instance, like Lawrence, Woolf was intrigued by the zeppelin raids. She never saw them as ushering in a new dispensation, but she does comment on how the raids provide a new way of seeing the city and its people. Details come into sharp focus as Woolf notes the shocked responses to the raids:

We saw the hole in Piccadilly this afternoon. Traffic has been stopped, & the public slowly tramps past the place, which workmen are mending, though they look small in comparison with it. (*D* 1:65)

She comments that "it always seems utterly impossible that one should be hurt" (*D* 1:32). Her inability to comprehend these foreign experiences extends to a German prisoner of war:

the existence of life in another human being is as difficult to realise as a play of Shakespeare when the book is shut. This occurred to me when I saw Adrian [Stephen] talking to the tall German prisoner. . . . The reason why it is easy to kill another person must be that one's imagination is too sluggish to conceive what his life means to him. (*D* 1:186)

Woolf's attempts to know the other, her sympathetic comments on the fragility of human existence, were not always present during the war. Some of her most impatient comments were reserved for women and the upper classes, who, in their motorcars, look like "portly jewels in satin cases" (*D* 1:17). The human race, she declares in January 1915, has "no character at all—sought for nothing, believed in nothing, & fought only from a dreary sense of duty" (*D* 1:19). This disillusionment extends to the women she sees in London, whose faces look "as senseless as playing cards; with tongues like adders" (*D* 1:149).

It is no wonder that Woolf later found the celebrations over the Armistice equally unattractive and insincere. As the guns and sirens of all England sounded around her, she felt "immense melancholy" and found the national rejoicing "very sordid and depressing" (*LL* 2:290, 292).

Woolf's dislike of nationalistic attitudes and her suspicion of women who participate in the social and political maneuverings of a patriarchal society begin during the First World War. Many years later, Woolf again expresses these opinions, but, with a Second World War portending, the emphases have changed and the style is more argumentative rather than contemplative, for Woolf's purpose is now not only to record her feelings but to persuade others to join her. It is now Woolf who openly argues for a political stand.

On the eve of the Second World War Woolf set forth her arguments against war and the patriarchal governments that encourage it in *Three Guineas*. She argues that a society fashioned by women careful to reject the old patriarchal forms of control and domination would be unlikely to indulge in warfare. However, Woolf never claims that women are physically or psychologically incapable of violence. For example, in *Mrs. Dalloway* the character of Miss Kilman suggests that women are as capable of force and coercion as are their male counterparts. And in *Three Guineas* Woolf wryly admits that war work provides a welcome relief for women tired of domestic tyranny.

For Woolf, the masters of the state are indistinguishable from the masters in the home. In *Three Guineas* she argues that domestic and national authoritarianism is one and the same:

> the public and the private worlds are inseparably connected.... the tyrannies and servilities of the one are the tyrannies and servilities of the other. (*TG*, 258)

Woolf assumed that "'the personal is political': personal relations are the mirror of the social system, and its crucible."[20] The tyrannical father in the home is also the authoritarian head of state; repressions within the family provide the basis for denial of civil liberties. In *Three Guineas* she comments drily, "Society it seems was a father, and afflicted with the infantile fixation too" (*TG* 245). Her statement refers to English domestic regulations during the First World War, when the will to control belonged to the *patria* as well as the *pater*.

Lawrence's own response to the First World War is marked by a similar fluctuation in position and emphasis. In a letter to S. S. Koteliansky of 5 August 1914, he exclaimed, "I am very miserable about the war" (*LL* 2:205). "Everything seems gone to pieces," he wrote Amy Lowell four days later (*LL* 2:206). Yet by 5 February 1915, his rage over the war's senseless bloodshed led him to a paradoxical position: "I feel so bitter against the war altogether, I could wring the neck of humanity for it" (*LL* 2:277). The desire for peace and the lust for murder frequently exist side-by-side. Although he considers the war a "colossal idiocy" (*LL* 2:212), he prepares to participate in a worldwide massacre: "I do want to kill. But I want to select whom I shall kill. Then I shall enjoy it. The war is no good" (*LL* 2:315).

Lawrence deplores the random slaughter at the front. His form of warfare is a carefully planned method of attack designed to destroy existing political and social structures. To use Stephen Greenblatt's phrase, Lawrence intends to fire "invisible bullets" into the English social system.[21] One basis for Lawrence's quarrel with Bertrand Russell rested in his belief that Russell's lectures on pacifism were too obvious, and, therefore, ineffective. In a letter to Russell of 29 April 1915, Lawrence sets forth his own method of attack:

> I cannot tell you . . . my utter hatred of the whole establishment—the whole constitution of England as it now stands. . . . But softly, softly. I will do my best to lay a mine under their foundations. . . .
>
> For I am hostile, hostile, hostile to all that is, in our public and national life. I want to destroy it. (*LL* 2:328)

The "bombs" Lawrence urges Russell to "fire" into "the herd" are verbal ones (*LL* 2:546). Lawrence regarded *Women in Love* as an explosive force that would knock "the first loop-hole in the prison where we are all shut up" and destroy the social and industrial structures he so detested (*LL* 2:663).

These plans for undercover violence disprove Paul Delany's statement that although Lawrence "claimed to hate the existing order . . . [he] insisted that nothing could be done against it."[22] Lawrence's position during the war was indeed "dubious," but not for the reasons Delany states. Lawrence argues that nothing could "be done against" society by using the acceptable weapons of debate and parliamentary action. Given his stance against the war, his desire for the destruction of the English democratic system, and his outspokenness on these issues in *England, My England* and *Women in Love*, it is no wonder that he was regarded with suspicion.

Despite his dislike of the traditionally fashioned, unrevolutionary pacifist organizations that sprang up during the war, Lawrence did send Philip Heseltine half a crown ($3.00) for the No Conscription Fellowship, which he considered "worthy" (*LL* 2:551). However, Lawrence constantly sneers at what he regards as the establishment morality of the pacifists: "I hate the reformers worst, and their nauseous Morrellity" (*LL* 3:270). For Lawrence, to fight or not to fight was a personal affair, a matter of private conscience not to be associated with any group cause. He considers the conscientious objectors as supporting the societal structures they seemingly reject. Lawrence's comments on Bertrand Russell show that he regards Russell as as much a conformist as those who stripped him of his Cambridge fellowship and put him in prison (*LL* 2:378, 392).

In his itinerant wanderings and his refusal to subscribe to the moral and political attitudes of his time, Lawrence acts as if he finds his country's laws beyond and even beneath him. In *No Man's Land: Combat and Identity in World War I*, Eric Reed describes the front veteran as a "'liminal' type," a declassified man who exists beyond the constructs of society.[23] Reed does not limit his description to the First World War veteran. He uses the term to describe all those who "practice transformations upon themselves, roles, medals, values, spiritual and physical states."[24] Those who live "'outside' the boundaries of domestic existence" risk persecution by contemporaries eager to appropriate the power possessed by the outsider:

> The "liminal type" has always provided the ground upon which those at home project their ambivalence toward the social order they inhabit: their fear of disorder and their fear of petrification.... [The liminal figure] embodies the anxieties, acts out the guilts, and attenuates the boredom native to domesticity.[25]

Lawrence is a perfect example of Reed's liminal type. Married to an alien, spied upon by fellow citizens, his writings censored officially and privately, his home raided and denied him, he was treated as a marked man, a maverick to be brought into and restrained by the dominion of the law.

In contrast to the disillusion that haunts Virginia Woolf's wartime writings, Lawrence's hopes for what will follow frequently carry a note of paschal jubilation. He perceives his struggle with Frieda as "a fight to the death. But being dead, and in some measure risen again, one is invulnerable" (*LL* 2:658). The theme of resurrection runs throughout the war letters. Lawrence anticipates "the new shoots of a new era: a great, utter revolution" following the war (*LL* 2:426). He calls for "a resurrection with sound hands and feet and a whole body and a new soul" (*LL* 2:454). He describes the war itself as ushering in "a new heaven and a new earth" (*LL* 2:455). In a well-known letter to Lady Ottoline Morrell of 9 September 1915, he describes German zeppelins as heralds of another apocalypse. The zeppelins usher in "a new heaven and a new earth" with their destructive power (*LL* 2:390). For Lawrence, the airships are "a strange new celestial body dominating the night heavens" (*LL* 2: 396). His description of raids reads like a second book of Revelation. He depicts the "big guns" as capable of shattering past and present, revealing a future brought about by the war (*LL* 2:396).

The destruction of an unsatisfactory past and the hopeful anticipation of a happier future is one of the themes that informs *Look! We Have Come Through!* (1917). The poems in *Look!*, especially the last poems in the sequence, result from Lawrence's belief in a joyful resurrection of the spirit. It is unheard of to refer to Lawrence as a war poet, probably because the quality of his wartime prose overshadows his poetic achievement during the period. However, his poetry is of interest, for it provides a concise record of his fluctuating attitude toward the war.

Although the opening poems of *Look!* were originally composed in 1912–13, the presence of the war can be felt throughout the collection, especially in the concluding poems "New Heaven and Earth" and "Manifesto." In "New Heaven and Earth," Lawrence sets forth the same egoism and lust for murder he had earlier portrayed in "Eloi, Eloi Lama Sabachthani," but this time he discovers these emotions in himself, rather than ascribing them to another. A similar attitude may be found in other poems in *Look!* such as "Manifesto" and "Craving for Spring," which share the common theme of the necessity of death and subsequent apocalyptic resurrection.

The rebirth of the self through encounter with the other, that which is not the self, is described in "New Heaven and Earth"

as an exploration of an unknown continent: "I am the first come! / Cortes, Pisarro, Columbus, Cabot, they are nothing, nothing!" (*CP* 1:259). Lawrence's attempts to portray the "rush of creation" that sweeps away the "exquisite, ghastly first-flowers" in "Craving for Spring" (*CP* 1:271), "New Heaven and Earth," and "Manifesto" are not entirely successful. Unfortunately, he cannot sustain the enthusiasm he wishes to convey. Although in "Craving for Spring" he conjoins images of color and vivacity, the gloom of a world at war is not forgotten. In "Autumn Rain," Lawrence captures the despair of the war. He compares the falling drops to seeds of pain harvested on the battlefields. The general pall cast by the war over the home front can also be seen in "People" and "Street Lamps." The atmosphere of wartime is conveyed by images of a dark, washed-out world illuminated by the sickly glow of artificial lights. In "Street Lamps," the partial gloom created by the lights communicates the misery and destruction of war. The poem's description of an autumnal world in which there is no hope of "new things coming" is in contrast to the jubilance expressed by Lawrence in many of his other letters and writings of the period. The vacillation in his attitude toward the war indicates the emotional and physical strain he suffered during this period. Oftentimes, he experienced hallucinations of destruction, a delirium of horror such as that conveyed in this letter to Lady Ottoline Morrell of 14 May 1915:

> I've got again into one of those horrible sleeps from which I can't wake. . . . Everything has a touch of delirium. . . . And when I see a snake winding rapidly in the marshy places, I think I am mad. (*LL* 2:339)

Lawrence's nightmarish hysteria results in a feeling of vertigo. He frequently complains of a falling into "blackness" (*LL* 2:313). In keeping with his tendency to bring war back to the individual, he blames humanity for his impressions of collapse and nullity. On 5 September 1915 he writes, "The persistent nothingness of the war makes me feel like a paralytic convulsed with rage" (*LL* 2:386). He despairs of ever publishing *Women in Love* in "the existing state of squilch" (*LL* 3:76). A vast "chasm" lies between "I" and "you"; between self and other rests "all heaven and hell" (*LL* 3:32). He assures E. M. Forster that "there is darkness between us all, separating us.

We are all isolated" (*LL* 2:347), a viewpoint Forster shared and that he had earlier explored in *Howards End* (1910).

Lawrence uses the image of a chasm to delineate his Cornish neighbors: "they are the very bottomless pit" (*LL* 2:552). His bitterness toward his fellow humans during the war may have partially resulted from a lack of food and money. Denied his audience by the stringent wartime censoring of *The Rainbow*, kept from moving to a country that might have been more accepting of his work, Lawrence was left to struggle against poor housing and inadequate rations. Although he received two grants from the Royal Literary Fund and gifts of cash from friends, he was perennially hard up during the war. He was forced to ask his agent for advances on unpublishable works and literally to beg for help from financially successful authors like Arnold Bennett. Lady Cynthia Asquith frequently sent him gifts of food, as did Lady Ottoline Morrell, Catherine Carswell, and S. S. Koteliansky.

Lawrence's worldview was significantly affected by the domestic troubles he experienced during the war. There were frequent arguments between Frieda and Lawrence, some of which ended in violence, as when Frieda hit her husband over the head with a stoneware dinner plate or when Lawrence threatened to strike her on the mouth. The internecine battle was fought by Frieda and Lawrence throughout their years together. Yet Lawrence did not regard his marriage as entirely hopeless. Like his attitude toward the war itself, his view of married life fluctuated between hope and despair. His confidence in a new world after the war is reflected in his aspirations for his problematic relationship with Frieda. Marriage, he told Middleton Murry on 11 October 1916, is a fight to unity, "the long and blood fight" until the two "are at one" (*LL* 2:662).

In his works, Lawrence extends the battle for definition between self and other to his characters. Unlike Woolf, who saw the war as mainly a masculine construct, Lawrence blamed women for its continuance. In "The Crown," he attests that the "attitude" toward death that stimulates the war is mainly held by "women who flutter round and peck at death in us" (*C* 294). Woman as vulture is also the topic of the poem "Frost Flowers." The disintegration of the order of things is represented by women, "the issue of acrid winter, these first-flower young women" (*CP* 1:270). The stylish but deadly "sharp, slim wagtails" (*CP* 1:269) recall Pussum in *Women in Love*, who personifies the "last fires of dissolution." The stench of wartime is a feminine perfume, a "scent of the fiery-cold dregs of corruption" (*CP* 1:270).

In 1917, Robert Mountsier, later Lawrence's American agent, asked him to write an essay on "women and the war, and labour" (*LL* 3:78). Lawrence declined the commission:

> I haven't the guts. All I can say is, that in the tearing apart of the sexes lies the universal death, in the assuming of male activities by the female, there takes place the horrid swallowing of her own young, by the women. . . . I am sure woman will destroy man, intrinsically, in this country. . . . I am sure there is some ghastly Clytemnestra victory ahead, for the women. (*LL* 3:78–9)

Lawrence's focus was on the domestic arguments between men and women. England's quarrel with Germany is transposed into the fight between Adam and Eve. Like Woolf, Lawrence traces the impetus to war back "home to the heart of the individual fighters" (*LL* 2:233). Both writers perceive war as an event occurring between individuals as well as countries. Like Woolf, he does not differentiate between personal and public states. In a letter to Gordon Campbell of 3 March 1915 he proclaims, "*I* am the English nation. . . . L'Etat c'est moi" (*LL* 2:301). The state rests within the individual; a single person is a country, even a continent, whole and isolated unto him or herself. Thus, the impulse to war manifested by England and Germany is also exhibited by their separate citizens: "it's at the bottom of almost every Englishman's heart—the war—the desire to war—the *will* to war—and at the bottom of every German's" (*LL* 2:233).

Eric Reed argues in *No Man's Land* that after the First World War "the language of contest and struggle became almost obligatory to anyone who wanted to communicate the seriousness of an issue."[26] Careful consideration of the fictions of Woolf and Lawrence reveals that both writers engaged in the language of conflict well before the outbreak of the Great War. The battles between Gertrude and Walter Morel in Lawrence's *Sons and Lovers* (1913) and the violence accompanying Rachel Vinrace's sexual discovery in Woolf's *The Voyage Out* are portrayed through metaphors of war and murderous conflict. For Lawrence and Woolf violence is as much a part of human relationships as are harmony and love. Both authors depict a polarity of emotions in their prewar novels. For them, human relationships are an imprisoning matrix in which conflict and violence are as essential as sexual attraction and affection.

2

The Battle between Them: Sexual Conflict in the Early Fictions

> ... [T]he artist is affected as powerfully as other citizens when society is in chaos, although the disturbance affects him in different ways. His studio now is far from being a cloistered spot where he can contemplate his model or apple in peace. It is besieged by voices, all disturbing.
>
> (*CE* 2:232)

In "THE ARTIST AND POLITICS" (1936), VIRGINIA WOOLF APPARENTLY recommends the artist's participation in political activity: "He [the artist] is forced to take part in politics; he must form himself into societies like the Artists' International Association" (*CE* 2:232). However, the language used by Woolf in this essay indicates neither conviction of the necessity of political action on the part of the artist nor belief in its benefits. The artist is "forced" unwillingly into the realm of politics, "besieged" by demanding voices. These voices are cause for concern: erratic ("some for one reason, some for another"), violent ("besieging"), ubiquitous and chaotic ("all disturbing") are the demands upon the artist during wartime. They cry of the cataclysmic destruction of the presumably more peaceful prewar existence. The voices recall the "questioning" wind and its "aimless gust of lamentation," which breaks up the Ramsay household and ushers in the First World War in *To the Lighthouse*.[1]

Woolf's equivocal attitude toward the artist's political role appears throughout "The Artist and Politics." She describes political themes in literature as if they were a deviation from the norm: "the poet *introduces* communism and fascism into his lyrics; the novelist *turns from* the private lives of his characters to their social surroundings and their political opinions"

(*CE* 2:230; emphasis added). Woolf dismisses any questions raised by "The Artist and Politics" and unconvincingly begs her argument: "that the writer is interested in politics needs no saying" (*CE* 2:230).

Throughout her writings, Woolf appears ambivalent toward what Gayatri Spivak has termed "our own elusive historico-politico-economico-sexual determinations."[2] For example, in a letter to Dame Ethel Smyth of 18 May 1931, Woolf writes,

> Now, about Causes. Of course, and of course, I'm not such a pacifist as to deny that practical evils must be put to the sword: I admit fighting to the death for votes, wages, peace *and so on:* what I can't abide is the man who wishes to convert other men's minds; that tampering with beliefs seems to me impertinent, insolent, corrupt beyond measure. (*VWL* 4:333; emphasis added)

Woolf claims she is willing to "fight to the death" for certain issues. At the same time, she condemns "the man who wishes to convert other men's minds." The evasive "and so on" suggests further topics over which Woolf would be willing to go to battle. Yet the phrase belittles Woolf's attested goals, reassuring her reader that her claim of violent action is overstated. Indeed, the whole passage assures the reader that *Woolf* would never attempt to convert "other men's minds."

However, the agenda of Woolf's art is her readers' conversion. Her texts have frequently been described as powerful feminist tracts;[3] they are compelling pacifist ones as well. Woolf continually links the terms *feminism* and *pacifism*. In *Three Guineas*, she rejects the label of "'Feminism'" as "futile and false" (*TG*, 248) and questions the morality of contributing to pacifist societies since war is "the man's habit, not the woman's" (*TG*, 13). In the Society of Outsiders liberty and equality for women would go hand in hand with the conviction "not to fight with arms" (*TG*, 193). In Woolf's vision, equal rights and pacifist aims are inseparable.

Like the markedly polemical *Three Guineas* and *A Room of One's Own* (1929), Woolf's novels center around the problems of aggression and violence. Insofar as they portray ongoing conflict between individuals, her novels can be termed war novels. Throughout her fictions, she depicts struggles for power. Military imagery, the illustration of physical violence, and sexual fear are means she uses to portray the dynamics of battle. She eliminates the supposed polarity between love and war so that the two concepts become inseparable. For her, all human communication seems doomed to discord and strife.

The theme of war in Woolf's fiction has its paradigm in her first, notably prewar novel, *The Voyage Out*. Completed before the outbreak of World War I, *The Voyage Out* fully displays Woolf's interest in a topic that was to dominate her later novels. The world described in the first pages of *The Voyage Out* is one of chaos and conflict. *The Voyage Out* is fashioned around threats and premonitions of danger, warnings that the world of the novel and its inhabitants may not be as innocuous as they first appear. "Angry glances" strike the backs of the Ambroses.[4] "Small, agitated figures" bestow "unfriendly" stares (*VO*, 1). Although Helen Ambrose is protected by her class, cloak, tears, and, supposedly, her husband, she is threatened by the mob around her: "the friction of people brushing past her was evidently painful" (*VO*, 2). Crying, she shields "her face from the curious" (*VO*, 2).

Ridley Ambrose turns to defend his wife. His gesture is not entirely benevolent. He flourishes his cane at a group of boys and they return abuse: "'Bluebeard!'... 'Bluebeard'" (*VO*, 2). The epithet is noteworthy. Bluebeard was, of course, the notorious husband who hid his murdered wives in a locked closet. Ambrose resembles Bluebeard in ways other than his beard. Onboard the *Euphrosyne* he resides in a secret room, forbidding others to enter under pain of his wrath. Although Ridley reaches over to comfort his wife on leaving their children, she notes that he lacks genuine sympathy: "she shut her face away from him, as much as to say, 'You can't possibly understand'" (*VO*, 3). Helen avoids confronting the feigned sympathy of Ridley's gaze. The accusation is unuttered, and she takes refuge in a silence loud in its condemnation. Misogyny, violence, and death, three elements essential to the story of Bluebeard, are also key concepts in *The Voyage Out*. Before Ridley's immense linguistic powers (he is a classicist and translator), fervent misogyny, and piercing glance, Helen responds with silence and absence. Like Bluebeard's castle, which is decorated with precious tapestries woven of gold and silver to disguise the horror within, the descriptive surface of *The Voyage Out* hides the unthinkable. "When one gave up seeing the beauty that clothed things, this was the skeleton beneath" (*VO*, 4).

The ship *Euphrosyne* is ironically named, for it affords no shelter from the chaotic world of the London docklands. Woolf describes the Ambroses' journey in a small boat to the moored

ship as if it were a passage through the underworld. The journey begins inauspiciously as the Ambroses are ferried away
from their children in a boat laden with ghosts of the past.
They barely escape death: "the cab stopped, for it was in danger of being crushed like an egg-shell" (VO, 6). Images of military machinery add to the ominous threat of violence lurking
beneath the semblance of stability: "The wide Embankment
which had room for cannonballs and squadrons, had now
shrunk to a cobbled lane steaming with smells of malt and oil
and blacked by waggons" (VO, 6).

Having accepted destruction, the Ambroses serve as harbin-
gers of death onboard the *Euphrosyne*. As Rachel sets the din-
ing table, Ridley, in his guise as Bluebeard, introduces the
subject of the novel:

> As she occupied herself in laying forks severely straight by the
> sides of knives, she heard a man's voice saying gloomily:
> "On a dark night one would fall down these stairs head fore-
> most," to which a woman's voice added, "And be killed."
> As she spoke the last words the woman stood in the doorway. . . .
> "Oh, Rachel, how d'you do," she said, shaking hands. (VO, 7–8)

In this initial meeting between aunt and niece, Woolf introduces themes that were to run throughout her later work. In
Jacob's Room, Jacob Flanders's death is augured not only by
his name, which suggests the fields in which he will die, but
also by the "bright knives" formed by tears in his mother's
eyes.[5] In *Mrs. Dalloway* and *To the Lighthouse* Woolf associates
knives with violence, particularly sexual violence. Rachel Vinrace's death is foreshadowed by the cutlery she arranges on
the table as well as by the voices foretelling her demise.

There are indications as to what the course of the novel will
be. Mr. Pepper complains of rheumatic pains while Helen Ambrose counters, "'One does not die of it, at any rate'" (VO, 8).
The conversation moves to Rachel's dead mother. Ridley audi-
bly moans, "'Ah! She's not like her mother'" (VO, 8). While
Helen takes up cut flowers and arranges them, the conversation continues:

> "You knew Jenkinson, didn't you Ambrose?" asked Mr. Pepper
> across the table.
> "Jenkinson of Peterhouse?"
> "He's dead," said Mr. Pepper. (VO, 9)

Recalling the name of Bluebeard, we are told that "Jenkinson of Cats" has had "the misfortune to lose his wife" (*VO*, 10). A few pages later, Rachel muses that her elderly maiden aunts would suffer little if the upstairs piano were to fall through the floor: "'but at their age one wouldn't mind being killed in the night?' she enquired" (*VO*, 14). These passages are noteworthy, for they are indicative of the tone of the novel. Sexual fear and violence accompany Rachel Vinrace throughout her voyage to South America.

For Rachel, the "voyage out" to South America and its jungles is also a voyage from the self's solitary room. In *The Voyage Out*, Woolf proposes that love consists of the movement of the self toward another through experience of the unknown. Yet for Rachel Vinrace the gaze of the other is akin to sexual aggression. For instance, after observing the Ambroses' embrace, Rachel envisions an undersea world inhabited by threatening sea monsters:

> Down she looked into the depths of the sea. . . . One could scarcely see the black ribs of wrecked ships, or the spiral towers made by the burrowings of great eels, or the smooth green-sided monsters who came by flickering this way and that. (*VO*, 23–24)

The juxtaposition of sexual embrace and oceanic monsters occurs again late in the novel, during Rachel's illness, which follows after her sexual encounter with and subsequent engagement to Terence Hewet: "While all her tormentors thought that she was dead, she was not dead, but curled up at the bottom of the sea" (*VO*, 416). Rachel's fear of being objectified by the gaze of others leads her to seek refuge within the privacy of the inner self. Yet the image she uses to characterize the secret self is one she had earlier found distasteful. Although safe from the gaze of others, Rachel looks within herself. She is at once both surveyor and surveyed. What she perceives in her self-conscious gaze is an image of horror.

Throughout the novel concupiscence is associated with human cruelty and international armed conflict, particularly when Rachel Vinrace first encounters male sexual desire in the form of Richard Dalloway. Richard's wife, Clarissa, fusses over his apparently selfless devotion to his work. "'You're not to think about those guns,' said Clarissa" (*VO*, 67). In order to keep his mind off "the guns of Britain" (metonymy for British imperialism, world conflict, and sexual desire), Clarissa reads from Jane Austen's *Persuasion* (1818), a novel about delayed gratification. Nevertheless, Richard cannot help thinking about guns as he engages in a suggestive political discussion with Rachel Vinrace. Significantly, his conversation opens with a bestial grunt. From this inauspicious beginning, Richard expresses himself in the language of power and authority. The language of cultural domination is uttered by a speaker also capable of subhuman sounds.

Woolf consistently explores the futility and violence of human communication. Dalloway's efforts to be understood take the form of a sexual assault in which there is a prurient pleasure in innocence attacked:

> "Girls are kept very ignorant, aren't they? Perhaps it's wise—perhaps—You *don't* know?"
> He spoke as if he had lost consciousness of what he was saying.
> "No; I don't," she said, scarcely speaking above her breath. (*VO*, 75)

The power play implicit in Dalloway's suggestion that women be kept ignorant of their own sexuality is successful, as evidenced by Rachel's struggling speech. Attacked with the notion of a sexuality denied her, she is placed on the defensive. With great comic flair, Woolf introduces the figure of the wife, who appears just in time to avert disaster. But, ironically, Clarissa distracts Richard's attention with the warships she had earlier persuaded him to forget: "'Warships, Dick! Over there! Look!'" (*VO*, 75). Within the context of *The Voyage Out*, sexual encounters between men and women in a patriarchal society frequently take on the dynamics of physical violence and international conflict. Dalloway closes in on Rachel Vinrace while the ships' predatory aspects suggest hunters in search of prey; the vessels are "sinister," "bald as bone," "with the look of eyeless beasts seeking their prey" (*VO*, 75). Dalloway, too, possesses feral qualities. His kiss is a method of attack:

> Holding her tight, he kissed her passionately, so that she felt the hardness of his body and the roughness of his cheek printed upon hers. . . .
> "You tempt me," he said. The tone of his voice was terrifying. He seemed choked in fight. (*VO*, 84–85)

Woolf describes this sexual encounter between man and woman as a pitched battle in which Rachel falls into a locked embrace both "hard" and "rough." Later in the novel, Rachel's search for a definition of love ends in preparation for a fight. "'What is it to be in love?' she demanded. . . . she rose, and with her two books beneath her arm returned home again, much as a soldier prepared for battle" (*VO*, 207). Following her engagement to Terence Hewet in chapter 21, love is again described by Rachel in terms of conflict: "'It will be a fight'" (*VO*, 345).

This concept of love as aggressive act is personified in the figure of Evelyn Murgatroyd. For Evelyn, love, marriage, and war go hand in hand. Evelyn imagines herself a woman of action, another Anna Maria Ribeiro da Silva fighting alongside her husband. Evelyn is a female Garibaldi and like the famous commander she regards life as a perpetual battle:

> "I don't call this *life*, do you?"
>   "What do you call life?" said St. John.
>   "Fighting—revolution," she said, still gazing at the doomed city. (*VO*, 151)

In her portrait of Evelyn Murgatroyd, Woolf chooses to ignore Garibaldi's later pacifist tendencies. Her emphasis is on women who engage in battle with others or who struggle to protect themselves from fear inspired by male sexual and political aggressiveness. Miss Allan's "parti-coloured button of a suffrage society" (*VO*, 314) is emblematic of her sexual isolation. For Woolf, the possibility of female suffrage holds out little hope that the conflict between the sexes can be resolved.

In *The Voyage Out*, as in all Woolf's novels, the vote is depicted as a particularly worthless masculine agent. Early in the novel (chapter 3) the vote is associated with aggression. Dalloway dismisses as hysterical the attack by a militant suffragette before the Houses of Parliament and pretends, but only for a moment, condescending gentlemanly concern. He threatens his own demise before women are allowed to vote. Rachel's father, Willoughby Vinrace, seems to relish any physical pain the suffragettes have to endure. Taken up by Lloyd George, dismissed by another M.P., and vilified by the male characters, the suffrage movement in *The Voyage Out* is very much controlled by misogynists.

Although Clarissa Dalloway exclaims, "'Aren't you glad to be English!'" (*VO*, 75), Woolf makes the point in *The Voyage Out*, as she does in *Three Guineas*, that countries are male entities and governments masculine constructs. Woolf ridicules the importance of parliamentary debates. She questions the apparently immutable position of such a masculine institution as the *Times* in a world of change: "The paper lay directly beneath the clock, the two *seeming* to represent stability in a changing world" (*VO*, 135; emphasis added). Just as the *Times* practices violence in cutting out part of the world upon which it pretends to report, so the government of England excludes part of the population it claims to represent. Although Clarissa is married to an M.P. and displays suitable patriotic fervor over the appearance of the Mediterranean Fleet, she is unable to take part in the government of her country. In *The Voyage Out*, Woolf amply demonstrates her position on a topic she was to write about for the next twenty years.

However, in *The Voyage Out* men and women often appear united despite political and sexual differences. Rachel Vinrace, Miss Allan, Evelyn Murgatroyd, Terence Hewet, and St. John Hirst share a common struggle to protect the self from destruction through extreme intimacy with another human being. As we have seen, Rachel responds with physical and emotional trepidation when embraced by Richard Dalloway. Regarding the depiction of the relationship between Terence and Rachel, James Naremore has astutely commented that "through a deep sense of sexual love, Terence and Rachel glimpse an elemental terror which Virginia Woolf suggests is the primitive biological force of life itself."[6] However, only Rachel is granted an extended vision of this "elemental terror." Following her brief physical clash with Richard Dalloway, she experiences a claustrophobic hallucination of masculine lust and aggression in which sexual desire is transmuted into the dynamics of hunter and prey, invader and defender.[7] Rachel is trapped by the sexuality denied her by her father and Dalloway. At the mercy of men who both deny her sexual identity and who aggressively place her in a sexual role of their own making, Rachel is forced to face the frightening aspects of her own unrecognized desire and those of the men around her.

Rachel Vinrace is imprisoned by forces of coercion and aggression. Whether male or female, young or old, each character in *The Voyage Out* has his or her own idea of who Rachel is, is not, or should be. Eventually, Rachel dismisses all acts of love and kindness as malignant. During her illness, she is oblivious to Hewet's affection and perceives only savagery and sexual violence: "She opened [her eyes] completely when he kissed her. But she only saw an old woman slicing a man's head off with a knife" (*VO*, 413). All of the female figures who restrict Rachel are represented by this vicious and menacing apparition. They, like their male counterparts, have forced Rachel to conform to their idea of her. Rachel's mother dies, leaving her to cope as best she can; her aunts have smothered her in Richmond. Helen Ambrose introduces Rachel to the daunting realm of adult sexuality. One of the women at the hotel chops the head off a chicken, thereby reinforcing the theme of violent brutishness that runs through the novel. Finally, even Rachel's nurse is transformed into an image of horror. Playing cards by candlelight, Nurse McInnis becomes a symbol of brutality and death, a deformed woman playing cards in an oozing, damp tunnel under the Thames.

At the conclusion of *The Voyage Out*, Woolf employs an image that suggests the self battling to escape pursuit and imprisonment:

> Every now and then the moth, which was now grey of wing and shiny of thorax, whizzed over their heads, and hit the lamps with a thud.
> A young woman put down her needlework and exclaimed, "Poor creature! it would be kinder to kill it." But nobody seemed disposed to rouse himself in order to kill the moth. (*VO*, 452)

Avrom Fleishman has pointed out that "the butterfly and moth are associated with the human soul in an emblem of long tradition."[8] Fleishman argues that in *The Voyage Out* the image of the butterfly symbolizes the meeting of the sexes.[9] In the passage quoted above it is clear that the moth smashing against the light will meet with nothing but destruction. Following the First World War, Woolf uses butterflies as symbols of malevolence. In *Jacob's Room*, butterflies are scavengers:

> The blues settled on little bones lying on the turf with the sun beating on them, and the painted ladies and the peacocks feasted upon bloody entrails dropped by a hawk. (*JR*, 35–36)

The wolfish characteristics exhibited by these butterflies have their prototype in the murderous intentions of the humans at the conclusion of *The Voyage Out*. Even before the advent of the First World War, Woolf displayed an interest in humanity's tendency to self-destruct. In *The Voyage Out*, as in all her fictions, she amply illustrates that war plays "a considerable part in determining the structure of the world."[10] Woolf proves that there is no time during which the artist is not besieged by "all disturbing" voices that announce conflict and destruction.

In a letter to Edward Garnett of 29 June 1912, D. H. Lawrence describes his new life with Frieda Weekley in terms of armed conflict:

> the great war is waged in this little flat on the Isarthal, just as much as anywhere else. In fact, I don't think the *real* tragedy is in dying or in the perversity of affairs, like the woman one loves being the wife of another man. . . . I think the real tragedy is in the inner war which is waged between people who love each other, a war out of which comes knowledge and—(*LL* 1:419)

Lawrence's equivocal attitude toward male/female relations is epitomized by the contrast he makes between the "knowledge" gained through the meeting of the sexes and "the *real* tragedy," the "great war" of domestic life. The battle waged in the small cottage is only one of the many skirmishes Lawrence either experienced himself or made the subject of his fictions. The dynamics of battle inform much of Lawrence's early work. In *The White Peacock, The Trespasser,* and "Once!—" (1912) Lawrence focuses on a theme prominent in his later writings: the cruelty inherent in human relationships, a destructiveness manifested through emotional, physical, and verbal clashes.

For example, in *The White Peacock,* sexual encounters are frequently transmuted into murderous collisions between hunters and their prey. Military imagery in *The Trespasser* suggests Siegmund's insistent desire and Helena's trepidation. In both novels, thwarted passion results in murderous fantasies.

Like the threatening cityscape described in the opening pages of *The Voyage Out,* the landscape of Nethermere in *The White Peacock* reveals an underlying savagery. There is a sharp distinction between Cyril's sentimental description of the "old papery nest" of "pretty field bees which seem to have dipped their tails into bright amber dust" and George's tormenting of the insects.[11] Distressed by his unfulfilled desire for Lettie, George releases his frustration through acts of brutality and murder. In chapter 2, the incident of the trapped black cat is representative of the human antipathies portrayed in the novel. Lettie discovers the cat hidden within an apparently paradisal landscape of "tall meadow-sweet" and elders (*WP,*

11). But beyond the elder's branches resides a frightening apparition:

> On the bank before us lay a black cat, both hind-paws torn and bloody in a trap. It had no doubt been bounding forward after its prey when it was caught. (*WP*, 12)

Lettie Beardsall resembles the injured cat, for in hunting her quarry she, in turn, is apprehended. The game of charades in chapter 9 is her method of drawing George into a battle in which sexual innuendos are the verbal spars. The repartee heightens Lettie's enjoyment of "the forbidden game." She complicates the intrigue by kissing Leslie "unobserved, delighting and exhilarating him more than ever" (*WP*, 116). Later in the novel, Leslie, teased beyond endurance, clenches his fists and grins with rage: "'You tantalising little————'" (*WP*, 170). Leslie is unable to complete Lettie's epithet; George describes her as a cat: "'She—she's like a woman, like a cat'" (*WP*, 90). Cyril admits that Lettie possesses "a kind of feline graciousness" (*WP*, 167).

Caught in the gamekeeper's trap, ignored by her partner, Mrs. Nickie Ben meets her end in George's hands. His indifference to physical cruelty attracts Lettie and, pale with apprehension, she watches George drop "the poor writhing cat into the water": "If we move the blood rises in our heel-prints!" (*WP*, 13). Lettie's sentimental philosophizing over the cat's demise gives voice to the subject of *The White Peacock*. Throughout the novel Lawrence portrays human gestures as acts of violence and brutality.

In *The Trespasser*, the Isle of Wight's sunny beaches conceal a surrounding viciousness. For instance, Siegmund's "game with the sea" results in injury.[12] The "insidious creeping of blood down his thigh" (*T*, 74) suggests that his play-fellow is neither innocent nor gentle. Nor are the two battleships that rest upon the horizon entirely guileless. They are "uncouth monsters lying as naive and curious as sea-lions strayed afar" (*T*, 109). Like the ships in *The Voyage Out*, the battleships in Lawrence's novel possess feral qualities. They are observant, "uncouth monsters" awaiting prey, keeping watch "along their sharp noses" (*T*, 56) as Siegmund and Helena act out their sexual conflict.

Siegmund's resemblance to the battleships is obvious; he, too, is a snuffling beast of prey. Throughout *The Trespasser*, the image of the throat and the act of strangulation represent human vulnerability and accompanying savagery. In a letter of 11 May 1910 to Helen Corke, Lawrence describes his dissatisfaction with their sexual relationship in a graphic image of ferocity:

> You see, I know Siegmund is there all the time. I know you would go back to him, after me, and disclaim me. I know it very deeply. I know I could not bear it. I feel often inclined, when I think of you, to put my thumbs on your throat. (*LL* 1:160)

Lawrence was fascinated by the attractiveness and vulnerability of the human throat. At one point during his life he was obsessed with a painting by Maurice Greiffenhagen called *An Idyll* (1891), which depicts a man moving to kiss a woman's bare throat. Partially clad, arms passive, she averts her eyes and mouth from her bare-toothed pursuer. In a long letter to Blanche Jennings of 31 December 1908, Lawrence presumably thanks her for the gift of a reproduction of Greiffenhagen's painting:

> [it] has made me kiss a certain girl till she hid her head in my shoulder; but what a beautiful soft throat, and a round smooth chin, she has; and what bright eyes, looking up! (*LL* 1:103)

Lawrence uses *An Idyll* in *The White Peacock* to represent the sexual attraction between George and Lettie. As they go through a pile of art books they come upon the painting:

> They turned on, chatting casually, till George suddenly exclaimed "There!"
> It was Maurice Greiffenhagen's "Idyll."
> "What of it?" she asked, gradually flushing. . . .
> "Wouldn't it be fine?" he exclaimed, looking at her with glowing eyes, *his teeth showing white in a smile that was not amusement.*
> "What?" she asked, dropping her head in confusion.
> "That—a girl like that—half afraid—and passion!" He lit up curiously. (*T*, 29; emphasis added)

In Lawrence's presentation of George, cruelty is equated with passion. Teeth bared as if to devour his prey, he grins with appreciation at Lettie's intermingled excitement and fear.

The numerous references to Greiffenhagen's work point to Lawrence's interest in sexual timidity, a subject he explored

in poems written well before he ever saw *An Idyll*. The image
of the throat and the theme of strangulation so prominent in
The Trespasser have their precursors in two of Lawrence's early
poems. In "Snapdragon" (1907), two lovers engage in mutual
acts of vicarious strangulation by squeezing the throat of a
flower:

> She laughed, she reached her hand out to the flower,
> Closing its crimson throat. My own throat in her power
> Strangled, my heart swelled up so full
> As if it would burst its wine-skin in my throat.
>
> (*CP* 1:123)

The male speaker of "Snapdragon" presses "the wretched,
throttled flower" between his fingers "till its head lay back, its
fangs / Poised" to attack the woman (*CP* 1:125). In "Love on
the Farm" (1907), the husband assaults his wife. She is a rabbit
caught in his trap:

> I know not what fine wire is round my throat;
> I only know I let him finger there
> My pulse of life, and let him nose like a stoat
> Who sniffs with joy before he drinks the blood.
>
> (*CP* 1:43)

Like a rabbit frozen with fear, the wife waits passively for the
death blow. To use Lawrence's expression, she is "a wee bit
frit," hesitating until the "strong teeth" settle (*CP* 1:43).

A similar relationship between hunter and prey exists in *The
Trespasser*. Throughout the novel Siegmund seeks comfort
against Helena's "soft, strong throat" (*T*, 63). He "crushes" her
to him in a grip "like steel," and just as she is released he moves
"his mouth over her throat, something like a dog snuffing her,
but with his lips" (*T*, 63–64). Like a predator, Siegmund seeks
his victim's most vulnerable area. His own throat is unpro-
tected, and Hampson finds its nakedness attractive: "his eyes
wandered over the wet hair, the white brow and the bare
throat of Siegmund" (*T*, 109). Showing his teeth in a laugh,
Hampson repeats his appreciation: he "glanced over [Sieg-
mund's] easy, mature figure and strong throat" (*T*, 111). Following his return from his holiday, Siegmund is asphyxiated
by the animosity of his family. He cannot utter articulate
sounds: "He believed he could remember the sound of inarticulate murmuring in his throat. Immediately he remembered,

he could feel his throat producing the sounds" (*T*, 199). Unable to speak, feeling as if he will suffocate, Siegmund strangles himself (*T*, 204).

In *Sons and Lovers*, the throat serves as a focal point for sexual desire. Paul Morel's innocence is represented by "his young throat almost like a girl's."[13] His sexual frustration is emblematized by repeated references to bare throats. Fascinated by Clara Dawes's white throat, Paul observes its every detail. He reveals his bare throat to his mother following his confession that "'I really *don't* love [Miriam]'" (*SL*, 252). She, in turn, confesses a similar deficiency of love:

> "And I've never—you know, Paul—I've never had a husband— not really—"
> He stroked his mother's hair, and his mouth was on her throat. (*SL*, 252)

Later, in chapter 11, Paul kisses *Miriam*'s throat and Lawrence uses an identical phrase to describe the act: "his mouth was on her throat" (*SL*, 327). In his fight with Baxter Dawes to establish sexual territory (as represented by Clara), Paul comes close to strangling the older man.

Lawrence consistently compares the rituals of sexual desire to rapacious attacks. In a letter to Louie Burrows of 17 December 1910, he writes,

> Oh dear—do say you love me—and don't be so restrained. Some savage in me would like to taste your blood. (*LL* 1:206)

Throughout his early writings, Lawrence dwells upon the fantasy of vampirism. In "Love on the Farm" the husband is a stoatlike creature "who sniffs with joy before he drinks the blood" of his wife. Leslie, in *The White Peacock*, indulges in a similar appetite as he admires Lettie's white forearm:

> "Can you remember," said Leslie, speaking low, "that man in Merimée who wanted to bite his wife and taste her blood?"
> "I do," said Lettie. "Have you a strain of wild beast too?" (*WP*, 118)

As in Lawrence's letter to Louie Burrows, love in Merimée's story, "Le manscrit du Professeur Wittembach" (1869), is associated with violence and bloodshed. Lying on her bridal bed, the young countess of Merimée's story dies, "la figure horriblement lacerée, *la gorge* ouverts, inondée de sang" (her "face horribly torn, *the throat* open, deluged in blood"; emphasis added).[14] A similar image occurs in chapter 6 of *The White Peacock* during George's courtship. He begs Meg to give him a kiss, for she is "like a ripe plum! I could set my teeth in thee, thou'rt that nice." (*WP*, 204). In their thirst for blood, Leslie and George resemble carnivorous, even cannibalistic, beasts. Their fearsome anthropophagy is partially echoed by the natural world. For instance, Lettie discovers a wood pigeon that has had its eyes pecked out by a rival. She then teases George that he and Leslie should also fight for her favor: "'I think a wood-pigeon must enjoy being fought for—and being won.'" (*WP*, 210).

The theme of cannibalism is also present in *Sons and Lovers*. Naked before Paul, Miriam Leivers resembles a creature "awaiting immolation" (*SL*, 333). Clara, too, gives herself to Paul in the spirit of blood sacrifice:

> He sunk his mouth on her throat, where he felt her heavy pulse beat under his lips. . . .
> When she arose, he, looking on the ground . . . saw suddenly sprinkled on the black wet beech roots many scarlet carnation petals, like splashed drops of blood. And red, small splashes fell from her bosom streaming down her dress to her feet. (*SL*, 355)

In sinking "his mouth on her throat," Paul acts as if to devour Clara. His obsession with Clara's throat conforms to their respective roles as hunter and prey. Clara as bleeding victim is not far removed from Clara as sustenance:

> He stood showing his teeth. . . . He suddenly caught her in his arms, stretched forward, and put his mouth on her face in a kiss of rage. She turned frantically to avoid him. He held her fast. Hard and relentless his mouth came for her. (*SL*, 371–72)

There are numerous descriptions of male vampirism in Lawrence's early writings. Through their bloodthirsty attacks, Lawrence's men assert their dominance over their ultimately compliant female victims.

In a letter to Blanche Jennings of 4 November 1908, Lawrence remarked, "Pah—I hate women's heroes. At the bottom women love the brute in man best" (*LL* 1:88). *The White Peacock* illustrates Lawrence's belief that women are attracted to masculine ferocity. Lettie's admiration of George's strength is

sparked by his treatment of Mrs. Nickie Ben. Her appreciation
of George's savage good health indicates her fascination with
the coarser side of his personality. While they dance around
the cottage, George's perspiring face appeals to her, and she
admires George's "wet and glistening" hair: "'You great brute,'
she said, but her voice was not as harsh as her words" (WP,
95). Lettie fashions her world around George's vulgarity and
coarseness. Her conception of life as "hairy, barbaric" condemns both her husband's personal habits and his Tory politics
(WP, 296). George's rough, "inflamed, barbaric hands" (WP,
229) epitomize her philosophy of life; for her, he is the supreme animal.

In *The White Peacock* and *Sons and Lovers*, the cruelty practiced by men and women upon one another often results in
self-injury. George's methodical alcoholism is a form of suicide
and his cruel treatment of his children a form of self-
flagellation. The whip he brandishes at his son, Wilfred, is indicative of his self-hatred. Frustrated in his love for Lettie,
married to a woman he despises, George is destroyed by un-
governable passions. In failure he turns to self-condemnation;
the brutal energy Lettie admired is used against himself. Paul
Morel, in *Sons and Lovers*, is gradually debilitated by the turmoil of unfulfilled passion. The violent conflict over physical
intimacy with Miriam leads him to treat her callously. Eventually, he becomes the victim of his own appetite.

Lawrence argues that the conflict between men and women,
the "battle between them which so many married people fight,
without knowing why," results in a form of knowledge.[15] This
knowledge is accompanied by a sense of terror, the nameless
apparition Lawrence refers to in his letter to Edward Garnett.
In *The Trespasser*, Siegmund and Helena's relationship is based
on fear. Incarcerated in Siegmund's "brute embrace" (T, 126),
Helena is terrified by "the secret thud, thud of his heart, the
very self of that animal in him" (T, 126). But Siegmund has no
integral self; he has been destroyed by Helena's false ecstasy
and his own unfulfilled desire:

> He felt detached from the earth, from all the near, concrete, be-
> loved things; as if these had melted away from him, and left him,
> sick and unsupported, somewhere alone on the edge of an enor-
> mous space. (T, 104)

Siegmund and Helena hate each other. As they regard one another at Waterloo before parting they each experience a vision

of horror. Siegmund cannot bring himself to look at Helena: "he could not see her; he could only recoil from her" (*T*, 196). Forced to regard one another, Helena and Siegmund perceive only their dismay before the threatening other.

In works directly preceding the publication of *The Trespasser*, Lawrence personifies the cruelty of love in the figure of the uniformed soldier. He enclosed his poem "The Young Soldier with Bloody Spurs" in a letter to Edward Garnett of 13 August 1912 (*LL* 1:434–37). The "spurs" of the title refer to the Bavarian soldier's cruel treatment of his horse and the female narrator. Just as the soldier camouflages his mistreatment of the horse, so he dismisses the young serving girl who carries his child. Although the woman fears an actual physical clash, the psychological cruelty the soldier inflicts upon her by his disregard provides a greater desolation.

In the short story "Once!—," Lawrence again explores a brief sexual encounter between a woman and a soldier. Like the serving girl of the poem, Anita's affair with a young officer lasts only one night. Passion is intermingled with cruelty and bloodshed:

> "All that night we loved each other. There were crushed, crumpled little rose-leaves on him when he sat up, almost like crimson blood! Oh and he was fierce, and at the same time, tender—!" (*LAH*, 158)

There is little difference between the act of love and an act of cruelty. Like the demented speaker of Browning's "Porphyria's Lover" (1842), the officer's tribute to Anita's beauty borders on the sadistic:[16]

> "—and he had a long gold chain, threaded with little emeralds, that he wound round and round my knees, binding me like a prisoner, never thinking." (*LAH*, 159)

The emotional paucity of this meeting is evident not only in the title but also in Anita's admission that her search for physical sensation is an insubstantial enterprise. Throughout Lawrence's work the soldier represents self-denial and sexual cruelty. Despite, and perhaps because of, her marriage to a German officer, Anita "has never really loved" (*LAH*, 153). She is attracted to the superficial, the sensational. She admits she was captivated by the young officer's "'figure in its blue uniform'" (*LAH*, 158), the way "'he unfastened his sword-belt and trappings from his loins'" (*LAH*, 159). In *Sons and Lovers*, Mrs. Morel rages against Arthur for joining the army and becoming a "'thing in a red coat,'" "'nothing but a body that makes movements when it hears a shout'" (*SL*, 219–20). In *The Rainbow*, the poverty of Anton Skrebensky's personality is represented by his uniform and by his acquiescence in the functions performed by the army.

The most powerful depiction of sexual cruelty occurs in the story "The Prussian Officer." What irritates the captain is the "free movement" of his orderly's limbs, "which no military discipline could make stiff" (*PO*, 5). Free within his uniform, Schöner reserves part of himself from the drudgery and demands of army life. This independence of self drives his commanding officer "irritably insane" (*PO*, 5). Unable to leave the army due to gambling debts, Herr Hauptmann takes refuge in the arms of successive mistresses. Such superficial relationships offer no solace: "after such an event, he returned to his duty with his brow still more tense, his eyes still more hostile and irritable" (*PO*, 2). No doubt the captain's sadistic sexuality prompted Edward Garnett to change the story's title from "Honour and Arms" to "The Prussian Officer" five weeks before the volume was published on 26 November 1914. It is likely that Garnett hoped the change would attract readers eager to learn of the enemy and of his supposed perversions.

In Lawrence's fiction, soldiers are associated with violence perpetrated through language. In "The Prussian Officer," Herr Hauptmann kicks Schöner for not disclosing the purpose of the pencil behind his ear. Unwilling to admit that he "had been copying a verse for his sweetheart's birthday-card" (*PO*, 7), Schöner can only utter a "dry, inhuman sound," an inarticulate "click" in his throat (*PO*, 8). In "The Thorn in the Flesh," Bachmann, too, is betrayed by language. The story opens with the young soldier trying to compose a letter to his mother. Like Schöner, he finds articulation difficult: "But he could write no more. Out of the knot of his consciousness no word would come" (*PO*, 22). It is this same letter that later betrays Bachmann and leads to his discovery.

In Lawrence's fictions following the publication of *The Prussian Officer and Other Stories*, the conflict between men and women is fought not only through physical force but also with the weapon of language. The "bloody battle" (*SL*, 22) between Walter and Gertrude Morel is brought about by the husband's falsehoods. The ongoing arguments between Birkin and Ursula in *Women in Love* substitute for the more physical, sexual clashes of Ursula and Anton Skrebensky. Throughout works written immediately before and during the First World War, Lawrence portrays the disintegration of language as a means of human communication. For Lawrence, the World War was also a word war of censorship, jingoism, and verbal misunderstanding.

3

The Prisonhouse of Language: Writings of the War Years

In *THE GREAT WAR AND MODERN MEMORY*, PAUL FUSSELL INSISTS that from its outset the First World War revealed the incapacity of language to relate the horror of battle: "The problem for the writer trying to describe elements of the Great War was its utter incredibility, and thus its incommunicability in its own terms."[1] Fussell cogently argues that "whatever the cause, the presumed inadequacy of language itself to convey the facts about trench warfare is one of the motifs of all who wrote about the war."[2] That those who attempted to describe the western front found existing literary forms indispensable but inadequate has been well-established.[3] What has gone unnoticed is the emphasis placed upon the role of language by those who remained at home during the war. Government authorities were clearly concerned with the power of the word throughout the conflict. Postal services were discontinued between England and Germany—Frieda Lawrence was forced to communicate with her relatives via Switzerland, and this correspondence aroused official suspicion.[4] Letters home were censored by officers at the front and domestic mail was inspected.[5] On occasion, Lawrence's mail went curiously astray. Paul Delany has suggested that several of Lawrence's letters might have been tampered with by authorities eager to find evidence of his supposed pro-German sympathies.[6] Virginia Woolf was well aware of the authority of language; several entries in her wartime diary acknowledge the force of Lloyd George's jingoistic orations and the propagandistic, anti-German sentiments of Lord Northcliffe's papers.

Keith Cushman has noted that much of the language of servitude present in "The Thorn in the Flesh" was added by Lawrence to the printed proofs in October 1914.[7] Cushman remarks that "this language seems rather questionable."[8] It may seem less questionable, however, if we remember that by the time Lawrence made the final revisions, the war had been in progress for two months. Throughout the war Lawrence was well aware of the invidious power of language. On 23 April 1915 he wrote to J. B. Pinker,

> I'm afraid there are parts of [*The Rainbow*] Methuen wont want to publish. He must. I will take out sentences and phrases, but I won't take out paragraphs or pages. . . .
> You see a novel, after all this period of coming into being, has a definite organic form, just as a man has when he is grown. And we don't ask a man to cut his nose off because the public won't like it: because he must have a nose, and his own nose too. (*LL* 2:327)

At the same time Lawrence was anticipating the upcoming skirmish with his publishers he was writing violence into his account of the second generation of Brangwens.[9] His disregard for his publisher and his nose thumbing at the government are simultaneous. It is as if Lawrence, aware of established authority's control of the printed word, needed to flaunt the freedom of his pen. The most striking example of Lawrence's bravado is found in a letter to J. B. Pinker of 31 May 1915:

> I hope you will like the book: also that it is not very improper. It did not seem to me very improper, as I went through it. But then I feel very incompetent to judge, on that point. . . .
> One other little thing: I want, on the fly leaf, in German characters, the inscription "Zu Else"—i.e. "[example in Lawrence's hand]." Put that in for me, will you. It is just "To Elsa." But it must be in Gothic letters. (*L* 2:349)

Although concerned that Pinker might find *The Rainbow* "improper" and therefore unprintable, Lawrence goes on to order a highly provocative dedication—an act comparable to waving a red flag before John Bull.[10]

Under the Defence of the Realm Act, private letters at home and from the front, business communications, cables, the press, and literary publications were all subject to inspection and censorship. In his biography of Lytton Strachey, Michael Holroyd has suggested that the prosecution of *The Rainbow* occurred "ostensibly on the grounds of obscenity but actually because of its denunciation of war."[11] His argument is founded upon a review of *The Rainbow* by James Douglas in *The Star*,

22 October 1915. Douglas's article is couched in terms comparable to the patriotic jingoism of Horatio Bottomley:

> Art is a public thing. It is a dweller in the clean homes and swept streets of life. It must conform to the ordered laws that govern human society. If it refuses to do so, it must pay the penalty. The sanitary inspector of literature must notify it and call for its isolation.
>
> The wind of war is sweeping over our life, and it is demolishing many of the noisome pestilences of peace. . . .
>
> Life is infinitely more precious than literature. It has got to go on climbing up and up, and if literature strives to drag it down to the nethermost deeps, then literature most be hacked off the limbs of life.[12]

The high irony of Douglas's indignation resides in the similarity of his opinion that war is "demolishing many of the noisome pestilences of peace" to Lawrence's comment to Arthur McLeod on 5 January 1915: "What do you mean by saying you'd go to war? No, the war is for those who are not needed for a new life" (LL 2:255). Although the emphases are different, both writers share a hope that England will be revitalized through the war's destruction.

Less vituperative, but more damaging, was Clement Shorter's review in *Sphere* (23 October 1915). Shorter disliked Lawrence's novel on account of the "Lesbianism" he spied in chapter 12. In his article, Shorter obliquely recommends "censorship" and "police prosecution." He closes by saying, "I can find no justification whatever for the perpetration of such a book."[13] Sir John Dickson, the prosecuting magistrate, took Shorter seriously and wondered why the publishers "did not take steps to suppress [*The Rainbow*] after the criticisms had appeared in the Press."[14]

The suppression of *The Rainbow* briefly became a Bloomsbury cause célèbre. This was partially due to Philip Morrell's questioning of the case in the Commons. Approached by Clive Bell and Lytton Strachey, J. C. Squire, writing as "Solomon Eagle" in the *New Statesman*, defended *The Rainbow* in terms that probably did more harm than good. Although Squire questions whether "censorship in this case was desirable," he goes on to hint that Lawrence might be "under the spell of German psychologists"—hardly an assessment that would calm a xenophobic court.[15]

Not every writer had to be silenced. Writers often published pieces of propaganda on their own accord. In his book *The Press in War-Time* (1920), Sir Edward Cook describes the press as the "*avant-couriers* of necessary policy."[16] Cook argues that the press must remain unfettered if it is to be an effective means of dispersal for propaganda. He emphasizes how extremely important the press was in maintaining the national patriotic fervor the government counted on during the war.[17] It is ironic that two of Lawrence's closest associates should have devoted themselves to advancing the cause of the government's control of language during the war. By 1915 Ford Madox Ford had changed his name and pro-German sentiments and begun work for C. F. G. Masterman, director of a secret propaganda bureau known as Wellington House.[18] John Middleton Murry was appointed chief censor in 1918, an honor of which he was understandably reluctant to inform Lawrence.[19]

A believer that "all good and evil comes from words" (*VWL* 1:274), Virginia Woolf was appalled by the power of the press to "form, express, and sustain [the] national will." In a letter to Duncan Grant of 15 November 1915 she notes the effect of war propaganda with horror:

> The revelation of what our compatriots feel about life is very distressing. One might have thought in peace time that they were harmless, if stupid: but now that they have been roused they seem full of the most violent and filthy passions. (*VWL* 2:71)

Woolf felt that the jingoism of the prowar press inflamed the public with irrational patriotic sentiment. Her dislike of the overtly patriotic atmosphere is apparent in another letter to Grant of 3 January 1915: "What hellish luck—to miss you—and all for the sake of a Queens Hall concert, where the patriotic sentiment was so revolting that I was nearly sick" (*VWL* 2:57).

The jingoism of the press annoyed not only Woolf but Lawrence as well. His particular *bête noire* was Horatio Bottomley, editor of the weekly *John Bull* and self-appointed friend of the people. Bottomley spoke out in favor of the war effort on his own initiative, or rather on his own behalf. One of his earliest biographers, and former sidekick, Henry Houston, claims that "H[oratio] B[ottomley] began his journalistic career with a propagandist motive, and throughout his association with the Press that motive remained dominant."[20] Houston goes on to point out that Bottomley "exploited his war boom so ably that he contrived to get himself looked upon as the popular exponent of the national spirit."[21] Lawrence, too, considered Bottomley as representative of the national spirit; the idea depressed him: "As for Horace Bottomley, a nation in a false system acting in a false spirit will quite rightly choose him" (*LL* 2:371). For Lawrence, Bottomley represented the falsity of "decomposing life" brought about by the war (*LL* 2:438). He regarded Bottomley as a very real threat and even considered the possibility of his becoming prime minister: "If we continue in our bad spirit, we shall have Horatio Bottomley for our Prime Minister before a year is out"(*LL* 2:379–80). No doubt Bottomley hoped that this would be the case. His immense power should not be ignored, nor should one make light of his oratorical skills. Bottomley's only rival as a speaker who could appeal to the masses was David Lloyd George.[22] The power he wielded by means of the editorship of the extremely popular *John Bull* and his very own "John Bull Exposure Bureau" must have intimidated many of his enemies.[23] He seems to have intimidated Lawrence successfully, for Lawrence did not publish his vitriolic attack against Bottomley in *Kangaroo* until 1923, one year after Horatio was safe in prison and serving a seven-year sentence.

Ironically, given his later efforts, Bottomley was caught completely off guard by Britain's declaration of war. The main article in *John Bull* of that notable week in August 1914 was entitled "To Hell with Serbia."[24] However, on 15 August 1914 *John Bull* made a swift about-face and appeared both with a new military cover and prowar content:

> look with calm confidence, and firm resolve, to the golden eventide—when the sound of battle shall be silenced, and with the women and children, we will foregather to talk of the victory—of our dear lost comrades—and the new-born world in which, at last, the Prince of Peace shall be King.[25]

It was his sentimental bombast and violent xenophobia that Bottomley's critics most disliked. However, they seem to have been few in number if we go by the number of people who crowded into the London Opera House on 14 September 1914. Five thousand people attended *"John Bull's* Great Patriotic Rally for Recruiting."[26] It was at this event that Bottomley first gave his famed "Prince of Peace" speech, one he was to deliver over and over again at paying lectures during the war:

> If the British Empire resolves to fight the battle cleanly, to look upon it as something more than an ordinary war, we shall one day realize that it has not been in vain, and we, the British Empire, as the chosen leaders of the world, shall travel along the road of human destiny and progress, at the end of which we shall see the patient figure of the Prince of Peace pointing to the Star of Bethlehem which leads us on to God.[27]

On 14 January 1915 Bottomley spoke at the Great War Rally at Albert Hall. The main theme of the evening, one of Bottomley's favorites, was the war as life-and-death struggle between the Anglo-Saxon race and the barbarous and base Teutonic horde. In fact, throughout the war Bottomley used his coined phrase "Germhun" to emphasize what he saw as the virulent nature of the enemy:

> For us and our Dominions this is a war of sentiment, a war for ideals. We are fighting all that is worst in the world—"the product of a debased civilization"; we are fighting the Germhun.[28]

On 14 March 1915 Bottomley's first article appeared in the *Sunday Pictorial,* an illustrated paper owned by Lord Northcliffe and his brother, Lord Rothermere, both of whom were jingoistic journalists in their own right. Bottomley received £150 pounds for each article that appeared in the *Sunday Pictorial.* He certainly gave his readers their money's worth of bombast and prejudice, as evidenced by this extract from an article devoted to the sinking of the *Lusitania:*

> And now comes the news of the *Lusitania* massacre. I want every German now in Britain to get away sharp—never mind how long he has been "naturalized." You cannot naturalize an unnatural freak—a human freak. *But you can exterminate it.*[29]

If D. H. Lawrence harbored a particular dislike for Horatio Bottomley, Virginia Woolf's irritation with the prowar press centered upon Lord Northcliffe. Her bitterness toward the prowar stance taken by the "Northcliffe papers" is evident throughout her diary. In an entry for 7 October 1918 she notes the German offer to begin peace negotiations and complains that "as the Times insists upon minimising it, not much exhilaration remains" (*D* 1:199). In the following entry, dated 12 October, Woolf records Lord Grey's first speech as president of the League of Nations Union. But again, her enthusiasm for a possible peace wanes in the light of Northcliffe's militarism:

> The Northcliffe papers do all they can to insist upon the indispensability & delight of war. They magnify our victories to make our mouths water for more; they shout with joy when the Germans sink the Irish mail; but they do also show some signs of apprehension that [Woodrow] Wilson's terms may be accepted. (*D* 1:200)

Woolf would have agreed with D. H. Lawrence that "Lord Northcliffe wants sinking to the bottom" (*LL* 2:357). Even those who did not side with the prowar preachings of the press were still overcome by the constant clamorings for victory. While Liberals such as Walter Runciman and Reginald McKenna pointed out that Great Britain was nearing economic collapse, Lloyd George used the press in order to raise "an enthusiastic response ... for 'the knock-out blow.'"[30] Both Woolf and Lawrence disliked the oratorical strategies of Lloyd George. In a letter to Lady Cecil of 25 October 1915, Woolf notes with pleasure that Leonard found Lloyd George's "appearance and views all very shocking" (*VWL* 2:69). Lawrence described Lloyd George as a "striving toad," "a clever little Welsh *rat*" (*LL* 3:46–8). Yet despite her cynical attitude toward jingoism, Woolf once fell victim to the orations of the prime minister. Before his call for his people's "prayers" and his assertion that "Britons must cling together," she felt sinisterly "whipped up" and manipulated by Lloyd George's rhetoric (*D* 1:127–28).

In spite or perhaps because of being writers, Woolf and Lawrence questioned the assumed benevolence of language and its efficacy in furthering human communication. In their works, and particularly their wartime writings, they question the altruism of linguistic acts. They portray language as simply another arena of conflict in which the self does battle with the threatening other.

Evidence of Woolf's and Lawrence's mutual questioning of language exists in their prewar fictions. For instance, in *The Voyage Out*, Woolf portrays the advance toward intimate knowledge of another as fraught with physical and verbal danger. As the steamer journeys up an Amazonian river, the country grows "wilder and wilder" until the trees and the undergrowth seem "to be strangling each other near the ground in a multitudinous wrestle" (VO, 327). The air is full of bestial screams. Words melt in the equatorial sun; there is no language but that of primordial, sexual desire, a language that in Woolf's novels signifies danger and violence. Conversation between Rachel and Terence becomes an interplay of repetitions, suggesting cries echoing throughout the jungle.

The difficulty of discourse is further portrayed in the character of Miss Allan. Her self-assigned task is hopelessly vast: she is determined to outline English literature, an ambition Woolf set herself as evidenced by her unfinished sketch, "Anon," and Miss La Trobe's play in Between the Acts. Working in her tidy room, Miss Allan reads and writes her way through English literary history, attempting to compress it into a single volume. Although her work is an attempt at communication, like all the characters in the novel she finds human discourse a threatening and potentially dangerous occupation. Her fear of intimacy, along with her suffragist's views, make her the prototype of Mary Datchet in Night and Day. Just as Miss Allan removes herself from any "human note" (VO, 211) through her academic endeavors, tepid suffragism, and undemonstrative kindness, Mary avoids physical and verbal intimacy by devoting herself to suffrage propaganda. Woolf's dislike of pamphleteers can be seen in Night and Day, a novel composed amid the wartime bombast of the jingoistic press.

Within the greater struggle against "the enemy" of suffrage is Mary's battle against herself. Like Miss Allan, who lies buried amid her history of English literature, Mary renounces emotional life. In abjuring human attachments she negates an essential part of herself. Her renunciation is a form of self-cruelty. Her decision to relinquish intimacy with Ralph Denham is described as a brutal hacking off of some vital part of the body, an image that presages the mutilated mackerel in the last section of To the Lighthouse. Politics becomes a shield against emotional vulnerability. To avoid thinking of her love for Ralph, Mary calls out "'Don't you think Mr. Asquith deserves to be hanged?'" (ND, 133). Both Miss Allan and Mary Datchet abandon emotional contact for the world of political discussion, a form of pseudocommunication. Woolf suggests that political movements and organizations are no substitute for human relationships, that they further increase the distance between individuals and lead, ultimately, to misunderstandings. Just as Rachel wishes to strike Miss Allan following her frustrated attempts at conversation, so Ralph Denham mistakes the verbal hints of Mary's affection and thereby causes her injury.

Verbal assaults and misunderstandings are prominent in many of Lawrence's prewar fictions, and, as in Woolf's fictions, these linguistic battles focus on sexual attacks and gender differences. For example, in "The Old Adam" (1911) the "battle of words" between Mr. Thomas and Edward Severn quickly leads to an actual physical scuffle (*LAH*, 83). In "New Eve and Old Adam" (1913), the chaffing between husband and wife quickly turns into an all-out argument in which the words *hate* and *love* are interchangeable. Duplicitous utterances inspire the battles of Walter and Gertrude Morel in *Sons and Lovers*. Morel lies about his finances, his property, and his drinking. His falsehoods set off the fearful, bloody battle of his married life. His insecurity before language—he can barely read or write—is aggravated by Gertrude's quick verbal wit. Throughout *Sons and Lovers*, arguments between husband and wife follow the pattern of first verbal accusation, then denial, followed by physical violence. Like his mother, Paul Morel is apparently master of the spoken and printed word. Indeed, he relies upon language to do his courting for him. Mrs. Morel drily observes that "his and Miriam's affair was like a fire fed on books—if there were no more volumes it would die out" (*SL*, 360). Language as a substitute for sexual relations is evident in Paul's reluctance to read aloud John 16:21. Aware of Paul's hesitation, Miriam takes the deletion as an announcement of gathering sexual tension: "She shrank when the well-known words did not follow. . . . she felt there was really something hostile between them, something of which they were ashamed" (*SL*, 268). Unable to express or act upon his sexual desire, Paul hurls a pencil, implement of language and phallic substitute, into Miriam's face. As in *The Voyage Out*, dysfunction of language in *Sons and Lovers* accompanies sexual violence. Paul cannot express his desire and, in frustration, his passion turns to cruelty. His attempts to communicate his desire for Miriam physically and verbally fail. His physical and verbal ineptitude serves only to alienate Miriam; he speaks "another language than hers. How it hurt her and deadened her very perceptions" (*SL*, 201). A voracious reader and amateur critic, Paul only injures others with his efforts at verbal communication.

Affiliations between sexual dominance and the authority of language are evident in both "The Prussian Officer" and "The

Thorn in the Flesh." Incapable of explaining the presence of the pencil behind his ear, and powerless to answer his captain's commands, Schöner eventually strangles the figure of corporeal and verbal power. However, the captain's death does not afford Schöner the power of speech. He possesses "no language with which to speak" to a passing woman. He shrinks from human utterance: "She would make a noise of words that would confuse him, and her eyes would look at him without seeing him" (*PO*, 19). In the end, Schöner is destroyed by language. Betrayed by the pencil that he uses merely to copy verses for his sweetheart, unable to respond to the commands of his captain or to cry for water, Schöner dies, his "open, black mouth" eloquent testimony to the malevolent nature of language in Lawrence's story (*PO*, 20).

Soldier Bachmann in "The Thorn in the Flesh" fares little better. He, too, experiences the poverty of language in his inability to find words with which to write his mother. He can neither manipulate language nor cope with words addressed to him. The sergeant's commands are obscure; they function as verbal missiles, rousing Bachmann to physical violence:

> The breath of the barking words was on his nose and mouth. . . .
> He raised his arm, involuntarily, in self-defence. . . . he felt his fore-
> arm hit the face of the officer a brutal blow. The latter staggered,
> swerved back, and with a curious cry, reeled backwards over the
> ramparts, his hands clutching the air. (*PO*, 26)

The sergeant's rank and authority are embodied in his words. His voice "lacerates" Bachmann; the breath of the words brushes against his face.

The difficulties associated with language during the First World War, the "prostituted" use of words by governments and the popular press, are reflected in Woolf's and Lawrence's writings of the period. In the stories that comprise *England, My England*, the prominence afforded the written and spoken word suggests wartime concerns with language. Furthermore, the difficulties engendered by linguistic acts point to the disintegration of communication between individuals. *Women in Love* consists of a series of conflicts in which language is the main weapon. In *Night and Day*, Woolf successfully portrays the collapse of language. For both Woolf and Lawrence, the word is an aggressive agent, a blade pointed toward the listener. In the meeting of self and other, language is the primary weapon and speech is a hostile activity.

The title story of *England, My England* epitomizes Lawrence's wartime preoccupation with language and the problems of authority. Winifred and Egbert do battle within the security bought them by her father's money. The tyranny of the past—represented by the hideous mass of coiled snakes at the bottom of the garden at Crockham—provides the setting in which Winifred and Egbert act out their hostilities. The site where the couple make their first home is "dark, like a lair where strong beasts had lurked and mated"; the destructiveness of their union has its correlative in the past (*EME*, 8). The world of "England, My England" is terrorized by the insidious presence of the "curious coiled brownish pile" of snakes that lurks at the end of Crockham's garden:

> One day Winifred hears the strangest scream from the flower-bed under the low window of the living room: ah, the strangest scream, like the very soul of the dark past crying aloud. She ran out, and saw a long brown snake on the flower-bed, and in its flat mouth the one hind leg of a frog was striving to escape, and screaming its strange, tiny, bellowing scream. . . . She gave a cry, and it released the frog and slid angrily away. (*EME*, 8)

This primeval relationship between hunter and prey suggests the destructive character of Winifred and Egbert's marriage. The image of snake and frog was used by Lawrence in "The Crown" to symbolize "the world of corruption" in which "one beast shall devour another" (*C*, 298). In "The Crown," Lawrence repeats a scene similar to the one in "England, My England." The disturbing image of a frog emitting "a loud terrible scream," a creature we do not normally consider capable of such a sound, is contrasted to the complete breakdown in communication between Winifred and Egbert. Unlike the frog's spontaneous, if surreal, "tiny bellowing scream," the couple are unable to express themselves. A similar perversion of communication exists in Virginia Woolf's *Between the Acts*. The hostilities between Isa and Giles Oliver are represented by the struggle between hunter and prey. When Giles finds a snake "choked with a toad in its mouth," he stamps out the "monstrous inversion."[31] His violent act reflects the storms of war gathering across the Channel and his own battles with his wife, who is verbally strangled and unable to express her innermost thoughts. Giles's unuttered animosity and frustrated desire find violent expression in his destruction of a choked snake.

Giles's act is analogous to the forces of destruction that haunt the world of *Between the Acts*. Egbert's battle, like that of Giles, is fought and lost long before he ever reaches the trenches of France. Hypnotized by past violence, Egbert nullifies the present. He is responsible for his daughter's injury, an event that gives the deathblow to his already disintegrating marriage. In a spontaneous urge to self-destruct, Egbert joins the army. His passivity is apparent even in this action since his decision depends upon the authority of Godfrey Marshall. Egbert's refusal to choose is reflected in his unthinking response to spoken commands. In his relationship with Winifred words are the chosen weapons. At the front Egbert is forced to use the actual machinery of war through the authority of the word: "He moved into a lightning-like mechanical response at the sharp cry from the officer overhead" (*EME*, 31). Sent by a word to his death, Egbert merely follows orders. His death is a negative act inspired by his disownment of self, self-negation, and subservience to established authority.

In the 1925 essay "Him with His Tail in His Mouth," Lawrence uses the image of the self-devouring snake to represent humanity's destructive dependence on the past and desire for obliteration.[32] In praying for Joyce's salvation Winifred uses her sexuality as a sacrificial offering. A victim awaiting immolation, Winifred submits to Egbert's physical desire: "Winifred waited for him in a little passion of duty and sacrifice, willing to serve the soldier, if not the man" (*EME*, 29–30). Winifred participates in the war effort by offering her body to a man she no longer loves: "Winifred now had a new duty towards him: the duty of a wife towards a husband who is himself performing his duty towards the world" (*EME*, 29). Duty, subservience, self-destruction: both Egbert and Winifred are nullified by their submission to authority past and present. Lawrence suggests that the couple mutually prostitute themselves before the power of *pater* and *patria*.

The juxtaposition of the battle between men and women and those of the World War provides the central structure and theme of "Tickets, Please." The general death wish Lawrence perceived in England during wartime is epitomized by the wild, careening trams filled with sensation seekers who risk death in return for diversion. Unwanted at the front, the "cripples and hunchbacks" who drive the trams create their own sense of danger (*EME*, 34). Lawrence's story illustrates Eric Reed's assertion that one of the results of war on the home front was the celebration of misrule.[33] Reed's equation of war and festival is revealed in the careening journeys of Lawrence's trams and the transformation of women from passive to active service. The young women are "fearless young hussies." In "their ugly blue uniform, skirts up to their knees, shapeless old peaked caps," they have "the *sang-froid* of an old non-commissioned officer" (*EME*, 35). These women warriors "pounce on the youths who try to evade their ticket-machine"; they are "peremptory, suspicious, and ready to hit first" (*EME*, 35). The female figures bear obvious similarities to male soldiers. They are comfortable with obscenities, they wear uniforms, and have a battle-weary air. Their enemy is not the German but man in general as personified by John Thomas Raynor. The significance of Raynor's Christian name—we are told that the women sometimes call him, "in malice, Coddy" (*EME*, 36)—cannot be neglected, particularly in light of the later *John Thomas and Lady Jane* (1928), the second version of the Lady Chatterley story.

The good-humored chaff that Raynor indulges in with Annie is a means of expressing the "subtle antagonism" they bear one another (*EME*, 37). Raynor's rejection of Annie for "pastures new" inflames her into all-out battle (*EME*, 39). The organized revenge of John Thomas's former conquests among the tram girls begins with a little gentle joking but grows more intense until, finally, the first blow is struck: "suddenly, with a movement like a swift cat, Annie went forward and fetched him a box on the side of the head that sent his cap flying and himself staggering" (*EME*, 42). The "darkness and lawlessness of wartime" is enacted in the savage attack by the women on John Thomas (*EME*, 40). Within their depot waiting room, the women create their own "Thermopylae" (*EME*, 35):

> Their blood was now thoroughly up. He was their sport now. . . . Strange, wild creatures, they hung on to him and rushed at him to bear him down. His tunic was torn right up the back, Nora had hold at the back of his collar, and was actually strangling him. . . . He struggled in a wild frenzy of fury and terror, almost mad terror. . . .
>
> He lay at last quite still, with face averted, as an animal lies when it is defeated and at the mercy of the captor. (*EME*, 43)

Hunter turned prey, John Thomas suffers the attacks of the women he once pursued. Garbed in her uniform and tasting victory, Annie demands that he "choose" (*EME*, 42) one of them and by doing so become an "all-round individual" rather than a shadowy "nocturnal presence" (*EME*, 39). However, none of the women wants to choose or be chosen by John Thomas. The physical loser, John Thomas is allowed to leave, battered but free.

John Thomas's cunning silence before Annie's demands that he choose suggests Joe's reluctance to speak in "Monkey Nuts." Throughout this story Lawrence explores the nature of male/female communication. Unable to express her desire for Joe, Miss Stokes sends a telegram. As in "New Eve and Old Adam" the signature on the telegram is an essential part of the story. Identified only by the initials "M. S.," when asked what they signify after a week of silence, Stokes replies, "Monkey nuts" (*EME*, 69). The initials and her quick witticism come back to haunt her. No longer "Miss Stokes," she now becomes "nuts" and "Major" (*EME*, 76). Lawrence's implication is that Stokes is suffering from delusions of grandeur, the result of rejecting traditional female roles. She is a wartime land girl, wears a uniform, and feels no compunction about expressing her desire both verbally and physically. Stokes epitomizes the type of female that Lawrence disparages in his postwar writings.[34] His antagonism toward working women is evident in both "Monkey Nuts" and "Tickets, Please." Lawrence's wartime short stories exemplify Gilbert and Gubar's point that "a major campaign in the battle of the sexes is the conflict over language and, specifically, over competing male and female claims to linguistic primacy."[35] In Lawrence's stories, the word serves as prime battle site between the sexes. To paraphrase Samuel Hynes, the rhetoric of sexual discourse is the rhetoric of war.[36]

In "Monkey Nuts," speech becomes a form of attack. The truthfulness of utterances is questioned. Miss Stokes doubts Albert's words. She lies about having seen Joe and Albert at the circus. During the sexual bantering between Stokes and Albert, Joe maintains an ominous silence. Alfred tries to encourage him by offering him a verbal weapon: "'What's got him? Is it Monkey nuts that don't suit him, do you think?'" (*EME*, 72). The quick repartee engaged in by Albert and Stokes is in strong contrast to Joe's almost pathological disinclination to speak. When he does make an utterance it emerges as a "bark" (*EME*, 73). He can speak to Stokes only through Albert.

He turns his words over to another and grants Albert the authority to talk for him. Albert, discomfited by Stokes's question about Joe's absence, also finds words difficult and turns to music to make his attack:

> Miss Stokes did not speak: she only stared with large, icy blue eyes at him. He became self-conscious, lifted up his chin, walked with his nose in the air, and whistled at random. So they went down the quiet, deserted grey lane. He was whistling the air: "I'm Gilbert, the filbert, the colonel of the nuts."[37]

Militarism, bantering, and malicious attack are combined in Albert's tune. The derision inherent in his speech leaves Stokes hurt, but Albert, who only sees her as an available woman, is puzzled by her tears. Joe, still unwilling to speak, allows his friend to express his emotions and fight his verbal battles. When Miss Stokes comes "no more with the hay," Joe "felt more relieved even than he had felt when he heard the firing cease, after the news had come that the armistice was signed" (*EME*, 76). The implication of "Monkey Nuts" is clear: "a sexual revolution is more threatening to men than conventional war can ever be."[38] For Lawrence, the battle between the sexes is more terrifying than the battle between nations.

The conflict between man and woman as fought on the front of language is the central theme of "Wintry Peacock." The story focuses on the intricate patterns of deceit between Alfred Goyte, his wife, the narrator, and the Belgian woman, Élise. Unable to read French, Mrs. Goyte submits a letter addressed to her husband to the narrator for translation. She tries to hide her unscrupulous act behind flirtatious glances, although the narrator notes her deception: "her gloomy black eyes softened caressively to me for a moment, with that momentary humility which makes man lord of the earth" (*EME*, 77). The flattery practiced by Mrs. Goyte has its parallel in the "trivial, facile French phrases" of Élise's letter (*EME*, 78). Lawrence underscores Élise's duplicity by comparing her "effusions" to "a bit of torn newspaper": "Nothing more trite and vulgar in the world, than such a love-letter—no newspaper more obvious" (*EME*, 78–79). Mrs. Goyte's duplicity is practiced upon her in turn by the narrator. In "reading" Élise's letter, he censors it and substitutes his own version of a text that he regards as deceitful. When the narrator assures Mrs. Goyte that the baby referred to in the letter is not her husband's, she repudiates his "translation" of the events: "'Don't you believe it,' she cried. 'It's a blind. You mark, it's her own right enough—and his'" (*EME*, 81). But the narrator continues to mistranslate what he later condemns by his laughter as a fine joke. His version of the letter provides a parody of the worst of wartime sentiment as found, for example, in *John Bull:*

> "If it had not been for you we should not be alive now, to grieve and to rejoice in this life, that is so hard for us. . . . The little Alfred is a great comfort to me. I hold him to my breast and think of the big, good Alfred, and I weep to think that those times of suffering were perhaps the times of a great happiness that is gone for ever." (*EME*, 82)

Throughout the translation of the letter Mrs. Goyte engages in chaff; the object of derision is the absent husband. At one point she sympathizes with the deceived Belgian girl: "'isn't it a shame to take a poor girl in like that'" (*EME*, 82).

Mrs. Goyte, too, is taken in. She protests that throughout Alfred's absence she has been "writing him such loving letters" (*EME*, 83). Lawrence hints that her letters may have lacked veracity like those of her rival. Abandoned by her husband for the army, left in the care of her parents-in-law, Mrs. Goyte takes the peacock, Joey, as the object of her affection. As in *The White Peacock* the bird is symbolic of vanity and duplicity. The disintegrating relations between husband and wife are manifested in Mrs. Goyte's bizarre cooing:

> She put her face forward, and the bird rolled his neck, almost touching her face with his beak, as if kissing her.
> "He loves you," I said. . . .
> "Yes," she said, "he loves me, Joey does,"—then, to the bird— "and I love Joey, don't I. I *do* love Joey."(*EME*, 80)

Mrs. Goyte's affection for the bird indicates the poverty of her marriage. The human characters in the story are no less pathetic and bedraggled than the helpless bird caught in the snow. Imprisoned by their mutual dislike and chilled love, Mr. and Mrs. Goyte, Élise, the narrator, and the bird engage in "a flapping and a struggle" to outwit one another (*EME*, 84).

The vindictiveness of the characters in "Wintry Peacock" is expressed through their treatment of one another's verbal artifacts. As Mrs. Goyte laughs over Élise's letter, she fears her own missives have been a source of mirth. The narrator reassures her: "'Nay,' said I. 'He'd burn your letters for fear they'd give him away'" (*EME*, 83). Although there is a "black look" on Mrs. Goyte's face at the suggestion, it is she who burns Élise's letter before her husband can look at it. At the conclusion of the story all utterance is suspect:

> "What was there in [the letter]?" [Alfred] asked.
> "Why?" I said. "Don't you know?"
> "She makes out she's burnt it," he said. . . .
> "Well," I answered slowly, "she doesn't know herself what was in it." (*EME*, 89)

The keenness of the deception brings a smile to the faces of the two men. Duplicity operates on several levels: the Belgian girl "says" that her baby is Alfred's; Mrs. Goyte is taken in by the deception of the narrator "as much as she took anything else" (*EME*, 89). Goyte regards the letter as "a plant" and insinuates that Élise is lying about her child's paternity. When asked what Élise said *"exactly,"* the narrator repeats the phrases of the letter *"as well as I could"* (*EME*, 105; emphasis added). The duplicity of language and all interlocutors is amply demonstrated. Alfred Goyte's desire for exactitude and truthfulness provides an ironic contrast to his subsequent dismissal of Élise's honesty:

> "They know how to pitch you out a letter, those Belgian lasses."
> "Practice," said I.
> "They get plenty," he said. (*EME*, 90)

The prevarications interlock like a set of Chinese boxes. The entire concept of language is questioned. Although the characters depend upon language to gather information about one another, the word is shown to be false. In protecting the falsity of language, the narrator and Alfred Goyte become comrades-in-arms. With a final shout of triumph, Goyte decides to "'do that blasted Joey in'" (*EME*, 91). The narrator shares Goyte's amusement: "I ran down the hill, shouting also with laughter" (*EME*, 91). The triumph of the two men over two similarly dishonest females underscores both the equivocal nature of language and the ongoing struggle between men and women as portrayed in Lawrence's fictions.

The significance of language in Lawrence's wartime stories is nowhere more evident than in "The Blind Man" and "The Thimble." Maurice Pervin is left blind after being hit by a piece of shrapnel. His injury results in a physical disfigurement that marks him as "pitiable" to others and "horrible" to himself (*EME*, 61). Pervin's scar and blindness represent "the final reduction under the touch of death" (*C*, 475).

Like Hepburn's speech impediment in "The Thimble," Pervin's blindness is indicative of what Eric Reed has described as the problematic nature of language for soldiers returning home from the front. Reed translates F. Schauwecker's remark from *Im Todersrachen* (1921) that "whoever comes home from the front is silent. He steps from a region ruled by the deed into a region where the word is everything."[39] The returning soldier's puzzlement over the word is comparably discussed by Robert Graves in *Good-bye to All That* (1929):

> England was strange to us returned soldiers. We could not understand the war-madness that ran wild everywhere, looking for a pseudo-military outlet. The civilians talked a foreign language; and it was newspaper language.[40]

Civilian bellicosity is expressed in language that is at once Graves's own as well as foreign to him. In a *Listener* interview of 1971, Graves recalled that his experiences at the front could not be transmitted through language:

> *Graves.* . . . the funny thing was you went home on leave for six weeks, or six days, but the idea of being and staying at home was awful because you were with people who didn't understand what this was all about.
> *Smith.* Didn't you want to tell them?
> *Graves.* You couldn't: you can't communicate noise. Noise never stopped for one moment—ever.[41]

For both Graves and Schauwecker, the battles of the First World War were the dividing point between a world where words are a viable form of communication and a land where language failed its expressive function. Many of the soldiers' songs collected by John Brophy and Eric Partridge in *The Long Trail* are nonsensical. The rhythm of the tunes and words provided a means of measuring off long and seemingly endless marches. Other songs, such as "I Don't Want to Be a Soldier" and "Far, Far From Ypres I Want to Be," cloak the soldiers' desire for peace in satire, thereby providing a bulwark against defeat and disappointment.[42] The glossary of soldiers' slang provided by Brophy and Partridge serves to underscore the differences in the use of language at the front compared to that at home.

Throughout "The Blind Man," acts of language are consistently depicted as problematic. The Pervins are a literary couple. Isabel reviews "books for a Scottish newspaper." They talk, sing, and read together "in a wonderful and unspeakable intimacy" (*EME*, 46). Despite his blindness, Pervin can "still discuss everything" on the farm with the hired man, Wernham (*EME*, 46). But the Pervins avoid unnecessary contact with the flimsiness of language. Their mutual, unspoken knowledge is favorably contrasted to the meaningless utterances of others:

> after their dark, great year of blindness and solitude and unspeakable nearness, other people seemed to them both shallow, prattling, rather impertinent. Shallow prattle seemed presumptuous. (*EME*, 47)

The "shallow prattle" that the Pervins find so discomfiting is personified by Bertie Reid. Immediately upon his arrival Reid introduces to the Pervin household the prattle that the couple had formerly tried to avoid:

> "You will be glad when your child comes now, Isabel," [Reid] said. . . .
> "Yes, I shall be glad," she answered. "It begins to seem long. Yes, I shall be very glad. So will you, Maurice, won't you?" she added.
> "Yes, I shall," replied her husband.
> "We are both looking forward so much to having it," she said.
> "Yes, of course," said Bertie. (*EME*, 57)

Reid is an intellectual who rejects the physical side of his nature, and his inquiry is inspired by politeness. A bachelor, "he could not marry, could not approach women physically" (*EME*, 58). Lawrence describes Reid as suffering from an "incurable weakness, which made him unable ever to enter into close contact of any sort" (*EME*, 58). Reid ensures his distance from others by barricading himself within legal and literary language.

Lawrence emphasizes the congruent paucity of speech and sight throughout his story. Maurice's blindness makes him dependent on Isabel to transform the printed word into sound.

He distinguishes himself by his lack of words, a characteristic that oppresses the literary Isabel:

> Sometimes . . . a sense of burden overcame Isabel, a weariness, a terrible *ennui*, in that silent house. . . . Then she felt she would go mad, for she could not bear it. (*EME*, 46)

On Reid's arrival, she cannot see him. Their conversation lacks emotional significance. Denied sight and meaningful speech, Isabel and Bertie demonstrate the essential poverty of the "visual consciousness" (*EME*, 54).

In "The Blind Man," the printed word, speech, and sight are depicted as insufficient means toward knowledge. Lawrence emphasizes the "blood-prescience" of touch, the "sheer immediacy of blood-contact" that Pervin possesses at the ends of his fingertips (*EME*, 54). This form of cognition frightens Isabel and Bertie, themselves so dependent on the printed and uttered word. Pervin's touch has "an almost hypnotizing effect" on Isabel (*EME*, 54). Bertie stands "as if hypnotized" beneath Pervin's hand (*EME*, 62). Although the war has destroyed Maurice Pervin's sight and left him disinclined to speak, it has accorded him discernment more reliable than any linguistic act.

"The Thimble" further portrays the deficiency of language during the war. Words are an inadequate form of communication for the Hepburns. Essentially strangers to one another, the problem of revealing themselves is compounded by Hepburn's war injury. He speaks with a "mumbling muffled voice" (*EME*, 196). Hepburn *is* his voice, a surreal, ghostly presence known only through distorted sound: "She had not yet looked at his face. The muffled voice terrified her so much. It mumbled rather mouthlessly" (*EME*, 195). Hepburn's smashed jaw is indicative of what Lawrence saw as the difficulties of communication between men and women during the war. Newborn, the Hepburns are resurrected from the death of the war years. Like Maurice Pervin, they must rely on touch to establish a connection:

> "Am I going to love you?"
> Again he stretched forward and touched her hand, with the tips of his fingers. And the touch lay still, completed there. (*EME*, 200)

Language is incomplete and open to misunderstanding. Hepburn's jaw is smashed, "the bottom teeth all gone" (*EME*, 196).

His mouth is "not a mouth," his speech "a disfigurement of speech" (*EME*, 196). The words he speaks bear no meaning for his wife: "She could not understand" (*EME*, 196). The Hepburns reject the word as symbolic of their false, prewar meeting.

The thimble referred to in the title also indicates the falsity of their prewar existence. On the thimble is an enigmatic inscription:

> There was an engraved monogram, an Earl's, and then Z, Z, and a date, 14 Oct., 1801. She was very pleased, trembling with the thought of the old romance. What did Z. stand for? She thought of her acquaintances, and could only think of Zouche. But he was not an Earl. Who would give the gift of a gold thimble set with jewels, in the year 1801? Perhaps it was a man come home from the wars: there were wars then. (*EME*, 195)

The letter *Z* signifies nothing to Mrs. Hepburn; it suggests no one in particular and, standing alone, it has no literal meaning. However, it is the last letter in the alphabet and as such it connotes the limitations of the spoken and written word. When Hepburn throws the thimble out the window he rejects the past, with its burden of history, and discards language. In "The Blind Man" and "The Thimble," Lawrence indicates that from now on the power of communication will lie in the sensation of touch, the correspondence of body to body. The importance Lawrence attaches to physical caresses in such stories as "You Touched Me" (1919) and "Samson and Delilah" (1916) would be further developed in *Fantasia of the Unconscious*, particularly in chapter 5, entitled "The Five Senses."[43]

In "The Mortal Coil" (1916), language becomes a means of self-identification. The story opens with Marta fingering the seal of her lover, Fritz Friedeburg (*EME*, 170). In touching Friedeburg's signature, Marta acts as if to know the man. Fritz's seal *is* him, his representative. Marta then attempts to delineate herself through her own signature:

> She went to the writing-table, and on a sheet of paper began writing her name in stiff Gothic characters, time after time:
> Marta Hohenest
> Marta Hohenest
> Marta Hohenest (*EME*, 172)

Identified in the story as Friedeburg's mistress, Marta lives and dies in his room. She seems to have no address of her own. Thus, her signature is an act of self-assertion. Following her death, the only things that remain of Marta are her name and her cast-off clothes.

Friedeburg, too, strives toward self-knowledge. Like Marta, he caresses the physical form of his identity, his seal:

> He saw the paper, where her name was repeatedly written. She must find great satisfaction in her own name, he thought vaguely. Then he picked up the seal and kept twisting it round his fingers, doing some little trick. And continually the seal fell on to the table with a sudden rattle that made Marta stiffen cruelly. He was quite oblivious of her. (*EME*, 173)

Marta and Fritz's fascination with their signatures indicates a self-absorption that fails to achieve self-knowledge and that is ultimately self-destructive. Her attempts to define Fritz are unsuccessful. He is deep in "self-mistrust," although he pretends to be "the free indomitable self-sufficient being" (*EME*, 175). He is characterized by his seal and the clothes he wears. Without his uniform he is nothing, just as at the end of the story there is nothing left of Marta but her "lustrous, pure-red dress" and "crimson silk garters" (*EME*, 189).

Incapable of circumscribing themselves, Marta and Fritz find communication with one another difficult. He regards her demand that he find self-significance as "raving" (*EME*, 178). Marta has "no more to say," and the argument disintegrates into a sexual power play. As Fritz claims "'I love *you*,'" he inflicts pain (*EME*, 181). There is a contrast between his words and his expression of "exultancy" and "power" (*EME*, 181). Words are no longer capable of bearing deceit; they are simply "meaningless" (*EME*, 182).

Throughout the stories that comprise *England, My England*, Lawrence depicts characters battling for dominance through the medium of language. In *Women in Love*, words are a means to self-identity, the ongoing struggle to communicate with the other yet be separate from it. Lawrence portrays the inevitable opposition of self to other as happening through dialogue. Birkin's arguments with Ursula are quests for definition. Dialogic battles between characters are frequently accompanied by actual physical violence.

Lawrence composed *Women in Love* while the conflicts of the First World War were being fought on the fields of Flanders and France. The deadly battles of the western front find expression in the verbal duels between his characters. H. M. Daleski has argued that in *Women in Love* the public is private; the war's encounters are acted out in the clashes between Birkin and Ursula, Gerald and Gudrun.[44] In a foreword intended to accompany the American edition, Lawrence suggests that *Women in Love*

> is a novel which took its final shape in the midst of the period of war, though it does not concern the war itself. I should wish the time to remain unfixed, so that the bitterness of the war may be taken for granted in the characters.[45]

Lawrence's account of the war's role in his novel is equivocal. The novel takes "its final shape in the midst" of war, yet "it does not concern the war itself." The time of the novel is "unfixed" only so that the "bitterness of the war may be taken for granted." His hints of the war's ominous presence in *Women in Love* read like a sphinx's riddle. In directing his reader to remember the war, he is able to focus the international conflict into battles between individuals. The verbal shells hurled by the characters across the no-man's-land of mutual distrust, dislike, and misunderstanding are analogous to the bombardments that occurred in France while he was writing his novel. As the offensives of the Somme raged with tragic effect during July 1916, Lawrence revised and typed the penultimate draft of *Women in Love*. For Lawrence, as for Lecercle, "words have literal violence"; in *Women in Love*, words whizz like metaphorical shells through the battlefield of discourse.[46]

In his foreword, Lawrence points to the dialectic that provides the essential structure and oscillating rhythm of his novel:

> In point of style, fault is often found with the continual, slightly modified repetition. The only answer is that it is natural to the author: and that every natural crisis in emotion or passion or understanding comes from this pulsing, frictional to-and-fro, which works up to culmination.[47]

H. M. Daleski has powerfully argued that "to establish a connection between the war and *Women in Love* helps to explain the structure of the novel. . . . what appears to be the dual motion of the book."[48] Lawrence's defense of his prose style points to the structure of conflict in *Women in Love*. Assertion, denunciation, reassertion—these are the attacks and counter-attacks that inform the novel.

In chapter 8, Lawrence describes the polite conversation of a summer's day at Hermione Roddice's country home in terms that bring to mind the armed conflict across the Channel:

> The talk went on like a rattle of small artillery . . . with a sententiousness that was only emphasised by the continual crackling of a witticism, the continual spatter of verbal jest. (*WL*, 84)

The entire chapter is composed of "verbal sallies" (*WL*, 84). Gerald, always eager for an argument, prepares himself for "action" (*WL*, 85). Throughout the chapter, Lawrence emphasizes the spiritual and verbal distances between his characters. Although attracted to one another, a "silence" exists between Birkin and Gerald, "a strange tension of hostility. They always kept a gap, a distance between them" (*WL*, 98). Lawrence's figures are like chessmen, restrained by the formal structure of the game, a game that he describes in terms reminiscent of his condemnation of the war in "The Crown":

> how known it all was, like a game with the figures set out . . . the same now as they were hundreds of years ago, the same figures moving round in one of the innumerable permutations that make up the game. But the game is known, its going on is like madness, it is so exhausted. (*WL*, 99)

His incantatory prose imitates the repetition that he censures in modern society. The strident reiterations of *Women in Love* are nowhere more apparent than in the discussion of an "American edition" of Turgenev's *Fathers and Sons* (1862). The violence of discourse, the futility of language, and the lust for cruelty are evident in the furor caused by a mistranslation:

> "There is a most beautiful thing in my book," suddenly piped the little Italian woman. "It says the man came to the door and threw his eyes down the street."
> There was a general laugh in the company. . . .
> "See!" said the contessa.
> "Bazarov came to the door and threw his eyes hurriedly down the street," [Miss Bradley] read.
> Again, there was a loud laugh, the most startling of which was the Baronet's, which rattled out like a clatter of falling stones. . . .

"An old American edition," said Birkin.

"Ha! Of course—translated from the French," said Alexander. . . .'Bazarov ouvra la porte et jeta les yeux dans la rue.' . . ."

"I wonder what the 'hurriedly' was," said Ursula.

They all began to guess. (*WL*, 86–87)

The Baronet's laughing "clatter of falling stones" recalls the "rattle of small artillery" that characterizes polite conversation at Breadalby. Lawrence points to the poverty of language both in the English mistranslation of the French idiom as well as in the inanity of an afternoon spent puzzling over what "hurriedly" was in an unavailable French translation of an even more inaccessible Russian original. The cruelty inherent in language and its failure as a mode of communication evident in the above passage culminate in Hermione's attack on Birkin. Reading becomes an act of hostility; Birkin takes up a "large volume" in order to ignore her. The tension between them results in Hermione's attacking Birkin with a "blue, beautiful ball of lapis lazuli that stood on her desk for a paperweight" (*WL*, 105). Birkin finds refuge within the cover of words:

> Hurriedly, with a burrowing motion, he covered his head under the thick volume of Thucydides, and the blow came down, almost breaking his neck, and shattering his heart. (*WL*, 105)

Ironically, Birkin shelters himself from the blow beneath a volume of Thucydides' history of the Pelopennesian Wars.

The languid play on words engaged in by the visitors of Breadalby is nothing compared to the big guns of Rupert Birkin's verbal sallies. His orations are attempts to define himself in opposition as well as in relation to an other. Hermione hits Birkin directly after he proclaims his otherness from her, a reaction to her argument for equality of spirit. The battle of the self to achieve an independence of identity from the other is at the center of Lawrence's novel.[49] This unending struggle between self and other can be seen in "The Prussian Officer" and "The Thorn in the Flesh." Lawrence himself points to the conflicts for self-identity in his two stories. In a letter to Edward Garnett of 13 October 1914, he suggests a title for what was later to become *The Prussian Officer and Other Stories:* "Shall they be called 'The Fighting Line'. After all, this is the real fighting line, not where soldiers pull triggers" (*L* 2:221). He indicates that the essential battle is fought between self and other, a struggle from which international conflicts arise. The conflict between nations as reflecting the struggle between individuals is a theme that recurs in *England, My England, Women in Love,* "The Crown," and "The Study of Thomas Hardy" (1914).

In "The Crown," Lawrence dwells at length upon what he perceived to be the dueling opposites necessary for equilibrium. The fight between lion and unicorn, self and other, is inescapable: "Is not the unicorn necessary to the very existence of the lion, is not each opposite kept in stable equilibrium by the opposite of the other?" (*C*, 253). The constant fight is the "*raison d'être* of our history" (*C*, 254). Without the struggle between opposites there is "a void, a hollow ache, a want" (*C*, 254). History, indeed time itself, is composed of this eternal struggle. Denied conflict, humanity will "leap back into the past, into a known eternity," rather than creating the present in its fight for definition (*C*, 260). Paradoxically, Lawrence believed that the First World War resulted from the breakdown of this warring duality. He thought his battling opposites were engaged in creative struggle, a battle distinct from the mechanical conflict of Germany and England to retain their national status quo:

> So we have gone to war. For a hundred years we have been given over to the slowly advancing progress of reduction, analysis, breaking-down, dissolution. . . . There remains only the last experience, the same to all men, and to all women, the experience of the final reduction under the touch of death. (*C*, 475)

For Lawrence, the First World War is an act of nostalgia, a looking back to what has been rather than an attempt to make something new. Like Woolf, who described the war as an "abyss" (*D* 2:73), he terms it a "void," a "bottomless pit" (*C*, 254). He perceives the war as a "frenzy of blind things dashing themselves and each other to pieces" (*C*, 259). Woolf uses a similar image in *Night and Day.* Frustrated over being incapable of professing his love to Katharine Hilbery, Ralph Denham turns for solace to an old man on a bench on the Embankment: "Ralph had a wild desire to talk to him; to question him; to make him understand" (*ND*, 417). In his attempt to communicate with another, Denham finds words insufficient.

Woolf portrays the meeting of self and other as destructive. In love, Denham's self-identity is threatened:

> And when the elderly man refused to listen and mumbled on, an old image came to [Ralph's] mind of a lighthouse besieged by the

flying bodies of lost birds, who were dashed senseless, by the gale, against the glass. He had a strange sensation that he was both lighthouse and bird; he was steadfast and brilliant; and at the same time he was whirled, with all other things senseless against the glass. (*ND*, 417–18)

Like moths drawn to a candle, the frenzied birds in *Night and Day* represent the self's contact with the other, a meeting that is both self-illuminating and self-destructive. In Hegelian terms, the self's supersession of the other results in certainty of "*itself* as the essential being." However, "in so doing [the self] proceeds to supersede its *own* self, for this other is itself."[50] Lawrence, in "The Crown," argues that the conflict between self and other results in a balance. The crown is the synthesis, the goal of the dialectic. Thus, the dialectical struggle between self and other may have positive results: a love relationship may be established, as between Katharine Hilbery and Ralph Denham, Ursula Brangwen and Rupert Birkin. But the conflict may end in destruction; consider the violent and ultimately fatal connection between Gudrun Brangwen and Gerald Crich.

The dialectic of "The Crown" is also the subject of the earlier "Study of Thomas Hardy." Lawrence was first invited to write a short book on Hardy by James Nisbet in early July 1914. The major portion of the writing was completed during the first months of the war.[51] By October 1914 the essay was essentially finished. In "Study," Lawrence establishes the dialectical rhythm he later employs in "The Crown" and *Women in Love*. The sexual polarities and conflicts apparent in Lawrence's pre-war work also find expression in "Study."

The battles between self and other are best illustrated by the arguments engaged in by Ursula and Birkin. Their dialogues are consistently described as "hostile" and in "opposition" (*WL*, 126). In "An Island," the argument follows the pattern of assertion, denunciation, and reassertion—a rhythm that forms the essential structure of the novel. Birkin's assertion that "'I abhor humanity, I wish it was swept away'" is countered by Ursula's remark that "'you'd be dead yourself, so what good would it do you?'" (*WL*, 127). Although Ursula finds Birkin's dream of a world without humans attractive, she argues against him. Birkin is particularly adamant in his rejection of the concept of love, a meeting and mingling that excludes the struggle for definition. In her attempt to understand and eliminate his position, Ursula is momentarily victo-

rious. However, her victory is a Pyrrhic one, for in winning
against the other she also negates herself:

> " . . . if you don't believe in love, what *do* you believe in?" she
> asked, mocking. "Simply in the end of the world, and grass?"
> He was beginning to feel a fool.
> "I believe in the unseen hosts," he said.
> "And nothing else? . . . Your world is a poor show."
> "Perhaps it is," he said, cool and superior now he was offended,
> assuming a certain insufferable aloof superiority, and withdraw-
> ing into his distance.
> Ursula disliked him. But also she felt she had lost something.
> (*WL*, 129)

The "duality in feeling" (*WL*, 129) between Birkin and Ursula
is the constant theme of the novel. The battle of opposing emotions is "a fight to the death . . . or to a new life" (*WL*, 143).
Hostility and love appear inseparable. Ursula is both attracted
and repelled by Birkin. His presence as the necessary other
affords the chance for the self's destruction and preservation.

The battle between self and other as fought on the front of
language is nowhere more apparent than in "Mino." As soon
as Ursula enters Birkin's quarters there is a "terrible tension"
in the room (*WL*, 145). Once again, the argument centers upon
the topic of love. Where Ursula seeks security and reassurance
from Birkin, he argues for self-definition and singleness of
being:

> "If there is no love, what is there?" she cried, almost jeering.
> "Something," he said. . . .
> "What?". . .
> "There is . . . a final me which is stark and impersonal and be-
> yond responsibility. So there is a final you. And it is there I would
> want to meet you—not in the emotional, loving plane—but there
> beyond, where there is no speech and no terms of agreement."
> (*WL*, 146)

Although Birkin appears to advance Hegelian "being-for-
itself," it is important to remember that Hegel does not distin-
guish between being-for-self and being-for-another.[52] The two
are one and the same: thus, the continual attraction between
Ursula and Birkin. In their verbal clashes self and other are
brought into identification, whatever their disagreement of
terms and the unsatisfactory realm of language in which their
battles are fought.

In "Mino," Birkin accuses Ursula of using linguistic "persiflage" against him, a kind of verbal buckshot that stings but does not hit home. The absurd yet painful raillery indulged in by the couple has its equivalent in the physical attacks of Mino on the female intruder. The struggle between Birkin and Ursula for ascendancy is reenacted in the animal world. Mino's physical offensive to achieve dominance has its correlative in Birkin's "fine words" (WL, 150). Described as a "noisy woman" (WL, 150), Ursula nevertheless questions Birkin's own use of language. He engages in "sophistries" (WL, 150); he is a "prevaricator" (WL, 151). Yet Ursula places value upon language even when she doubts its veracity. Her emphasis upon "love" is not on the concept of intimate relationships; what she wants is simply to hear the *word:* "'Say you love me, say "my love" to me,' she pleaded" (WL, 154). The term she now begs to hear she had previously questioned Birkin's use of only a page before: "'Proud and subserved, then subservient to the proud—I know you and your love. It is a tick-tack, tick-tack, a dance of opposites'" (WL, 153).

The continual oscillation between an acceptance of the veracity of the other's utterances and subsequent repudiation results in a tense situation in which hostilities lie seething beneath the surface of verbal expression. Before Hermione hits Birkin she experiences a "terrible tension . . . like being walled up" (WL, 104). Unable to express her anger, oppressed by Birkin's apparent sang-froid, Hermione takes recourse in physical violence. In "Creme de Menthe," the battle of dialogue between Pussum and "a young man" is consummated in an act of brutality. With one wave of a knife, she attacks both her antagonist and Halliday, the lover whom she despises but to whom she always returns.

Gerald Crich similarly expresses his dual feelings toward Gudrun through bloodshed. His mistreatment of his horse is directed against her. "Half-smiling," Gerald forces the horse to endure the noise of the passing train (WL, 110). Gudrun stands looking at him while Ursula shouts at Gerald. The dynamics of cruelty and attraction are clear. As Gudrun observes Gerald's abuse of his horse she experiences a decidedly sexual pleasure:

> Gudrun looked and saw the trickles of blood on the sides of the mare, and she turned white. And then on the very wound the bright spurs came down, pressing relentlessly. The world reeled

and passed into nothingness for Gudrun, she could not know any more. (*WL*, 112)

Her "poignant dizziness" before his brutality penetrates "to her heart" (*WL*, 111). Gerald is like the blade wielded by Pussum. He strikes with a similar viciousness: "A sharpened look came on Gerald's face. He bit himself down on the mare like a keen edge biting home . . . keen as a word pressing in to her" (*WL*, 111). The opposition between Gerald and Gudrun is one of attack and feigned defense culminating in a perverse sexual union that resembles murder more than a creative joining. Physical intimacy serves only to drive them further apart.

In "Rabbit," Gudrun and Gerald participate in a travesty of the *Bludbruderschaft* ritual of "Gladiatorial." Their mutual bloodletting drives them in abhorrence from one another. The "obscene recognition" of their "initiate" is simply another form of attack: "He felt again as if she had hit him across the face—or rather, as if she had torn him across the breast, dully, finally" (*WL*, 243). Similarly, their lovemaking in "Snowed Up" is an aggressive act, one in which they are bent on mutual self-destruction. Although they each desire to be self-sufficient, Gerald and Gudrun are locked in a battling relationship from which neither can extricate him- or herself. In their union, they discover what they are, and, more importantly, what they are not.

Throughout the novel the oppositional tension so many critics perceive as comprising the essential structure of Lawrence's works collapses.[53] Dialogues remain unresolved, utterances are dismissed or condemned as false. Whatever the topic, discussion ends not so much in a stalemate as a void in which the word possesses no sound or echo of meaning. The dissolution of a world at war brings with it the decomposition of language. Graham Holderness has argued that what is interesting about *Women in Love* is what is left unsaid.[54] Although Lawrence asserts that the war is present in his text, he never refers to it directly. Within the silent heart of the novel rage the battles of the World War, a conflict apparent within the dialogic struggle of the characters. In a letter of 1 May 1916 to Barbara Low, Lawrence points to the silence engendered by the war:

> I would write to you oftener, but this life of today so disgusts one, it leaves nothing to say. The war, the approaching conscription, the

sense of complete paltriness and chaotic nastiness in life, really robs one of speech. (*LL* 2:602)

However, despite his disillusionment with language, Lawrence continued to work on *Women in Love*, an eloquent depiction of the social context in which it was conceived.

It is customary for critics to disparage *Night and Day* as an Edwardian exercise that purposefully ignores the events of the First World War. In his biography of Woolf, Quentin Bell describes *Night and Day* as "a deliberate evocation of the past ... a very orthodox performance.[55] Andrew McNeillie has termed the novel "very traditional."[56] These assessments echo Katherine Mansfield's contemporary judgment of the novel. Mansfield was outraged by Woolf's apparent disregard of the war. In a letter to John Middleton Murry of 10 November 1919, she complained:

My private opinion is that it is a lie in the soul. The war never has been: that is what its message is. I don't want (G. forbid) mobilisation and the violation of Belgium, but the novel can't just leave the war out. . . . we have to take it into account and find new expressions, new moulds for our new thoughts and feelings.[57]

In a diary entry for 27 March 1919, Woolf herself notes the traditional form of her novel. Yet she also comments on its general tone of "melancholy" and her search for a new method that could express this world-weariness:

I suppose I lay myself open to the charge of niggling with emotions that don't really matter. . . . And yet I can't help thinking that, English fiction being what it is, I compare for originality & sincerity rather well with most of the moderns. L[eonard] finds the philosophy very melancholy. . . . Yet if one is to deal with people on a large scale & say what one thinks, how can one avoid melancholy? I don't admit to being hopeless though—only the spectacle is a profoundly strange one; and the process of discarding the old, when one is by no means certain what to put in their place, is a sad one. (*D* 1:259)

The problem of presenting a world busy discarding old methods is evident in *Night and Day*. The novel's irresolute conclusion suggests Lawrence's later *Women in Love*. Like *Women in Love*, *Night and Day* depicts communication as an aggressive act. Many of Woolf's contemporaries, such as Katherine Mansfield, failed to perceive that the supposedly prosperous and secure world of *Night and Day* is in the process of disintegration. In her *Athenaeum* review of 21 November 1919, Mansfield wrote:

> We had thought that this world was vanished for ever, that it was impossible to find on the great ocean of literature a ship that was unaware of what has been happening. Yet here is "Night and Day" fresh, new, and exquisite, a novel in the tradition of the English novel. In the midst of our admiration it makes us feel old and chill; we had never thought to look upon its like again![58]

Mansfield's disagreement with *Night and Day* rests on her opinion that Woolf had written a novel of manners in the tradition of Jane Austen. However, like *The Voyage Out, Night and Day* reflects, or rather embodies, the very conflicts of battle. Taking into account Mikhail Bakhtin's assertion that social situation determines the structure of utterance, and in keeping with his theory of the interdependence between social milieu and discourse, in *Night and Day* "discourse does not reflect a situation, it *is* a situation." *Night and Day* is neither orthodox nor aloof. In its contradictions and ambivalence the novel embodies the clashes of a society at war, a society that is in the course of questioning its values and cultural tropes. Mansfield complained that the "message" of *Night and Day* was that "the war has never been." However, Woolf in her novel portrays conflict as ever present, indeed one of the few constants in an unstable world. Like *The Voyage Out, Night and Day* undermines the concept of the traditional novel through conflict and contradiction. In a letter to her former Greek tutor, Janet Case, Woolf comments at length upon her intentions:

> Its the conflict [of going into society and not wanting to] that turns the half of [Katharine Hilbery] so chilly . . . and then there's the whole question . . . of the things one doesn't say; what effect does that have? and how far do our feelings take their colour from the dive underground? I mean, what is the reality of any feeling?— and all this is further complicated by the form, which must sit tight, and perhaps in Night and Day, sits too tight; as it was too loose in The Voyage Out. And then there is the question of things happening, normally, all the time. (*VWL* 2:400)

The tumult within these two novels is in opposition to the form that seeks to contain the uncontainable. In *Night and Day* the distressing silence of "the things one doesn't say" confronts the words Woolf provides for her characters. She suggests that there is an uneasy juxtaposition of "things happening, normally, all the time" with the "reality" of "feeling" and "the dive underground." Finally, there is tension within the form itself. She intends to enclose these unexpressed words and dubious emotions, yet she never quite manages to encircle her subject properly: the form is either "too loose" or "too tight." The difficulties engendered by the disintegration of societal structures, personal animosity, and the poverty of communication are all contained within a narrative form that suggests "business as usual" but that, at closer glance, reveals itself as self-questioning and ultimately self-destructive.

In the Bakhtinian vocabulary of verbal conflict, *Night and Day* exemplifies "the constant struggle between the centripetal forces that seek to close the world in system and the centrifugal forces that battle completedness in order to keep the world open to becoming."[59] This Manichean struggle is evident in all aspects of *Night and Day*, as the title suggests. Woolf commented to Lytton Strachey that "dialogue was what I was after in this book" (*VWL* 2:394). *Night and Day* is, in effect, about dialogue, the undelineated self (night) attempting to communicate with the delineating other (day). This effort is not invariably successful. Consider Woolf's famous dedication: "To Vanessa Bell, but, looking for a phrase, I found none to stand beside your name." Although it must be said that *Night and Day* "stands beside" Vanessa's name, Woolf's fruitless search for a dedicatory passage suggests that attempts at articulation do not always succeed. Oftentimes, in venturing to span "the space between men that can be bridged by the word," language lapses, and we take refuge in "the things one doesn't say" or which cannot be said.[60]

In *Marxism and the Philosophy of Language* (1929), Bakhtin argues that "the immediate social situation and the broader social milieu wholly determine—and determine from within, so to speak—the structure of an utterance."[61] The antipathies of dialogue in *Night and Day* have their social correlative in the First World War. Controversies are rife throughout the novel, and contests of affection form a context for more significant battles. Bakhtin suggests, in "Discourse in the Novel" (1934–35), that language resides within the struggle between unification and disunification, centralization and decentralization, centripetal and centrifugal forces. This conflict "animates every concrete utterance made by any speaking subject."[62] These struggles inform the structure and very dialogue of *Night and Day*.

Woolf takes pains to emphasize the cloistered artificiality of the Hilbery household: "a thousand softly padded doors had closed between [Denham] and the street outside.... this drawing-room seemed very remote and still" (*ND*, 2). With the appearance of Ralph Denham, an outsider to the Hilbery world, hostilities develop. The "awkwardness which inevitably attends the entrance of a stranger" is seemingly camouflaged by "sentences" (*ND*, 2). Immediately, Ralph is distinguished as out of "harmony with the rest" (*ND*, 3). His aggression toward the Hilberys is symbolized by his "compressing his teacup, so that there was danger lest the thin china might cave inwards" (*ND*, 3). This image amply illustrates the Bakhtinian dichotomy of centripetal and centrifugal forces that are at war in the novel. Like the teacup, which relies on the centripetal force of porcelain and glaze to hold it together, so Woolf's novel is built around a structure of plot, narrative, characterization, and dialogue. However, just as the china cup is threatened by the crushing external force of Ralph Denham (who is also "within" the same text), so *Night and Day* encloses the collapse of the novelistic tradition from which it springs, the social order that it portrays, and the communicative, signifying ability of the dialogue of which it is composed.

Hostilities are manifest throughout the dialogues of the novel. Denham reflects that Katharine embodies qualities of her parents that are "oddly blended" (*ND*, 5). There is a hint that he finds "her, or her attitude, generally antipathetic to him" (*ND*, 5). Woolf accompanies Denham's developing animosity with talk of war. Katharine's attitude toward Denham is correspondingly antagonistic. Unwilling to follow established patterns of discourse, Katharine and Ralph find communication difficult, especially given their incompatible binary positions:

> They were further silenced by Katharine's rather malicious determination not to help this young man, in whose upright and resolute bearing she detected something hostile to her surroundings, by any of the usual feminine amenities. They therefore sat silent. (*ND*, 6)

Female and male, upper and middle class, they are incapable of bridging the space between them with words. When they

do speak, it is in antagonistic terms that echo their mutual
dislike. Katharine's guided tour of the mementos of her grandfather, Richard Alardyce, irritates Ralph and underscores the
couple's differences. Although Alardyce is characterized as a
major English poet, a superb wielder of words, his memory
does not inspire the pair. Their conversation is a belligerent
hurling of accusatory stereotypes:

> ". . . I don't think I should find you ridiculous," Katharine added,
> as if Denham had actually brought that charge against her family.
>   "No—because we're not in the least ridiculous. We're a respect-
> able middle-class family, living at Highgate."
>   "We don't live at Highgate, but we're middle-class too, I
> suppose." . . .
>   "You sound very dull," Katharine remarked, for the second time.
>   "Merely middle class," Denham replied. (*ND*, 11–12)

This passage exemplifies what Bakhtin regards as the context
of utterance that "may be fought out as a duel of two social
codes within a single sentence—indeed within a single word."[63]
Denham reflects middle-class scorn for its own respectability;
Katharine suggests Woolf's combined apprehension and appreciation of a society built around communal rites and literary inheritances. Her doubtful claim that her family is "middle
class" suggests that she does not understand the term as Ralph
does. For Ralph, the phrase connotes financial worries, over-
crowding, and discomfort.

Ironically, this dialogue occurs under the auspices of language. Mr. Fortescue, a caricature of Henry James, speaks in
very long sentences. A dialogue evolves around the question
as to whether an unnamed cousin of the Hilberys should learn
Persian in Manchester (*ND*, 2–3). Denham is compared to Rus-
kin; presiding over the scene is the spirit of Richard Alardyce.
Despite this overwhelming verbal inheritance, Katharine is
denied language. Despite, or perhaps because of, Alardyce's
influence upon the Hilbery household, words no longer suffice.

The fictional present's poverty of language is evident
throughout *Night and Day*. Unable to create a printed text,
Mrs. Hilbery fashions an oral discourse from texts gone by.
Whereas Katharine concentrates on the tools necessary for
writing in the present—supplying her mother with work
schedules, paper, pens, and rubber bands—Mrs. Hilbery pre-
fers to search for inspiration among words from the past. She
carefully polishes the outward shell of language as if it were a

crystal ball that could provide her a vision of the past. Unable to fashion her own text, she is also incapable of deleting those of others and deciding "the radical questions of what to leave in and what to leave out" (*ND*, 35). Ironically, it is Mrs. Hilbery's professed admiration of language that renders her incapable of using it. Her paragraphs are "unfinished, and resembled triumphal arches standing upon one leg." (*ND*, 36). Although her scattered sentences are "brilliant," "nobly phrased, so lightning-like in their illumination," "they produced a sort of vertigo" in which "the dead seemed to crowd the very room" (*ND*, 35). Depending upon the past to give them significance, Mrs. Hilbery's words fail within the present of the novel.

Ralph Denham's dealings with his family resemble a pitched battle. His communications with his mother take the form of a threat, and his rebellion against family custom is "fought with every weapon of underhand stealth or of open appeal" (*ND*, 20). Even consumption of food is an aggressive act: "He set [his plate] down in a chair opposite him, and ate with a ferocity that was due partly to anger and partly to hunger" (*ND*, 20). Denham's defense against the invasions of his family is "a prolonged campaign" (*ND*, 22). He wants to step beyond conflict, but his evasions are unsuccessful. He attempts to communicate "OUT" when he is "in," and his efforts deceive no one.

Discourse as assault is particularly evident in the fourth and fifth chapters of *Night and Day*. Chapter 4 opens with Mary Datchet musing on the difference between war and art, and as the chapter progresses, the distinction between these two activities diminishes. William Rodney's talk on "the Elizabethan use of metaphor in poetry" becomes an act of provocation (*ND*, 47). Rodney shakes his paper aggressively; his reading goes forth in "repeated attacks" (*ND*, 48). Although Rodney's own speech is contentious, he is dismayed to hear his listeners mutilate what he regards as his private language. Discussion becomes a violent activity in which words hew apart words in an attempt to isolate and truncate meaning. Like Mrs. Hilbery, William Rodney in his efforts to produce a text paradoxically produces no text at all. Or rather, the texts produced have little significance for their audience. Mrs. Hilbery's biography completely escapes the bounds of traditional narrative. The chaos of her efforts contrasts with Rodney's long pastoral drama, in which he clenches language into rhythmic patterns. Yet his exertions to reorganize language systematically leave

Katharine cold and unresponsive. Mrs. Hilbery and William Rodney represent a dialectical view of language: her production is joyously disunified and threatens to explode into paragraphic fragments; his drama labors under the pressure of an imposed, tyrannical structure that portends its logical collapse. Although Woolf indicates that these texts fail in the world of her fiction, they reside within the success of *Night and Day*. Her novel embodies the bankruptcy of language while at the same time representing her victory over linguistic and social chaos.

In *Night and Day*, misunderstandings are frequent. The novel presents a series of exchanges in which the characters are unable to bridge linguistic space. Katharine Hilbery's express purpose in approaching her father is to discuss the case of her cousin, Cyril Alardyce. Cyril's cohabitation with a woman who has borne him two illegitimate children is revealed in two letters. Katharine's father, too, is involved in considering the vagaries of love, but the couple he contemplates is safely interred in the past. Interested only in past entanglements, Mr. Hilbery does not address the problems of the present, and his solution to family discord is to disown it linguistically: "'the less talk there is the better'" (*ND*, 111). Cyril's indiscretion is further obscured by the fictions of Aunt Celia and Cousin Caroline. The dialogue between the two women is a pitched battle: "Cousin Caroline puffed," "Aunt Celia intervened," Cousin Caroline responds "with some acerbity" (*ND*, 124). Unable to face the becoming of an event into fact, the women weave verbal fictions to escape the unpleasantness of reality.

The struggle between "truth" and "fiction," the fluctuation of meaning between two points of view, is an essential element in the relationship of Mary Datchet and Ralph Denham. Woolf indicates that their dialogue will be informed with misunderstanding:

> Purposefully, perhaps, Mary did not agree with Ralph; she loved to feel her mind in conflict with his, and to be certain that he spared her female judgement no ounce of his male muscularity. (*ND*, 229)

Ralph certainly does not spare Mary, nor does Mary spare herself. Incapable of expressing the reality of her emotion, she is subject to the brutality of his egoism. He neither plays the part allotted him in Mary's fiction, nor does he speak the truth.

Mary, in turn, lies to Ralph and insists that she will go to America, a subterfuge to hide her disappointment. She accuses Ralph of duplicity, but she herself is not entirely candid. Ralph's infliction of suffering seems boundless. He utters Katharine's name surreptitiously, observes Mary impatiently, and returns to his incantatory evocation of the woman he loves but to whom he will not speak. Although Ralph is unable to bring himself to shoot birds, he is perfectly capable of wounding Mary.

Despite her avowal that "'I've none of your passion for . . . for the truth" (*ND*, 241), Mary spies the unspoken meaning of Ralph's affections for Katharine Hilbery. The dialectic between truth and falsehood that occurs throughout the novel is particularly evident in the dialogues between Mary and Ralph, William and Katharine in chapter 18. The professed relations of attachment and engagement are only part of a tragedy of errors. Outside the quotation marks of speech reside unuttered, contradictory emotions. Ralph's insistence that "'I'm a liar'" is countered by Mary's obstinate reply: "'I love the truth a certain amount—a considerable amount—but not the way you love it'" (*ND*, 241). For once, Ralph tells the truth about his character, an utterance negated by his false proposal to Mary. And whereas Mary professes her admiration of candor, the truth of her love for Ralph remains unspoken, communicated only by uncontrollable emotional reflexes. Ralph's own "alienation" is also evident only through physical "signs." Since language appears incapable of communicating significance, the observer must attend to the body's idiom.

Verbal communication is suspect throughout *Night and Day*. Each disseminating act inflicts anguish. Every utterance, every gesture becomes a blow. Caught within the web of signs, Mary and Ralph are unable to convey their emotions. Mutual understanding is temporarily achieved only to be followed by misery. Woolf suggests that discourse itself is a futile activity. Thus, Mary replies to another of Ralph's delusions "with anger": "'we don't agree; I only wanted you to understand'" (*ND*, 265). And Ralph turns in bitterness "to the illogicality of human life"; the enemy, logos, is faced (*ND*, 266). Words, the very tools of expression, are deficient. Unlike Bakhtin, who argued that "a word is a bridge thrown between my self and another. . . . [It] is territory shared by both addresser and addressee," Woolf seems to suggest that words serve only to emphasize division.[64]

Night and Day is about conflict. Ambivalences of language lead to misunderstandings between individuals and result in suffering. In the contentions involving her characters, Woolf not only reflects the hostilities of the First World War, but she also re-creates discord within the dialogic situation of her novel. Georg Lukács has argued that in the novel "certain crises in the personal destinies of a number of human beings coincide and interweave within the determining context of an historical crisis"[65]. Yet Woolf is not content simply to portray the "determining context of an historical crisis." The historical situation becomes a linguistic one as well. For Woolf the tensions of the World War are integral to the conflicts of her novel.

The writings of Bakhtin provide us with a new method of discussing the nature of conflict in *Night and Day*. The battles within the novel exemplify Bakhtin's assertion that discourse both reflects and creates a situation. The war during which the novel was written is not merely echoed in dialogue; dialogue is itself a contentious activity. However, in addition to creating conflict, language in *Night and Day* also illustrates the joyous freedom of Bakhtinian dialogic. Because of the continual conflict of utterance, meaning is never ossified or tyrannized. In the concluding scene of her novel, Woolf emphasizes the vitality of language and the gladsome undefinability of the other. Light and dark, night and day—these images suggest the antipathetical and yet complementary relationship between the self and other. Although these antipodal images symbolize the alienation invested in modern society by the Great War, they can also be seen in the light of Bakhtin's alterity, a similar structural situation but, unlike alienation, a friendly condition. As Katharine Hilbery fleetingly fashions her self in correspondence with Ralph,

> it seemed to her that the immense riddle was answered; the problem had been solved; she held in her hands for one brief moment the globe which we spend our lives in trying to shape, round, whole, and entire from the confusion of chaos. (*ND*, 533)

From out of chaos comes unity, from discord, love. In *Night and Day* binary opposites are momentarily brought together. We are reminded of Woolf's remark to Clive Bell: "the great battle is between those who think it unreal and those who think it real. (What do they mean?)" (*VWL*, 2:403). The conflict within meaning, between real and unreal, true and false, is encapsulated in the final image of *Night and Day:*

> Katharine pushed the door half open and stood upon the threshold. The light lay in soft golden grains upon the deep obscurity of the hushed and sleeping household. For a moment they waited, and then loosed their hands. "Good night," he breathed. "Good night," she murmured back to him. (*ND*, 538)

The novel concludes with a meeting of utterance. Yet the phrase "Good night" bears different intonations: Ralph "breathes"; Katharine "murmurs." Ralph's own phrase is sent "back to him"—a verbal missive bearing new meaning. In the end, the verbal sallies of *Night and Day* remain unresolved.

4

The Senseless Boxing of Schoolboys: The Sport and Comradeship of War

> I wish you were out of London. The bombs are getting much
> too close to one's friends. . . . Its odd, though, that one cant
> take it altogether seriously. Its like a very dreary game of
> hide and seek played by grown ups. Twice while playing
> bowls raiders have come over and been shot down in full
> view. One day they hedge-hopped over the tree at the
> gate. . . . They circle round like airy omnibuses: I wish they
> weren't going to you. (*VWL* 6:431–32)

In this letter to William Plomer of 15 September 1940, Virginia
Woolf transforms aerial dogfights into child's play, "a very
dreary game of hide and seek played by grown ups." Beneath
this deadly sport, Woolf herself is playing bowls. She further
engages in a play of language so that the bombers caper about,
engaged in a game of leapfrog as they "hedge-hopped over the
tree." The game overhead, the game on the ground, and the
revel of language seem to defuse any danger from the planes
overhead. Yet the frolic of Woolf's imagination also emphasizes
the deadly nature of the cargo circling in the sky.

Woolf frequently compares the activities of war to child's
play. On 13 April 1918 she discounts the promises and jingo-
isms of politicians as "an elaborate game": "If one didn't feel
that politics are an elaborate game got up to keep a pack of
men trained for that sport in condition, one might be dismal;
one sometimes is dismal; sometimes I try to worry out what
some of the phrases we're ruled by mean" (*D* 1:138). Wartime
propaganda is a "game" indulged in by "a pack of men." In
a diary entry for 7 August 1938, she directly compares male
participation in war to the sport of schoolboys: "Yesterday I
saw 6 tanks with gun carriages come clambering down the

109

hill & assemble like black beetles at Rat Farm. Small boys playing idiotic games for which I pay" (*D* 5:160). The irony of dimension, the comparison of world war to an "idiotic game," distinguishes her comments on war. War is a game both ludicrous and horrifying:

> All these grim men appear to me like grown ups staring incredulously at a child's sand castle which for some inexplicable reason has become a real vast castle, needing gunpowder & dynamite to destroy it. (*D* 5:167)

The child's amusement takes on less innocent connotations when workmen are buried alive while digging experimental sloping trenches in Hyde Park (*VWL* 6:284). Hitler himself is reduced to a bizarre, animated toy: he is "that insignificant insect" that pulls "all the guns" (*VWL* 6:271) and chews "his little bristling moustache" (*D* 5:142). In contrast to Roger Caillois's assertion, in *Man, Play, and Games,* that "play is essentially a separate occupation, carefully isolated from the rest of life," Woolf makes of game a deadly activity that is all too much part of daily existence.[1] Elaine Scarry has commented on the obscenity of war = game equation.[2] However, she points out that the matrix of war centers around the structure of contest, that the concept of "winner" and "loser" goes hand in hand with the very activity of war.[3] In writing war as game, Woolf underscores both the pathos and the obscenity of war.

Woolf was not the first woman to make the condemnatory comparison between boys' games and men's wars. In a letter to the Countess of Bute on 10 June 1757, Lady Mary Wortley Montagu remarked,

> I cannot think we are older, when I recollect the many palpable follies which are still (almost) universally persisted in: I place that of war as senseless as the boxing of school-boys, and whenever we come to man's estate (perhaps a thousand years hence) I do not doubt it will appear as ridiculous as the pranks of unlucky lads.[4]

Woolf compares adolescent violence to the sport of war in the character of Percival in *The Waves.* She underscores the brutality of Percival's childish imperialism: "He breathes through his straight nose rather heavily. . . . He would make an admirable churchwarden. He should have a birch and beat little boys for misdemeanours" (*W*, 37). In youth Percival is a leader among his peers, a battlefield commander in miniature:

> Look now, how everybody follows Percival. He is heavy. He walks clumsily down the field, through the long grass, to where the great elm trees stand. His magnificence is that of some mediaeval commander. A wake of light seems to lie on the grass behind him. Look at us trooping after him, his faithful servants, to be shot like sheep, for he will certainly attempt some forlorn enterprise and die in battle. (*W*, 39)

Percival's organization and leadership is also apparent on the playground of India. "By applying the standards of the West, by using the violent language that is natural to him," Percival subjugates the "innumerable natives in loin-cloths," rights the overturned "bullock-cart," and proves himself "a God" (*W*, 147–48). Percival "is conventional; he is a hero" (*W*, 133). The imperialist leader dies after suffering a fall from his horse during a race. Woolf mocks the self-centered imperialism represented by Percival. Although he is admired by the other six characters in *The Waves*, the stability and order that he epitomizes is destroyed on the sportsground. Percival is neither as admirable nor as infallible as his peers believe him to be. In destroying Percival and calling into question English imperialism, Woolf refuses to participate in the game of mythologizing colonial rule. She is "the nihilist who denounces the rules [of the game] as absurd and conventional, who refuses to play because the game is meaningless."[5] Denied significance, the game of imperialism and domination played by Percival is revealed to be a folly no different from the play of children. In deriding the authority Percival represents, Woolf scorns its rules.

In her biography of Roger Fry, Woolf dwells at length upon the violence of childhood. She devotes several pages to Fry's account of the savagery he witnessed and was forced to participate in during his school years at Sunninghill House. As first or second in school, Fry had to assist at floggings and hold down the miscreant while the headmaster, Mr. Sneyd-Kynnersley, indulged in a frenzy of brutality. These beatings often drew blood. Schoolboy misbehavior and adult perversion culminate in Fry's recollection of a boy flogged to the point of involuntary defecation.[6] He insists that these childhood episodes were responsible for his fervent pacifism and lifelong dislike of violence: "'my horror of these executions was certainly morbid and it has given me all my life a morbid horror of all violence between men'" (*RF*, 34–35).

The parallel between violence experienced during childhood either as sport or punishment and the armed battles indulged in by adults was also noted by Woolf's nephews, Julian and Quentin Bell. During their years at the farm at Wissett, the two boys played a series of war games. Like the aerial hide-and-seek their aunt observed while playing bowls during a later war, the small-scale military activities of the Bell brothers took place while the Great War was being fought in France and Flanders. Thus, the game often took on macabre proportions, given the context in which it was played:

> The war game, which grew increasingly complex and took a variety of forms over the years, originated with Quentin, with Julian as an enthusiastic and inventive collaborator. In one version it was played on a board, moving counters about; in another it was played "life-size."[7]

The Bell brothers' playing of military games holds a particular interest in that the battles were acted out within the pacifist circle of Bloomsbury. In "Notes for a Memoir," written before setting off to fight in the Spanish Civil War, Julian Bell suggests that his war games were "a reaction" to the vehement pacifism of his home. He attests that the game was never based on topical events: "the enemy was never German . . . frequently the setting was classical."[8] But, as Woolf suggests in her fictions, the historical past always inhabits the present. Julian's war games quickly progressed from "Alexander's phalanx with twenty-two—at least twelve-foot—'sarissas,'" to "modern sets with naval battles."[9] He acknowledges that the war games developed into a life-long interest in war and physical violence:

> This gave a background to widespread reading of military histories. . . . By the time I left Owen's [School] I had a considerable stock of military ideas.
> Another very important influence . . . was my fencing and wrestling. . . . I also learnt to box. . . . I was able to beat off individual bullies, and even, on occasion, intimidate mobs. My natural nervousness . . . is consequently counteracted by a belief in the efficiency of force and the offensive. . . . I have acquired and retained a taste for fighting.[10]

Reenacting historical battles, fencing, wrestling, boxing—all of these activities confirmed Bell's conception of war as game. In his poem "Vienna," he unflinchingly compares the two activities.[11] Disregard of fear, a schoolboy's bravado, informs his letters home from Spain. He writes that "all's boy-scoutish in the highest'"; "it's all very definitely a picnic."[12] He calls his journey to the fighting line "this preposterous holiday" and suggests he might still come home if "there's real danger or real boredom."[13] These remarks indicate that for Bell war is an exciting outing; the dangerous "reality" is as easily dismissed or as much to be feared as the deadliness of boredom.

Following Julian's death on 18 July 1937 in Spain, Virginia Woolf wrote a memoir of her nephew in which she worried over their "lapses in communication." She admits her puzzlement over Julian's determination to go to war:

> I have never known anyone of my generation have that feeling about a war. We were all C.O.'s in the Great war. And though I understand that this is a "cause," can be called the cause of liberty & so on, still my natural reaction is to fight intellectually: if I were any use, I should write against it: I should evolve some plan for fighting English tyranny. The moment force is used, it becomes meaningless & unreal to me.[14]

Eventually, Woolf did write against conflict. Her dislike of force and tyranny, her intellectual fight against war is the subject of *Three Guineas*. Given her stance, it is not surprising that she found Julian's fervor "meaningless" and "unreal." In his equivocal introduction to a collection of memoirs written by conscientious objectors about the First World War, Julian wrote, "I believe that the war-resistance movements of my generation will in the end succeed in putting down war—by force if necessary."[15] Bell's oxymoronic attitude toward war is evident from the logic of his sentence: "war-resistance" needs to resort to "force" in order to "put down" war.

Julian Bell shared his sportsman's appreciation of war and his paradoxical belief in a war to end all war with H. G. Wells. The irony of Wells's position is clear if we consider two volumes published within a year of one another. In 1913 Wells produced a volume entitled *Little Wars: A Game for Boys from Twelve Years of Age to One Hundred and Fifty and for That More Intelligent Sort of Girls Who Like Boys' Games and Books*. It is a purely militaristic and, as the title indicates, sexist manual for what Wells describes as "playroom warfare," the "mere setting up and knocking down of men. Tin murder."[16] "'Little

Wars,'" says Wells, "is the game of kings—for players in an inferior social position. It can be played by boys of every age . . . by girls of the better sort, and by a few rare and gifted women."[17] Wells strives for realism and spends many pages suggesting ways of decorating blocks of wood to represent houses in order to lay out a suitably true-to-life "Country" for attack.[18] Moving toward verisimilitude, Wells eventually describes his tin soldiers as "men" who "inevitably kill each other"; he calls in "Captain M., hot from the Great War in South Africa," to assist in getting the details right.[19] The aim, Wells insists, is to achieve "just that eventfulness one would expect in the hurry and passion of real fighting."[20] He urges that what we want in playing "Little Wars" is "the real thing" happening in "real life."[21]

Julian Bell and H. G. Wells desire and avoid the reality of war. Although they enthuse over imaginary conflict, when presented with real danger, home seems the safest place. In the conclusion to *Little Wars* Wells restates his earlier enthusiasm for "the real thing." Although fine for children, war games are unsuitable in a larger, adult arena: "All of us in every country, except a few dull-witted, energetic bores, want to see the manhood of the world at something better than apeing the little lead toys our children buy in boxes."[22] Wells insists that far from warmongering, "Little Wars" will show "what a blundering thing Great War must be."[23] At the same time, "Little Wars" offers the opportunity to perfect Great War so that it can be played as humanely as possible: "I see no inconsistency in deploring the practice while perfecting the method."[24]

Ironically, within a year of *Little Wars'* publication, the Great War opened upon the sportsfields of France. Wells's reaction to the event became a jingoistic catchphrase. In *The War That Will End War* (1914) Wells declares, "this is now a war for peace. . . . it is the last war!"[25] Woolf disliked Wells's prowar and anti-German stance. In a diary entry for 17 June 1918 she recounts a meeting of the League of Nations, at which Wells was present:

> last Friday we went to the League of Nations meeting. The jingoes were defeated by the cranks. It was a splendid sight to see. The chief jingo was H G Wells, a slab of a man formidable for his mass, but otherwise the pattern of a professional cricketer. (*D* 1:157)

Author, gamester, pacifist, nationalist—Wells summed up his personal attributes in the character of Mr. Britling. Wells ad-

vances himself as a representative national speaker in the fictional figure of Britling. In chapter 4 of *Mr. Britling Sees It
Through* (1916), Britling's soliloquy records his expansion from
individual to national stature: "He had a vicarious factor. He
could slip from concentrated reproaches to the liveliest re-
morse for himself as . . . England, or for himself as Man."[26] In
Little Wars, Wells similarly describes an imaginary expansion
of himself from weakly author into stereotypical war-monger,
a military version of Dr. Jekyll and Mr. Hyde.[27]

The war, which opens with "a very loud report" in" a
cramped Oriental city," is enacted within the "Old England"
of Britling's country home.[28] At first, the two countries are
contrasted: "There was a tremendous commotion amongst
that brightly-costumed crowd, a hot excitement in vivid contrast to the Sabbath calm of Matching's Easy."[29] However, the
resemblance between the tossing of a bomb at the Archduke
Francis Ferdinand and the hockey game of Matching's Easy is
all too apparent. The players take sides, there is danger and a
forward line. Injuries, struggles, and defensives are all part of
the sport: "in everybody's eyes shone the light of battle."[30] As
war opens in Sarajevo, so the battle begins in Matching's Easy.

Like Wells, Woolf explores the various aspects of little wars.
War as game informs the opening scene of *Orlando*. Orlando's
play is a macabre parody of the battles engaged in by his
forefathers:

> He . . . was in the act of slicing at the head of a Moor which swung
> from the rafters. It was the colour of an old football, and more or
> less the shape of one. . . .
>
> Orlando's fathers . . . had struck many heads of many colours
> off many shoulders, and brought them back to hang from the raf-
> ters. So too would Orlando, he vowed. But since he was sixteen
> only, and too young to ride with them in Africa or France, he would
> steal away from his mother . . . and go to his attic room and there
> lunge and plunge and slice the air with his blade. . . . The skull
> swung to and fro, for the house, at the top of which he lived, was
> so vast that there seemed trapped in it the wind itself, blowing
> this way, blowing that way, winter and summer. The green arras
> with the hunters on it moved perpetually. (*O*, 15–16)

Orlando's play with the Moor's head is a grotesque imitation
of adult war. He hits the head, "an old football," during his
adolescent sport. The endless series of battles engaged in by
his ancestors (neither of Orlando's parents figure in the novel—

he is an unsupervised child at play) are mimicked in the repetition of his "lunge and plunge." The head swings "gently, perpetually" back and forth in the breeze and under the force of Orlando's own "slice" just as his fathers traveled to and fro to battles against the barbarians in Africa. The repetition of these games of war is further exemplified by the breeze that blows endlessly "this way . . . that way" within the ancient house throughout the recurrent rhythm of winter and summer. The green arras with hunters on it sways in the wind—the hunters endlessly pursue their game. Like these hunters, Orlando's ancestors chase their prey, the infidel, on "fields of asphodel" and bring back the trophies of "many heads of many colours off many shoulders" to hang from the rafters.

The oscillating motion within the fictive play of Orlando and his military ancestors recalls the principle of repetition set out by Freud as an element of child's play in *Beyond the Pleasure Principle* (1920). Freud observes that "children will never tire of asking an adult to repeat a game that he has shown them or played with them, till he is too exhausted to go on."[31] Repetition in play indicates the child's pleasure in his or her game. But Freud argues that "the compulsion to repeat also recalls from the past experiences which include no possibility of pleasure."[32] Orlando's game indicates his wish to be grown up. He vows to strike many heads off many shoulders, and to satisfy this desire he steals "away from his mother" into his secret "attic room" to practice mock murder. Through his play Orlando reenacts his separation from his father. The perpetual striking of the Moor's head is a substitute for actual warfare. The mock battle implies the warriors' return: they "had struck many heads of many colours off many shoulders, and brought them back to hang from the rafters." Orlando never does go to war, despite his vow. The cord upon which the trophy is hung is cut, thus breaking the rhythm of journey and return. Orlando is presented not with the homecoming of a parent but with the horrific, grinning emblem of death. Although an attempt to recall the father, Orlando's game underscores the absence of progenitors and the problem of identification of the subject in the novel.

In *Jacob's Room*, child's play is a brutal pantomime of the search for the self and the father. Jacob does not want to play with his elder brother, Archer. Like Orlando, Jacob is shown as being quite content playing on his own. The object of his play, the victim of his game, is "an opal-shelled crab" that he captures and takes prisoner in a bucket:

> The child's bucket was half-full of rainwater; and the opal-shelled crab slowly circled round the bottom, trying with its weakly legs to climb the steep side, trying again and falling back, and trying again and again. (*JR*, 19)

Caught within a bucket like the Moor's head on its string, the crab repeats its efforts to break free. Throughout the opening pages of *Jacob's Room* images of prisoner and captor recur. The crab is caught within a bucket that itself is entrapped within the beam of light that "blazed out across the patch of grass" (*JR*, 18). Like the bucket, the Flanders family is encircled by the violent wind "tearing across the coast, hurling itself at the hills, and leaping, in sudden gusts, on top of its own back" (*JR*, 18). The wind, in turn, is part of the "muddle and confusion" of the world in which the Flanders are placed (*JR*, 18). The chaos and violence of the Great War, in which Jacob is to die, is foreshadowed by the storm, by "something yellow-tinted and sulphurous in the darkness" (*JR*, 18). The patterns of imprisonment in the novel suggest the difficulty of capturing the subject. Makiko Minow-Pinkney suggests that "Jacob is a lacuna in the consciousness of the text, an absent centre, a fissure in the novel round which the other characters gravitate."[33] As we shall see, Jacob participates in games and war in an attempt to find himself through conflict with the other.

Jacob's dead father sets the precedent for his son's game playing. Seabrook Flanders is described by his wife as a "merchant of this city" (*JR*, 21). But other definitions ascribe him a childish role. He was immature, a gamester: "as many still remembered, he had only sat behind an office window for three months, and before that had broken horses, ridden to hounds, farmed a few fields, and run a little wild" (*JR*, 21–22). Seabrook Flanders is incapable of being captured by titles of occupation, and he fails to be enclosed by the role of the father.

The games Jacob and his brothers play enact their search for and their desire to replace their dead father. Archer offers his mother his toy knife to protect her from the attacks of the rooster that "had been known to fly on her shoulders and peck her neck":

> "Wouldn't you like my knife mother?" said Archer.
> Sounding at the same moment as the bell, her son's voice mixed life and death inextricably, exhilaratingly.

> "What a big knife for a small boy!" she said. She took it to please him. (*JR*, 22–23)

Archer's offer comes just at the moment his mother is re-minded of the father's death. His phallic gift to his widowed mother promises male protection from male assault. Woolf uses a similar image in the first section of *To the Lighthouse*. James Ramsay and his father engage in a battle for the sympa-thy and attention of the mother. James dreams of seizing an "axe . . . a poker, or any weapon that would have gashed a hole in his father's breast and killed him" (*TL*, 12). Mr. Ramsay meets aggression with aggression: he stands "lean as a knife, narrow as the blade of one, grinning sarcastically" (*TL*, 12). James plays at cutting out the picture of "a pocket knife with six blades which could only be cut out if [he] was very careful" (*TL*, 31). Incapable of killing his father or protecting his mother, James's frustrated aggression expresses itself through child's play.

The uselessness of the child's efforts to play at being adult is illustrated by Archer's choice of "a paper-knife" from Mr. Floyd, "because he did not like to choose anything too good" (*JR*, 31). John chooses "Mr. Floyd's kitten, which his brothers thought an absurd choice" (*JR*, 31). Like the small knife, Topaz, the kitten, also proves an unsuccessful male substitute. After reading in "the *Scarborough and Harrogate Courier*" that "poor Mr Floyd was becoming Principal of Maresfield House," Mrs. Flanders caresses the by-now-elderly cat Topaz (*JR*, 32–33). The motif of the disposable male in *Jacob's Room* is then reiterated:

> "Poor Topaz," she said (for Mr Floyd's kitten was now a very old cat, a little mangy behind the ears, and one of these days would have to be killed.)
> "Poor old Topaz," said Mrs Flanders, as he stretched himself out in the sun, and she smiled, thinking how she had had him gelded, and how she did not like red hair in men. (*JR*, 33)

Old and sterile, Topaz is soon to be killed—all of Mr. Floyd's gifts are useless.

Small, young, and immature, Betty Flanders's sons cannot take the place of their dead father. Archer's knife is only a toy. The game of "tea" John plays, "trotting up and slapping down in her lap grass or dead leaves," is a sterile occupation even though he strews "the grass and leaves . . . as if he were sowing

seed" (*JR*, 27–28). The children's frustration over their inadequate play-role breaks forth in overt aggression. Using the remains of a Roman fortress to shield them, a memento in its
own right of the ancient attacks of their precursors, "Archer
and Jacob jumped up from behind the mound where they had
been crouching with the intention of springing upon their
mother unexpectedly" (*JR*, 28). But even this mock offensive is
unsuccessful—the Flanders family proceeds "to walk slowly
home" (*JR*, 28).

Jacob's hobby of butterfly collecting further exemplifies the
attempt to capture the absent, delimiting figure of the father
and contain the self. Throughout Woolf's fictions the butterfly
serves as emblem for the self. In identifying butterflies Jacob
attempts to recognize himself. But this process of self-
identification is not unequivocal: Morris, the butterfly expert,
"is sometimes wrong" (*JR*, 34). The figure of authority is dismissed once again. Furthermore, Jacob's hobby necessitates
murder, presaging his own death in the Great War. To capture
and collect the butterflies, Jacob must kill them. His sport
emphasizes the essential viciousness of much of child's play.
The death of butterflies is related to more significant deaths:
"The tree had fallen the night he caught it. There had been a
volley of pistol-shots suddenly in the depths of the wood. And
his mother had taken him for a burglar when he came home
late" (*JR*, 34). The death in the forest, the pistol shot, the imprisonment and death of the butterfly all point to Jacob's future demise. The young man residing in *Jacob's Room* is not
an innocent. He is captor and executioner: he collects living
crabs and butterflies. He willingly embraces death in the form
of a sheep's skull and subsequently eradicates the self's emblem, the butterfly. In an attempt to find himself, Jacob is self-
destructive.

In *Jacob's Room* and *Orlando* the problem of defining the
subject is paramount. Orlando is both male and female; a lover
of women and men; a nearly eternal youth whose passing years
are recorded not by progressive physical decrepitude but in
sartorial evolutions and mutable love affairs. Although *Orlando* purports to be "A Biography," the biographer's preroga-
tive to the truth is questioned. The biographer/narrator of
Orlando appears to be serious in her pursuit of her subject.
She identifies "the first duty of a biographer, which is to plod,
without looking to right or left, in the indelible footprints of
truth" (*O*, 62). But this pursuit of truth is later mocked. Truth

of character is neither indelible nor obvious: "the truth being that a quality often lies just on the other side of the wall from where we see it" (O, 99).

The identification of Jacob as subject is also problematic. Unlike the evanescent portrait of Orlando, the subject of *Jacob's Room* is not so much the figure named in the title but his room. Yet the chamber lacks its owner's presence. Full of possessions, it is nevertheless "an empty room" (JR, 61). The absent subject creates an eerie nonpresence: "One fibre in the wicker arm-chair creaks, though no one sits there" (JR, 61). Jacob's belongings are not distinctive. His "photographs from the Greeks, and a mezzotint from Sir Joshua" are dismissed as stereotypical: "all very English" (JR, 60). The books, too, identify character in terms of another's taste. Jacob is consistently presented through the eyes of others. Mrs. Norman regards him as a potential rapist. Fanny Elmer considers him a Greek god, a "battered Ulysses" (JR, 279). All attempts to encapsulate character are dismissed: "Anyhow, this was Jacob Flanders, aged nineteen. It is no use trying to sum people up. One must follow hints, not exactly what is said, nor yet entirely what is done" (JR, 47).

In *Marxism and the Philosophy of Language*, Bakhtin argues that the self can only be defined in relation to the other, that utterance has meaning only when directed to an audience.[34] In *Jacob's Room*, Jacob and his aptly named friend, Bonamy, engage in a political discussion that rapidly disintegrates into boyish fisticuffs:

> Mrs. Papworth . . . did for Mr. Bonamy . . . and as she washed up the dinner things in the scullery she heard the young gentleman talking in the room next door. Mr. Sanders was there again: Flanders she meant. . . . she listened: heard Sanders speaking in a loud rather overbearing tone of voice: "good" he said, and "absolute" and "justice" and "the will of the majority." . . . "Objective something," said Bonamy; and "common ground" and something else— all very long words, she noted. . . . she . . . heard something—might be the little table by the fire—fall; and then stamp, stamp, stamp— as if they were having at each other—round the room, making the plates dance. (JR, 165–66)

In an effort to mark out their philosophical positions and to fashion self-identity, Flanders and Bonamy turn a political discussion into physical assault. In battle with the other, the existence of the self is made known. The clash between selves stakes out the claims of possession (Bonamy's broken coffee-pot) and delineates the boundaries of utterance (the definition of "good," "absolute," "justice"). Only when utterance is directed toward another and the sally returned is understanding achieved. Thus, the boyish roughhousing between Jacob and Bonamy illustrates both the assertion of the self and the violence of discourse. In *Jacob's Room* Woolf, like Bakhtin, suggests that "understanding strives to match the speaker's word with a *counter word*."[35] Political arguments are a form of violent play. The exchange of terms becomes the exchange of blows.

Thus, both utterance and game playing contribute to self-definition. If, as Bakhtin argues, "the structure of an utterance" is determined by "the immediate social situation," then the structure by which the self responds to the other is drawn "not from within, not from the depths of one's personality, but from the outside world."[36] Game as assertion of the self's autonomy is not an individual expression but a structure created by society in general. In *Orlando* and particularly *Jacob's Room* war as game is not only a brilliant adolescent invention that helps to acknowledge the other and fashion the self; it is also a fiction perpetuated by an older generation eager to camouflage its militaristic expansionism and warmongering. From the safety of his armchair, H. G. Wells was able to regard "little war" as a necessary and human preparation for the "Real Thing." He was capable of comparing tin soldiers to living men. A similar comparison occurs in *Jacob's Room*:

> *Like blocks of tin soldiers* the army covers the cornfield, moves up the hillside, stops, reels slightly this way and that, and falls flat, save that, through field-glasses, it can be seen that one or two pieces still agitate up and down like fragments of broken matchstick. (*JR*, 254; emphasis added)

The immobile "nonchalance" of a dozen sailors who meet their death, the mechanical accuracy of a gunner, all suggest that the battle being fought involves tin soldiers rather than living men. The "composed faces" of the young men who die "uncomplainingly together" resemble the toy soldiers knocked down in Wells's and Julian Bells's nursery games (*JR*, 254).

In her diaries and letters Woolf appears eager to dismiss war as a game played by overgrown boys. Yet the game of war in *Jacob's Room* has tragic connotations that cannot be discounted. If war is only a game, then the master players need feel no compunction. Woolf's description of the men who organize conflict suggests that their attitude is of players who sport with innumerable lives on distant battlefields. Both Woolf and Wells portray war as a game set up and played by a group of men too old for military service. The game acted out on the battlefield is directed by behind-the-liners, whom Siegfried Sassoon attacked in his poem "The General."[37] As in Sassoon's poem, Woolf's fictional elders display a certain resentment toward the younger generation, which they sentence to death. The leaders are "burdened" and weary, "manfully determined" to "impose some coherency" upon the chaos of the battlefield and win the game (*JR*, 281–82).

Game playing as expression of an older generation's resentment against displacement by youth is portrayed in *Between the Acts*. As his grandson George shreds the flowers in infantile destruction, Bartholomew Oliver advances, a horrifying "peaked eyeless monster moving on legs, brandishing arms" (*BA*, 17). Bart's attack is similar to Jacob and Archer's offensive against their mother. However, whereas their play expresses their desire for manhood, Bart's stratagem suggests the resentment of one generation toward another. Both games are violent, surprise attacks that articulate the aggression of the players.

Bart calls his Afghan hound, Sohrab, a "brute"; yet Bart himself displays brutish characteristics. Isa Oliver refers to him as "the old brute, her father-in-law" (*BA*, 26). There is a distinct similarity between Bartholomew Oliver and his dog; both prove to be threatening figures. Bart is presented as a frustrated soldier. Unable to release his aggressions upon a more suitable enemy, his unsuccessful game is a substitute for grander offensives. He yells at his dog "as if he were commanding a regiment" (*BA*, 18) and dreams of

> himself, a young man helmeted; and a cascade falling. But no water; and the hills, like grey stuff pleated; and in the sand a hoop of ribs; a bullock maggot-eaten in the sun; and in the shadow of the rock, savages; and in his hand a gun. The dream hand clenched; the real hand lay on the chair arm, the veins swollen but only with a brownish fluid now. (*BA*, 24)

The failed attack finds expression in Bart's dreams of youth and imperialism. The theme of play as a form of war and war as growing out of child's play has a curious development in *Between the Acts*. Rather than providing a youthful means of self-definition and rejection of authority, game allows the grandfather to see himself as young and a soldier. He plays at being a figure of military authority; his frustration and failure lead him to revenge himself on those around him, whether it be his dog, his sister, or his grandson.

Thus, throughout Woolf's fictions games in general and the game of war in particular provide male self-definition (what the male self would like to be) and destruction of what the self is not (the threatening other). Orlando affirms himself as not-Moor by striking at the suspended skull. The assault upon the foreign otherness of the Moor results in the shaping of Orlando. Bakhtin asserts that "each and every word expresses the 'one' in relation to the 'other.' I give myself verbal shape from another's point of view."[38] In Woolf's fictions, male game playing is a monologic version of dialogic utterance, since the other is often silenced in some way.

In *Mrs. Dalloway*, Septimus Warren Smith is molded by the conflict of the Great War. The war provides Septimus an opportunity to construct himself through conflict with the other. In battle with the enemy and through "the attention, indeed the affection of his officer, Evans," Septimus is defined.[39] In *Jacob's Room*, two badgers staking out their territorial claims are compared to two boys fighting. In *Mrs. Dalloway* the image is reversed. The relationship between Septimus and Evans resembles "two dogs playing on a hearth-rug." The younger snarls, snaps, "giving a pinch, now and then, at the old dog's ear" (*MD*, 131). As with Jacob and Bonamy, the playful antagonism between Septimus and Evans is the means by which the territory of the self is marked out: "They had to be together, share with each other, fight with each other, quarrel with each other" (*MD*, 131). The battle is on two levels. Septimus and Evans fight together against the Germans; they also take on one another in their play. However, with the death of Evans, Septimus loses self-definition. His dependence upon Evans to delineate his character is evident. Through quarrel and armed battle he pits himself against the other to assert his own being. The effort succeeds: "He was right there." But to be fashioned the self needs unending confrontation, the disappearance into the fray and the successful return. Unfortunately, the conflict with the other is ultimately self-destructive. Soon after Evans's death and the conclusion of the war, Septimus's sense of self-definition begins to falter. He is defined only by the company he keeps: observing the Italian girls, he retains himself. Alone at night the self threatens to lose coherence. Without the continual relay of self, to other, back to self, Septimus is doomed to self-loss and eventual self-destruction.

In order to avert this catastrophe, Septimus marries Lucrezia, one of the Italian hatmakers. Yet, ultimately, this attempt to regain selfhood is unsuccessful. Freud argues that the "traumatic neurosis" usually associated with "severe mechanical concussions, railway disasters and other accidents involving a risk to life" was suffered by many who endured the "terrible war."[40] He points out that this neurosis is a "subjective ailment" in which the patient's conception of himself is impaired in some way (Freud compares the illness to hypochondria or melancholia). Septimus's illness is similar to the war neuroses Freud describes. He, too, suffers from impaired self-perception. Depending upon Rezia to fill Evans's place, Septimus observes the unhappiness caused by his insecurity: "His wife was crying and he felt nothing; only each time she sobbed in this profound, this silent, this hopeless way he descended another step into the pit" (*MD*, 137). The momentary identity Septimus achieves during the war and in play with Evans evaporates before the reality of day-to-day communication rather than confrontation.

As in *Mrs. Dalloway*, the articulation of character in *Jacob's Room* and *Orlando* is problematic. Like the Moor's head, Orlando's heart and self-image are on a string: "he felt the need of something which he could attach his floating heart to; the heart that tugged at his side. . . . To the oak tree he tied it and as he lay there, gradually, the flutter in and about him stilled itself." (*O*, 20). Throughout the novel Orlando always returns to the symbol of the oak tree and his never-finished poem by that name. The oak tree affords the amorphous, androgynous, illogically timeless Orlando a sense of identity. Appropriately, Orlando, who exists within English history, is associated with the oak tree, symbol of England. He is the very oak tree to which he looks for support.

However, like his work-in-progress, Orlando is incomplete. The novel, in addition to tracing Orlando's movements through history, is the chronicle of his many love affairs. From his encounter with Queen Elizabeth onward, Orlando's association with the opposite sex (whether female or male) is characterized by violence. As in *The Voyage Out*, relations between

the sexes in *Jacob's Room* and *Orlando* are described in terms
of war and cruelty. For example, in Orlando's meeting with
Queen Elizabeth affection and lust are equated with war and
death. His innocent "dark head" and "heart of gold" are cou-
pled with the Queen's fear of murder and conflict: "The sound
of cannon was always in her ears. She saw always the glistening poison drop and the long stiletto. . . . she heard the guns
in the Channel; she dreaded—was that a curse, was that a
whisper?" (*O,* 24). Orlando's biographer comments that "violence was all" (*O,* 28) in the Elizabethan age. Violence also
dominates Orlando's Jacobean affair with Sasha. He names
her for a former pet and in doing so describes the very savagery
of love:

> he called her [Sasha] for short, and because it was the name of a
> white Russian fox he had had as a boy—a creature soft as snow,
> but with teeth of steel which bit him so savagely that his father
> had it killed. (*O,* 43)

"Nothing thicker than a knife's blade separates happiness from
melancholy," asserts Orlando's biographer (*O,* 44). The image
is an apt one for the injury caused by Sasha's disappearance
is portrayed as murder. She is "like the fox that had bit him,
now cajoling, now denouncing" until Orlando is incapable of
defining the truth: "Orlando believed her one moment. . . . the
next was the more violent with anger at her deceit" (*O,* 49).
Orlando's need to believe in Sasha, and thereby find meaning
for himself, is unsatisfied. His resentment and frustration find
fictional relief in *Othello:* "The frenzy of the Moor seemed to
him his own frenzy, and when the Moor suffocated the woman
in her bed it was Sasha he killed with his own hands" (*O,* 54).
Once again, the figure of a Moor affords Orlando the opportunity of acting out his fantasies.

The violence he desires to perpetrate is performed upon Orlando himself. Sasha's departure is accompanied by death and
disaster. The river upon which Orlando and Sasha had traced
their love becomes a channel of destruction. He sends his love,
his self, out to Sasha, but in the end nothing is returned. As in
the marriage of Septimus Warren Smith, the reciprocal relationship between self and other fails. Orlando's abuse of Sasha
is unheard and, therefore, empty of meaning.

His encounter with the Archduchess Harriet Griselda follows the sequence established in his affair with Sasha. For-

sworn of human company, surrounded by crowds yet alone, Orlando is briefly defined in the company of the Archduchess. In fitting "the gold shin case" to Orlando's leg, the Archduchess Harriet encloses him (*O*, 107). But Orlando's brief discovery of the self through contact with the Archduchess brings with it the seeds of its own perverse destruction. Love is Janus-faced; it is both tranquil and violent, white and black:

> It has two hands, two feet, two tails, two, indeed of every member and each one is the exact opposite of the other. Yet, so strictly are they joined together that you cannot separate them. . . . Orlando's love began her flight towards him with her white face turned, and her smooth and lovely body outwards. . . . All of a sudden . . . she wheeled about, turned the other way round; showed herself black, hairy, brutish; and it was Lust the vulture, not Love, the Bird of Paradise, that flopped, foully and disgustingly, upon his shoulders. (*O*, 108)

Like Septimus, Orlando discovers the absence of love and the violence of sexual brutishness through confrontation with the other and, therefore, with the self. That sexual lust is equivalent to violence is evident in *Mrs. Dalloway* and *Orlando*. For Septimus, sexual brutality and absence of meaning are synonymous. The language of Shakespeare "had shrivelled utterly," and Septimus now recognizes "how Shakespeare loathed . . . the getting of children, the sordidity of the mouth and the belly" (*MD*, 134). The only message humanity utters is one of cruelty and violence, of "loathing, hatred, despair" (*MD*, 135). Like Orlando's love, Septimus's message to the world is twin-natured. Although Septimus fantasizes about the "profound truth" of "universal love," he regards humans as essentially brutal (*MD*, 103).

Throughout *Mrs. Dalloway* and *Orlando* Woolf questions the nature of love, its cruelty, and its capacity to (de)limit the self. The rhythm of conflict and conquest in play as a means to define the self informs the sexual game. For example, Jacob's awakening sexuality is accompanied by the revelry of Guy Fawkes Night (the celebration of a murder averted) and the violence of the mob. Florinda expresses her unhappiness by flinging a glass at a young man's head. Later, her violence finds expression in Jacob's seduction. His own desire is reflected in the confusion of the crowd and the flames of the bonfire. The game of sex takes on further savage connotations in the description of the prostitutes which follows the account of Jacob's first dinner with Florinda:

> The voices, angry, lustful, despairing, passionate, were scarcely more than the voices of caged beasts at night. Only they are not caged, nor beasts. . . . What does one fear?—the human eye. At once the pavement narrows, the chasm deepens. There! They've melted into it—both man and woman. (*JR*, 131)

In meeting "the human eye," the self is paradoxically both identified and destroyed. The terror of self-identification through sex is illustrated by the consummation of Jacob's affair with Florinda. Woolf does not portray this event: its very absence suggests the obliteration of the self. Following intercourse with Florinda, Jacob is no longer his mother's son: "the heart was torn by the little creak, the sudden stir. Behind the door was the obscene thing, the alarming presence" (*JR*, 148). Jacob's subsequent betrayal by Florinda is also described in terms of absence. The self, no longer delineated by its relationship to the other, is expunged: "It was if a stone were ground to dust . . . as if the switchback railway, having swooped to the depths, fell, fell, fell" (*JR*, 153).

"So violent, so dangerous" is love (*JR*, 192) that Woolf compares sex with war. Woolf was not the first to parallel sexual lust and the desire for war. In his Epistles, Saint James states that the root of all wars is the lust of possession (4:1–2). Woolf juxtaposes the desire for sexual possession and armed conflict in part 8 of *Jacob's Room*. Ironically, the desire of young men and women is cut short by a more fatal engagement:

> Male beauty in association with female beauty breeds in the onlooker a sense of fear. . . . have you ever watched fine collie dogs couchant at twenty yards' distance? As she passed him his cup there was that quiver in her flanks. . . . I find it exceedingly difficult to interpret songs without words. And now Jimmy feeds crows in Flanders and Helen visits hospitals. Oh, life is damnable, life is wicked. (*JR*, 156–57)

Compared in this passage are the quiver of sexual power and the energy expended on the battlefield. Both activities end in death or disappointment: Jimmy dies on the fields of Flanders, Helen wets her pillow with tears. The narrator complains that the game is silent—it is a song "without words." The silence of the lovers is similar to the disappearance of Jacob into his

room with Florinda or the unspoken message of Septimus Warren Smith. Sexual lust is that eyeless beast seeking its prey
(*VO*, 75), a destructive force parallel to the obliteration of war.

In writing war as game into her fictions, Virginia Woolf sub-
tly transforms the reader's concept of war. Like Saint James,
Woolf regarded war as the lust for possession on an international scale. She asks the question of whether recreational conflict encourages war, if sexual desire inspires armed conflict.
For Woolf, war is a boy's game, and she contrasts it to such
feminine activities of creation as Mrs. Ramsay's knitting and
Clarissa Dalloway's sewing. In connecting war to the dynamics
of sexual relations, she questions the traditional concept of a
history that separates war from domestic events. In fact, in
underscoring the interconnection between war and the correspondence between men and women, Woolf challenges the construct of the romance of sexual love.

> The ignominy is horrible, the humiliation. And even this terrible
> glamour of camaraderie, which is the glamour of Homer and of
> all militarism, is a decadence, a degradation, a losing of individual
> form and distinction, a merging in a sticky male mess. It attracts
> one for a moment, but immediately, what a degradation and a
> prison, oh intolerable. D. H. Lawrence to Dollie Radford, 29 June
> 1916 (*LL* 2:618)

In the above letter, Lawrence reveals a twofold response to
the business of soldiering. He is at once attracted and repelled
by his fellow conscripts; the "terrible glamour of camaraderie"
holds an equivocal pleasure for him. Throughout his fictions,
he reveals a double reaction to the concept of the soldier. On
the one hand, he is envious of the man of action and the special
relationship formed between troops. Yet he disapproves of
those who don a uniform and compliantly obey the orders of
others. The soldier epitomizes, for Lawrence, the male companion he never had and whom he sought throughout his life.
He longed for a spiritual *Bludbruder* whom he could fight with
and against, a figure with whom he could identify. His search
for the supreme male friend led him into various stormy, short-
lived friendships, such as those with Bertrand Russell and J. M.
Murry. The friendship Lawrence depicts between Gerald and
Birkin in *Women in Love* exemplifies the type of totally male
connection he desires for himself. After proposing to Ursula,
Birkin feels "a complete fool" and takes refuge in the company
of Gerald. Gerald, in turn, finds Birkin a relief from "the stress

of his own emptiness" (*WL*, 266). Distressed and bored, the two men engage in a "jiu-jitsu" match to relieve the pressures of existence (*WL*, 268). Lawrence equates this physical combat with love. The naked struggle of the men affords physical intimacy (*WL*, 270). Through their wrestling, Birkin and Gerald attempt to establish a confraternity. At the conclusion of their skirmish, Birkin falls prostrate on top of Gerald's naked body. When he notices his position, Birkin is "surprised" (*WL*, 271). His astonishment suggests that their effort at intimacy has failed. Despite their nakedness and physical closeness, Birkin and Gerald are no nearer one another than they were before their battle. Their attempt at physical and spiritual oneness does not succeed; words, too, fail them: "There were long spaces of silence between their words. The wrestling had some deep meaning to them—an unfinished meaning" (*WL*, 272). Their struggle is "unfinished"; their fight has no conclusive "meaning." They remain as separate as before, unbonded by their physical confrontation. Birkin, who consistently regards words as endowed with special significance, is uneasy about his own efforts to substantiate verbally the success of the fight: "'I don't know why one should have to justify oneself'" (*WL*, 272). Gerald's speech is broken and indistinct. "I mean that— that—I can't express what it is, but I know it'" (*WL*, 275). He admits to Birkin that their personal languages are different: "'I don't use the same words as you'" (*WL*, 276). Birkin and Gerald exist within two separate worlds that are further isolated by the failure of discourse. Although they have shared the comradeship of battle, they lack the mythical bond such an experience supposedly affords.

In contrast to Woolf's belief that war is a predominately male activity, several critics have suggested that Lawrence's postwar leadership novels reflect his difficulties in relating to women's changing roles following the war years.[41] Although Lawrence's fictional leaders of the 1920s may be seen as his response to the ever-strengthening political and social position of women, they may also be considered as a revolt against the established political system of England at the time. Throughout the First World War, he perceives himself as hounded and betrayed by government authorities. He is a Christ who suffers the Judas kiss of censorship, eviction, and police harassment. In turn, he bitterly condemns the established order. In a letter to Catherine Carswell of 13 February 1917, he denounces his homeland: "I curse it, I curse England, I curse the English, man, woman, and child, in their nationality let them be accursed and hated and never forgiven" (*LL* 3:92). His volatile exclamations are particularly powerful since they come from a man who described himself as "one of the most intensely English little men England ever produced."[42] The tension between his nationalist self-identity and his desire to destroy the political status quo is to be found in his attitude to the soldier.

The dichotomy of Lawrence's position toward the companionship of the front line is particularly evident in "The Crown." In this essay, he juxtaposes the figure of a wounded soldier, stunned by his injury and flattered by a crowd of bloodthirsty women, to the biblical David, who represents the glory and egoism of youthful militarism. Lawrence regards the injured soldier as the epitome of horror and death. Priding himself on his wounds, the soldier attracts women greedy for a new kind of sensual pleasure, a communion with death:

> They wanted him, they wanted him so badly, that they were almost beside themselves. They wanted his consummation, his perfect completeness in horror and death. They too wanted the consummation. . . . And he . . . like a bridegroom just come from the bride, seemed to glow before the women. (*C*, 291)

The figure of the soldier represents the craving for destruction Lawrence perceived as characterizing the First World War. Amazed by his injuries, the soldier attracts those who are titillated by physical suffering and mutilation, who find "sensational experiences" in "death, hurt, horror" (*C*, 285).

Conversely, at first glance, the figure of David manifests a balance between law and love. However, his self-admiration is an unconquerable weakness. David asserts "his own oneness, the one infinity, *himself*, the egoistic God, I AM" (*C*, 268). His narcissism is self-destructive. He remains "barren," "sterile," "blasted with unfertility" (*C*, 268). His "seed" is "too impure, too feeble in sheer spirit, too egoistic" (*C*, 268). In the 1915 variant of "The Crown," Lawrence bluntly spells out the homosexuality he spies in David. He argues that the "reduction" of war leads men away from women. Horrified by "his own mangled, maimed condition . . . woman becomes repulsive" to man (*C*, 472). He asserts that any homoeroticism at the front comes out of a nostalgia for the self-image of the arcadian, prewar days: "[Man's] ideal, his basic desire, will be to get *back* to a state which he has long surpassed. . . . *This* is the

reason for homosexuality, and of connection with animals. . . .
This is David turning to Jonathan, Achilles to Patroclus" (*C*,
472).

Lawrence envisages the sexual impulses of men at the front
as embodying a feral quality. He condemns what he believes
to be military homoeroticism. In a letter to Lady Ottoline Morrell of 20 April 1915, he complains,

> Yesterday, at Worthing, there were many soldiers. Can I ever tell
> you how ugly they were. . . . I like sensual lust—but insectwise,
> no—it is obscene. I like men to be beasts—but insects—one insect
> mounted on another—oh God! (*LL* 2:331)

The terms Lawrence uses to describe what he sees as the bestial perversions of men in uniform are similar to those he applies to J. M. Keynes and Duncan Grant in March 1915. In a
letter to Lady Ottoline of 19 April 1915, he asserts that the
witty Bloomsbury conversation of David Garnett and Francis
Birrell makes him "dream in the night of a beetle that bites
like a scorpion" (*LL* 2:319). In *Women in Love*, Lawrence portrays the beetle as emblematic of an overweening drive to
perversion.

It would be simplistic to argue that because Lawrence associates fighting men with beetles, he wishes to portray soldiers
as merely repugnant. Throughout his fictions, Lawrence displays a dual attitude toward his military characters. Schöner
and Bachmann may appear essentially weak. Yet both these
characters achieve brief moments of self-assertion. Schöner is
condemned to die with his captain; he is bound to him by the
unalterable relationship of victim to oppressor. However, for
an instant, he takes his destiny into his hands and breaks Herr
Hauptmann's neck. Bachmann, too, finds a temporary release
from his military servitude during his night with Emilie. Both
men are condemned; they must obey the wills of others. In
Sons and Lovers, Mrs. Morel's condemnation of soldiers sums
up the inherent weakness that Lawrence ascribes to all his
military figures: they are "nothing" but bodies that make
"movements" when they hear a "shout" (*SL*, 220). It is the reluctance to take responsibility for the self, the desire to relinquish the privilege of self-determination that Lawrence
disapproves of in the soldier. In "England, My England," Egbert escapes from the chaos of his domestic life by volunteer-
ing for the trenches. In embracing death, he is freed from the

prison of the self: "Let the black sea of death itself solve the problem of futurity. Let the will of man break and give up" (*EME*, 33). His death absolves him from the conventions of marriage and fatherhood, allowing him to escape into the quietude of death: "No Winifred, no children. No world, no people. Better the agony of dissolution ahead then the nausea of the effort backwards" (*EME*, 33). In "The Mortal Coil," Freideburg avoids self-accountability, his gambling debts, and any possible future with Marta by relinquishing himself to the rhythm and nullity of the military march. He loses himself in "beer and yesterday's tobacco," "hunks of grey bread," and the soldiers' coarse "chaffing" with the serving women (*EME*, 186–87). Soon, however, "his own cold-thawing mud of despair" returns (*EME*, 187). He condemns the "mock warfare" of military maneuvers and wishes for the deliverance that real warfare would bring (*EME*, 187). Ironically, in the end it is Marta who dies, thereby leaving Freideburg with yet more problems to solve.

The feebleness of Egbert and Freideburg is also evident in Captain Herbertson in *Aaron's Rod*. Significantly, Herbertson appears only in the chapter entitled "War Again." He is destined to relive his war experiences. The war is "at the back of his mind, like an obsession" (*AR*, 113). His conversational tactics take on the movements of the battlefield: his talk is a "rattle," his conversation a "skirmish" (*AR*, 113). In speaking of his experiences, Herbertson hopes to expiate his memories. Unable to break away from his vision of war, he no longer lives within the present or for the future but only in the past. He is a living victim, the carnage's physical embodiment. Unlike some of Lawrence's soldier-heroes, such as Dionys in "The Ladybird," Herbertson has no vision of a postwar life. Instead, he relies on his embattled past and the friendships he formed at the front to define himself. He is sentenced to commune only with the dead who inhabit his memories. His relationship with Lilly is that of sinner to confessor. In telling of his war experiences, Herbertson hopes to expunge them. Yet the verbal expression serves only to make his recollections absolute in the present.

Lawrence frequently holds the special bonds formed at the front up to ridicule. In "Eloi, Eloi, Lama Sabachthani," he compares a soldier's relationship with his enemy to that of bridegroom and bride. His description of battle is a vicious parody of sexual intercourse:

>   And I knew he wanted it.
> Like a bride he took my bayonet, wanting it.
> Like a virgin the blade of my bayonet, wanting it,
> And it sank to rest from me in him,
> And I, the lover, am consummate. . . .
>
>   (*CP* 2:742)

Lawrence's attraction to the idea of a companion-in-arms is peculiarly evident in his use of the image of physical marriage. His captivation with the special relationship between the self and the enemy is simultaneously linked with a repulsion from the self-destruction implicit in the very act of "going over the top." However, Lawrence's soldier-figures are not always defenseless nor wantonly inhuman. Fascinated by the character of the fighting man, he centers many of his shorter fictions around mysterious, faunlike warriors.

For example, in "The Fox" (1923), Henry Grenfel personifies the wild, vibrant animal against which the liberated female farmer, March, does battle. For March, the fox is an indispensable enemy. If she were to shoot him she would destroy some part of herself and eradicate the object of her desire. She is particularly attracted to the fox's physical qualities: the glistening of his hair, the color of his eyes, his odor. She finds similar qualities in Grenfel, whose beard looks like the fox's white brush against his "ruddy cheek-bones."[43] The wildness and mysterious otherness of the fox is characterized by Grenfel's personal "odour" (*F*, 18). Grenfel is the wild animal, the darkness of spirit against which March struggles to protect herself. Like his emblem, Grenfel lies in wait to attack her:

> For the youth, sitting before the fire in his uniform, sent a faint but distinct odour into the room, indefinable, but something like a wild creature. March no longer tried to reserve herself from it. She was still and soft in her corner like a passive creature in its cave. (*F*, 18)

Grenfel's "odour" identifies him with the fox against which March takes out her gun. Grenfel, too, knows how to wield a gun. Home from the Turkish front, he returns immediately to the weapon that had given him so much pleasure before the war. Like the fox who overpowers March with his yellow stare, Grenfel is the victim turned hunter. He describes the connection between hunter and prey as a oneness of being:

> Your own soul, as a hunter, has gone out to fasten on the soul of the deer, even before you see any deer. . . . It is a subtle, profound

> battle of wills, which takes place in the invisible. And it is a battle
> never really finished until your bullet goes home.... It is your
> own *will* which carries the bullet into the heart of your quarry.
> (*F*, 24)

The terms Grenfel uses to describe the relationship between
hunter and prey bring to mind the sportsmen in Ernest Hemingway's short stories who stalk their victims as if they were
searching for themselves. In many of Hemingway's stories man
and animal fight their battles in solitude. In collections such
as *In Our Time* (1924) and *Men without Women* (1927), battles
between man and beast provide an opportunity for blood shar-
ing, an initiation ritual similar to the failed struggle between
Gerald and Birkin. For example, in "The Big Two-Hearted
River," Nick Adams searches for the center of himself while
fishing for the elusive trout, the other "heart" of the river. Grenfel's pursuit of March and March's hunting of the fox resemble
Adam's ritualistic fishing, for in chasing their respective victims they look for themselves. Lawrence portrays both March
and Grenfel as lacking in self-definition. March has abandoned
the traditional female roles. She farms, carries a gun, does
heavy labor, and protects the highly strung Banford. Grenfel,
on the other hand, is without a home. Expelled by his grandfather, he has wandered across the globe. Like the fox, he is an
outsider banished from society. The villagers condemn Grenfel
as "a good-for-nothing" who never does any "steady work" (*F*,
37).
  March is hypnotized by the fox. For her, he represents a
vicious, wild masculinity that she finds attractive, despite the
supposed emancipation from male domination represented by
her gun and land-girl's trousers:

> He was looking up at her. His chin was pressed down, and his eyes
> were looking up.... And he knew her. She was spell-bound—she
> knew he knew her..... He knew her, he was not daunted. (*F*, 10)

When March meets Grenfel she believes he is the fox. Yet the
unequivocal knowledge the fox has of March is not granted to
Grenfel. Unlike the fox, Grenfel is unsure of himself. March
dreams of the fox lyrically singing; the animal is a vicious
Siren that simultaneously bites and kisses its victim. Grenfel's
spoken proposal is hesitant, stumbling:

> "I want you to marry me. I want you to marry me. You know that,
> now, don't you? You know that, now? Don't you? Don't you?"

"What?" she said.
"Know," he replied. (*F*, 26)

Grenfel does not possess the fox's hypnotic power. March still turns to respond to the peevish calls of her housemate, Banford.

Grenfel is representative of the strong, feral male heroes of Lawrence's postwar novels. Like Don Ramon and Mellors, he has an instinctual knowledge that is garnered from a dark, animal world beyond the intellectual consciousness. However, like that of all of Lawrence's leader-figures, Grenfel's quest does not entirely succeed. In taking up his gun, his failure with March is predestined. The gun is symbolic of his position as returned soldier and social outcast. By killing the fox, Grenfel effectively murders that part of himself that March finds most attractive. The fox's death is Grenfel's attempt to capture and make a present of himself to March. In smelling the animal's "foxy smell," Grenfel inhales his own scent (*F*, 39). The body he offers to March is his. Grenfel eradicates his own power with the death of the fox. His ongoing courtship of March is continually thwarted by Banford. Like a fox jumping down upon a chicken, Grenfel eventually breaks Banford's neck. At the moment of her death, he observes her "as he would watch a wild goose he had shot" (*F*, 65).

Grenfel appears to succeed in capturing March. However, the connection he seeks with her is never established. His attempts to dominate her fail. He remains undefined, alienated from the other who would give him shape and whom he seeks to conquer: "He chafed, feeling he hadn't got his own life. He would never have it till she yielded and slept in him" (*F*, 70). Grenfel's last hope to dominate March and fashion her into "his own life" rests with Canada. He looks forward to building a utopia of the self outside England:

> He believed that as they crossed the seas, as they left this England which he so hated . . . she would go to sleep. She would close her eyes at last, and give in to him. (*F*, 70)

The "sleep" Grenfel wishes for March is similar to the death he imposed on Banford. His domination of March is another murder. The battle between Grenfel and March is a life-and-death struggle. But in the end, power is illusory. Lawrence's story concludes with Grenfel's struggle unresolved. The new world he desires is yet, if ever, to come. Grenfel epitomizes the contradictions found in all of Lawrence's soldier-figures. Although instinctive and powerful, Grenfel's strength turns against him. He wields his gun too freely, killing his personal totem, the fox, and fails to establish his superiority over March.

Count Johann Dionys Psanek, of "The Ladybird," resembles Grenfel. Like him, Dionys possesses feral qualities. Lady Daphne is entranced by his "fine black hair" and "his small, animal ears."[44] She notes "his strong white teeth, that seemed a little too large, rather dreadful" (F, 181). Dionys's frightening, carnivorous attitude toward Lady Daphne eventually turns self-destructive. He is the epitome of the soldier as social and spiritual outcast in Lawrence's fictions. A prisoner of war, he lies in an English hospital hundreds of miles away from his native Austria. His surname signifies his position as an outlaw: "'Psanek means an outlaw'" (F, 172). He embraces his position as "a little outsider" (F, 182): "'I will be Psanek, Lady Daphne. I will not be Johann Dionys any more. I will be Psanek. The law shot me through'" (F, 172). He lives beyond the social and natural rules of existence. He looks to a place beyond "the yellowness of sunshine" to where "the sun is dark" (F, 180). As a prisoner and political outsider, he longs to escape the natural limits of bodily existence.

Dionys's prophecies of a new world fail to materialize. The postwar utopia he foresees is a land of death. Although, at first glance, Dionys appears to welcome a new creation, his tendency is more toward destruction. When visited by Lady Daphne and her mother, Lady Beveridge, Dionys proclaims his wish to die. This death wish informs his visions of the future. He sees himself as "the king of Hades" and Daphne as his Persephone (F, 216). His realm will be "the afterlife" and Daphne will act as his "night-wife" (F, 216–17). The life-in-death foreseen by Dionys will come about only by destroying the established order. He proclaims that his god is "'the blessed God of Destruction. . . . The God of anger'" (F, 186). Ultimately, Dionys's god of apocalyptic power resides within himself.

Although Dionys appears to be an unequivocal Lawrentian leader, his advancement of the world's destruction eventually turns against him. He embodies the decadence against which he rages. His family crest is the ladybird: "'On our linen we had no crown: only the ladybird'" (F, 174). The sentence is significant. For Lawrence, the "crown" represents an equilibrium between such binaries as love and law, unicorn and lion. On the other hand, he considered beetles symbolic of decadence, dissolution, homosexuality, and the type of underground world represented by the Pompadour Club in *Women in Love*.

Dionys's position outside of the law eventually leads him beyond life itself. The words he speaks are a call for destruction. The song he sings in the secret of the night is an indecipherable ballad of bereavement:

> half-conscious, he would croon in a small, high-pitched, squeezed voice . . . . It was a curious noise: the sound of a man who is alone in his own blood: almost the sound of a man who is going to be executed. (*F*, 212)

His singing resembles that of a night animal. Daphne hears "the small, bat-like sound of the Count's singing to himself" (*F*, 212). Although Daphne perceives no meaning in the Count's song, she receives his music as a "call from the beyond," a voice speaking from outside the world of "father and mother, brothers and husband and home and land and world" (*F*, 213). Her response to the Count's ballad is similar to Ursula Brangwen's reawakening after her encounter with the horses in the last chapter of *The Rainbow*. Like Ursula, Daphne feels remade outside the bonds of family, marriage, and national affiliations. However, the vision of light and color granted Ursula at the end of *The Rainbow* is denied Daphne. Her new life exists only in darkness:

> She never *saw* [Dionys], as a lover. When she saw him, he was the little officer, a prisoner, quiet, claiming nothing in all the world. And when she went to him as his lover, his wife, it was always dark. She only knew his voice and his contact in darkness. (*F*, 219)

The tensions that reside within Lawrence's soldiers are summarized in the above passage. Count Dionys is at once soldier and dark god, prisoner and king. His utopian vision of a new world necessitates the apocalyptic destruction characterized by the First World War, a conflict that has, in turn, led to Dionys's death and rebirth in darkness.

The dichotomies inherent in Lawrence's soldiers also find expression in "The Captain's Doll." The title of Lawrence's tale indicates the infinite methods of incarceration portrayed in the story. The "captain's doll" is a puppet, a mannequin portrait of Captain Alexander Hepburn. In looking at the doll, Hepburn sees an uncanny reflection of himself:

> He sat gazing with curious, bright, dark, unseeing eyes at the doll which he held by one arm. It was an extraordinary likeness of himself, true even to the smooth parting of his hair and his peculiar way of fixing his dark eyes. (*F*, 80)

The doll is the handiwork of Countess Johanna zu Rassentlow, the mistress of Hepburn, and in this sense his "doll." The Captain, too, functions as a living puppet. He is compelled to obey the orders of his commanding officer, who, in effect, pulls Hepburn's strings. The Captain is also the puppet of his wife. He is reliant upon her for money. Mrs. Hepburn is, in turn, her husband's plaything. Lawrence hints that her fall from a balcony to her death may have come about with a little push from her husband (*E*, 110). In eulogizing his deceased wife, Hepburn describes her to Johanna as if she had been a clever pet:

> "English was never her language. It bubbled off her lips, so to speak. And she had no other language. Like a starling that you've made talk from the very beginning, and so it can only shout these talking noises, don't you know. It can't whistle its own whistling to save its life. . . . All its own natural mode of expressing itself has collapsed, and it can only be artificial." (*F* 111)

Hepburn's wife has no language except that which she has learned from him. Like a parrot in a cage, she can only mimic his mode of expression. Hepburn ascribes his wife's problem with language to the fact that she is Irish and a linguistic outsider. He also manipulates Johanna through language. She is required to speak to him in English rather than her native German. Late in the story, Hepburn unexpectedly comes upon Johanna swimming; her joyous sense of freedom at having escaped his presence can be seen in her naked limbs and heard in her natural speech.

In "The Captain's Doll," everyone is the plaything of one another. The cages of existence regress infinitely. Hepburn insists that all humans reside in prisons: "'There *is* no life outside, for human beings'" (*F*, 113). Ultimately, he argues that the prison exists within the self. Although he believes that he alone can reach freedom through his telescope, he is as much a prisoner as his birds, his wife, and Johanna. He is imprisoned by his belief in the paucity of his existence. He is an absolute "nothing" (*F*, 94) who embodies the complete "meaning-lessness" of being (*F*, 84). The Chinese boxes of imprisonment are exemplified by the figure of the doll. Mrs. Hepburn tries to buy the doll created by Johanna. It is eventually sold to Theodor Worpswede, a Munich painter. Worpswede, in turn, includes it in a study of "a doll, two sun-flowers in a glass jar, and a poached egg on toast" (*F*, 118). Hepburn purchases the still life in order to repossess himself. Like Grenfel's fox and Dionys's ladybird, Hepburn's doll is a totem: "This new version of himself along with the poached egg and the sun-flowers was rather frightening" (*F*, 118). Significantly, all three of these former soldiers are ascribed personal emblems, as if their self-identity is in need of mystical reinforcement.

Like Count Dionys, Hepburn, too, is a figure of darkness. Just as Daphne responds to Dionys's singing, so Johanna is affected by the sound of her lover's voice:

> She had forgotten it—forgotten his peculiar slow voice. And now it seemed like a noise that sounds in the silence of the night. Ah, how difficult it was, that suddenly the world could split under her eyes, and show this darkness inside. (*F*, 123)

The human skin encloses an essential emptiness. The "darkness" Johanna perceives inside Hepburn is symbolized by the "foolish empty figure" of his doll (*F*, 137).

Johanna is included in Hepburn's utopian dream of a new marriage. Yet although Hepburn insists that Johanna verbally promise to honor and obey him, she avoids speech. At the close of the story, it is not Johanna who obeys Hepburn but Hepburn who minds Johanna:

> "Oh," she said, turning round, "give me that picture, please, will you? I want to burn it."
> He handed it to her.
> "And come to-morrow will you?" she said.
> "Yes, in the morning."
> He pulled back quickly into the darkness. (*F*, 153)

Hepburn retreats into the darkness that he hides within himself. His request that Johanna verbally abase herself remains unanswered.

The re-formation of male/female connections preached by Grenfel, Dionys, and Hepburn fails to occur. At one time soldiers who followed commands, they are now unable to take the lead. Their attempts at achieving intimacy serve only to underscore alienation. Although envious of what he termed "the camaraderie, that is so glamorous—the Achilles and Patroclus business" (*LL* 2:644), Lawrence worked to destroy the myth of Homeric military heroism. He was at once attracted to the figure of the soldier and repulsed by what he considered the unthinking obeisance essential to military life. Perhaps his dualistic attitude toward military figures can be explained if we consider Lawrence's postwar need to place the individual into a system that would create order out of the chaos engendered by the First World War. The life of a soldier provides a sense of community. Although Lawrence had reservations about what he regarded as the imposed servitude of military life, he had fewer qualms over a concept of history that would connect the individual to the recurring cycles of cosmological time. As evidenced in his broken soldier-figures, Lawrence despaired over the fragmentary postwar present. Through his concept of a cyclical history, he hoped to fashion a place for the individual in the midst of disorder and destruction.

5

The Silver Globe of Time: War and History in the Postwar Fictions

> Life makes its own great gestures, of which men are the substance. History repeats the gesture, so we live in it once more, and are fulfilled in the past. Whoever misses his education in history misses his fulfilment in the past.[1]
> —D. H. Lawrence, *Movements in European History* (1921)

THAT D.H. LAWRENCE WROTE A HISTORY BOOK FOR ADOLESCENTS should come as no surprise given that within his postwar texts the presence of a historical past is integrally associated with the present. In his fictions, Lawrence attempted to overcome the barrenness of the postbellum world by delving into the richness of antiquity. For him, the war was a cataclysm that required explanation and placement within a historical structure. By fitting the Great War into a concept of history, he hoped to make its appalling destruction comprehendible.

Within Lawrence's texts the war serves as both a dislocating and unifying experience. The dual purpose performed by the war is only one of the many tensions within Lawrence's historical concept. He is not interested in tracing the progression of history, but rather of cyclical movements within time; between these movements is a continuity in which the past is inseparably connected to the present. Evelyn Hinz has suggested that Lawrence perceived an organic relationship between humanity and history.[2] He illustrates the interaction between the individual and the past in his history text as well as his novels. In the introduction to *Movements in European History*, he emphasizes the strength granted to individuals in the present by the power of the past. Lawrence is unable to explain how history transmits energy to the modern human. Individuals gain force from the cause of history, from the very fact (or fiction) of the past's nebulous existence. Thus, we embody all of history's events, whether peaceful or bellicose, and reenact them in our daily lives. If we are aware of the cause of history we are, Lawrence argues, condemned to repeat its gestures.

Much has been written on Lawrence's interest in ancient religions.[3] However, his concept of history is not merely a theory of how significant and emotive symbols pass from one generation to the other by means of an interflowing consciousness. He perceives the historical past, present, and future as forming a whole. He sees the essentially timeless nature of history as a reconciled dualism. Past and future come vibrantly together in the consummate present. They meet in a "clash of the two in one, the foam of being thrown up into consummation" (C, 260). Lawrence insists that the antagonism between the two time frames of past and future is reconciled in the present. He believes that "Timelessness" can be achieved by combining past and future within the now (C, 261). A peace treaty can be imposed eventually upon the divisive factions of time within history and the individual, so that history becomes the now made manifest in the body and mind of the writer and his or her reader.

Like Yeats and Joyce, who were influenced by the thought of Giambattista Vico, Lawrence was interested in the philosophy of history. He was acquainted with most of Nietzsche's writings by 1909. Throughout his life he read widely in history and anthropology. His ideas concerning history were constantly developing and under revision. Although his definition of history changes from work to work, the difference is one of emphasis rather than interpretation. In his wide reading Lawrence may have encountered the work of his contemporary, Oswald Spengler. Spengler presages contemporary neo-historicism by arguing that definitions of history are extremely personal narratives, and he shares with Lawrence the opinion that the individual embodies the historical moment:

> A thinker is a person whose part it is to symbolize time according to his vision and understanding. . . . Truth in the long run is to him the picture of the world which was born at his birth. It is that which he does not invent but rather discovers within himself . . . his being expressed in words; the meaning of his personality formed into a doctrine which so far as concerns his life is unalterable because truth and his life are identical. This symbolism is the one essential, the vessel and the expression of human history.[4]

The writer and reader as "vessel and expression of human history" follows Lawrence's earlier claim that the individual is history, as argued in *Movements*.

Despite various changes in expression and emphasis, Lawrence always favored a cyclical view of history. Like Nietzsche, he read Heraclitus and approved of him.[5] Lawrence, like Nietzsche and Heraclitus, viewed the individual as representative of the entire culture. In contrast to the shallowness of wartime characters such as Egbert, Winifred, and Bertie Reid, Lawrence's postwar writings grant the individual a cosmic significance. In *Fantasia of the Unconscious*, he suggests that the individual gathers strength from the universe. Concomitantly, he argues that heavenly bodies derive their power from human beings. In chapter 4 of *Fantasia*, Lawrence uses the image of the tree with its "vast, lissome life in air, and primeval individuality" to illustrate the interdependent connection between life and the individual.[6] He had used this image earlier in the "Study of Thomas Hardy." He regards the individual as relying on the past for energy, just as a tree uses its older cells to provide nourishment for the growing leaves.[7] Lawrence claims that the glory of mankind resides not in the authority-abiding masses but "in the few or more fine, clear lives, beings, individuals, distinct, detached, single as may be from the public" (*STH*, 47). In *Movements in European History*, he develops his concept of the worthy outlaw. He finds history comprised of distinct individuals who stand out and above the spirit and attitudes of their times and embody the energy and events of history.

During the second year of the Great War, Lawrence attempted to explain the occurrence of the conflict in "The Crown." The essential warring dualism within society between love and law, unicorn and lion had come to a standstill; one factor had taken prominence over the other. In "The Crown," Lawrence argues that the struggle between polarities is eternal. The battle between love and law, the individual and authority is a struggle for precedence between past and future. Ideally, these dualities should come together and form "the Crown, the Absolute" of the present (*C*, 259). He claims that the difficulties of the modern world stem from our "seeing in part," our desire to privilege authority over the individual, the past over the future (*C*, 258).

The duality of and conflict between attraction and opposition is explored further in *Movements in European History*.

Lawrence identifies two great currents in mankind: the desire for war and glory and the unification for production. Evelyn Hinz notes that Lawrence's argument for the oneness of history is based upon similes rather than direct comparison.[8] For example, the antagonism of the ancient Roman and Germanic races is likened to the enmity between the present peoples. The conflicts of the past inform the conflicts of the present:

> it is from this intermingling of the two opposite spirits, two different and opposite streams of blood, that modern Europe has arisen. The fusion of the two opposites brought us the greatness of modern days: just as the hostility of the two brings disaster, now as in the old past. (*MEH*, 52)

Despite this linguistic emphasis on duality, Lawrence argues for the metaphorical unity of history. The cycle of European history repeats and completes itself, moving from difference to unity: "So Europe moves from oneness to oneness, from the imperial unity to the unity of the labouring classes, from the beginning to the end" (*MEH*, 252). Out of cultural and racial animosities, Lawrence creates a linguistic balancing act in which unity is emphasized, disparity ignored, and conflict resolved.

In many of his works, D. H. Lawrence presents western European civilization as doomed; to survive, the European must break into a vital future through recourse to the life forces of previous cultures. His urging of present civilizations to look to the past has been erroneously described as "chronological" or "cultural" primitivism.[9] His nostalgic back tracking is not conscious theory; it is an impulsive search to metamorphize history and mitigate the disunity of the present.

For Lawrence, the rise and fall of civilizations is a cyclical process. He sees modern Western civilization as at the end of its cycle. He envisages a return to the old gods of the past, not just through the mimicking of ancient rituals or anthropological studies, but by an instinctive understanding of what our distant predecessors were attempting to encapsulate in their religious beliefs and the representations of their gods.

Lawrence sees civilizations as driven by fear to destroy the older cultures with which they come into contact. The desire to destroy is its own death wish. If modern society is to endure successfully into the next era, it must find within itself the older form of consciousness that still lingers in its blood. For him, modern man's recovery rests in his older consciousness, a knowledge bereft of mechanical attitudes and desires. Man must turn back and rediscover that which gave him allegiance to the gods: "We've got to get them back, for they are the world our soul, our greater consciousness lives in them."[10] Lawrence assumes that it is possible for our present civilization to return to an older, more vital attitude toward the world around us.

In *Sea and Sardinia* (1921), he looks at the world through an ancient's eyes. Hearing the name of Mount Eryx, he experiences the roar of the past, a verbal déjà vu of the blood consciousness:

> I confess my heart stood still. But is mere historical fact so strong, that what one learns in bits from books can move one so? Or does the very word call an echo out of the dark blood? It seems so to me.[11]

Lawrence continued to search for this violent yet beneficent past and to represent it in his writings. During the years that followed the Great War, he strove to assure himself of history's continuity in the midst of dislocation.

On 28 January 1915, Lawrence wrote to E. M. Forster, "it is time to gather again a conception of the Whole ... a conception of the beginning and the end" (*LL* 2:265–66). The difficulty for Lawrence was to devise a holistic vision not only of the present but also of the past and future as he worked in a fragmented society. The search of the protagonists in *The Rainbow* and *Women in Love* is for self-definition, an attempt to come to terms with the individual's place in a society exploding from the center. The quest for selfhood is a difficult one since Lawrence forces his characters to experience the horrors of a world at war and strips them of their identity. The historical movement of *The Rainbow* is neither chronological nor dynastic. It is the history of selfhood. Lawrence traces the phases of growth and occasional regression in each central Brangwen character. The rhythmic movements of the novel are felt not only through the temporal changes of season but within the characters themselves.

Although Lawrence places little emphasis on actual dates or topical events, the reader never experiences a sense of stasis. In *The Rainbow*, time moves through individuals. Instead of underscoring political movements or contemporary events, he emphasizes a series of important moments in the lives of his characters. For instance, Ursula's relationship with Skrebensky is illuminated and defined in vivid scenes that chart her progress toward the formation of selfhood, such as the wedding dance among the moonlit corn stacks and the beach scene in chapter 15. Both of these episodes mark Ursula's development; they foreshadow her rejection of the hollow, mechanized Skrebensky. The portrait of Ursula's advancement is the last in a series of such accounts, for the reader previously has encountered the phases of Tom and Anna Brangwen.

The development of generation after generation of Brangwens and their search for identity propel the reader through the novel. Just as the year passes in seasons, Lawrence's characters, too, have the winter and spring of the soul. Like the rain, the Brangwens are part of history's recurrent, timeless cycle. Each generation influences the following, for better or worse. If the stability of culture represented by Marsh Farm were to disappear, the Brangwens would lose none of their identity. The Brangwens are able to write history. They look beyond the fragments of their daily lives toward a temporal whole. They stand upon a Pisgah mount overlooking the entirety of their time. They reject the "smell of grave-clothes," the New Testament obliteration of the self; they embody the force that will bring about the resurrection of the individual, a positive bodily apocalypse. In their historical presence, the Brangwens resolve the conflict between present and past.

Although most of the members of the Brangwen family are outlaws who seek refuge at Marsh Farm from the little people who wield political authority, it is Ursula who particularly disengages herself from parental and national domination. In the last chapter of *The Rainbow*, the horses represent Ursula's external self. The animals are fenced in by the power that Ursula herself must escape. She perceives the horses as "clenched narrow in a hold that never relaxed . . . pressing for ever till they went mad, running against the walls of time, and never bursting free" (*R*, 452). The horses attempt to instill fear into Ursula, the outsider. She escapes from the struggling herd and drops beyond the boundaries of authority. Unlike the horses, Ursula escapes the walls of time; she falls free from the construct of conventional, progressive history, a model of time used by established power to justify its existence. She successfully peels away the constricting husk imposed by the external world and penetrates to the kernel of her intrinsic self. She cares no more for extraneous things and the restrictions they bring with them: "Why, must she be bound, aching and cramped with the bondage, to Skrebensky and Skrebensky's world?" (*R*, 455). In rejecting the tropes of her former world, Ursula defines herself as a cultural outsider:

> "I have no father nor mother nor lover, I have no allocated place in the world of things, I do not belong to Beldover nor to Nottingham nor to England nor to this world, they none of them exists, I am trammelled and entangled in them, but they are all unreal." (*R*, 456)

Even language is denied Ursula, for her death and rebirth is narrated as a painfully solitary experience in which she speaks to no one but herself. At last, Ursula emerges, free from restraints, reborn into a history that is not history, a contradiction of time's passage: "the kernel was free and naked and striving to take new root, to create a new knowledge of Eternity in the flux of Time" (*R*, 456).

In quest for her self, Ursula finds the other, the unknown: "It was the unknown, the unexplored, the undiscovered upon whose shore she had landed, alone, after crossing the void, the darkness which washed the New World and the Old" (*R*, 457). Her discovery of the new continent of the unknown self, unexposed to history's definitions, owes much to her predecessors, the "fresh, blond, slow-speaking people" who always looked as "if they were expecting something unknown" (*R*, 9). She is heiress to a wealth of generations, a continuity of individuals who avoid the confines of the mass and exist within a time construct of their own making. *The Rainbow* traces the history of the development of the self through a series of generations. Ultimately, Lawrence's novel is the history of humankind. It possesses a timelessness that owes less to his neglect of chronological happenings or to his use of Old Testament metaphor than to his careful portrayal of the history of the self as given in the saga of the Brangwens. *The Rainbow* is a troubling, apocalyptic work. It recommends the destruction of order, the blasting of time, the reassertion of the individual as the maker and measure of all things. It should come as no surprise that Lawrence's novel was banned during the First World War. A frank discussion of the violence of sexual relations, a call for the elimination of authority and the historical construct upon which authority bases its right to rule, and a book dedicated to a German, *The Rainbow* is one of the more subversive texts to have been published in England during the war.

In the story of its publication and subsequent censorship, *The Rainbow* checks Stephen Greenblatt's claim that texts are a revolt against authority that authority contains within itself.[12] *The Rainbow, Women in Love,* and *Lady Chatterley's Lover* (1928) were effectively exiled by the powers of authority. Lawrence's struggles to publish these novels are well known. *The Rainbow* was burned by court order; *Women in Love* was finally published in America over two years after completion; Lawrence printed privately *Lady Chatterley's Lover* in France and mailed it to buyers from Italy. Like their author, these texts were sent wandering, condemned and silenced by the expurgation of publishers and official censorship. Even in our supposedly permissive time, *Lady Chatterley's Lover* is a byword for the undermining of established morality, a fearsome example of sexual misrule.

Lawrence's rejection of modern society, its modes of power, and historical representations was not without its moments of regret. In a letter to Cynthia Asquith of 9 November 1915, he writes,

> When I drive across this country, with the autumn falling and rustling to pieces, I am so sad, for my country, for this great wave of civilisation, 2000 years, which is now collapsing, that it is hard to live. (*LL* 2:431)

He expresses a similar emotion to Edward Marsh in a letter dated 10 November 1915. He notes that his "horrible feeling of helplessness" results from his conviction of the approaching end of civilization, "as if ours was the age only of Decline and Fall" (*LL* 2:433). He mourns the destruction of a society from which he is eager to escape—in both letters he discusses his plans to sail to America. In keeping with his wartime vision of a new community rising from the ashes of the old, Lawrence's lamentation for the passing of the established order contains within it his plans for a New World formation.

The duality of world-weariness and hope for a new order is evident in *Women in Love.* In an early "Prologue" chapter, Lawrence outlines the simultaneous processes of disintegration and construction of society in which the individual will rule.[13] The individual as the bedrock of a new society is the primary theme of *Women in Love.* Unlike *The Rainbow, Women in Love* does not depict the historical movement of generations. Lawrence represents his definition of history through characters who possess the future within themselves. By their actions, his characters make their own history and in doing so define themselves. In addition to the linguistic confrontations between Gerald and Gudrun, Birkin and Ursula, tensions are created by the opposition of their self-made destinies.

In an article entitled "Myth and Fate in the Characters of *Women in Love,*" Donald Eastman suggests that the characters in the novel experience a sense of "historical chaos," an inability to relate past to present.[14] Written during the First World War, *Women in Love* offers no vision of historical unity. In contrast to her unique historical perspective in *The Rainbow,* Ursula, in *Women in Love,* is alienated from the past: "it seemed she had no identity, that the child she had been, playing in Cossethay churchyard, was a little creature of history, not really herself" (*WL*, 390). The world of *Women in Love* exists within a historical gap, a space between two world systems.

One's definition of history is one's definition of self. Gudrun accepts a traditional view of history comprised of the ongoing development of men. The characters of history are her playthings. Although she may laugh at them, in bringing them to herself she acknowledges their power over her:

> [Gudrun and Loerke] played with the past, and with the great figures of the past, a sort of little game of chess, or marionettes, all to please themselves. . . . As for the future, that they never mentioned except one laughed out some mocking dream of the destruction of the world by a ridiculous catastrophe of man's invention. (*WL*, 453)

Loerke and Gudrun regard their present and their future as being as laughable as the past. In playing with "the great figures of the past," they perpetuate the debacles of history. Their dismissal of the future brings about the cataclysm they predict.

In contrast to Gudrun's self-destructive mockery, Halliday and Libidnikov approve a form of primitivism. Halliday's simplistic nostalgia for the primeval past is epitomized by the carved figure of the woman in labor. Birkin pronounces the figure "'art'" (*WL*, 78). Yet he also insists that the sculpture is "'an awful pitch of culture, of a definite sort'" (*WL*, 79). The figure represents the apex of a culture that cannot be fully

comprehended. Like his contemporary Oswald Spengler, Lawrence suggests that people of one culture cannot escape their
world perspective. When they borrow elements from another
culture they only obtain the outward form, never the inward
feeling. Lawrence and Spengler share the view that to claim
intimate kinship with an alien culture is self-deceiving
sentimentality.

For all their modern bohemianism, the Pompadour crowd
desperately seek to lose themselves in the remnants of past
civilizations. The sensationalism of Halliday's interest in the
past is personified by Pussum. She is the perfect example of
what Lawrence describes in "The Crown" as wartime society's
tendency to turn back to the past, to the known self. Several
of the characters in *Women in Love* seek to return to the naïveté
of the past, a compulsion that Lawrence perceives as akin to
joining the "one mass" in its search for destruction (*WL*, 118).

The thrill Gudrun and Gerald find in death, their desire to
return to the childlike being of a past era, and their acceptance
of the future's disintegration are in direct contrast to Birkin's
vision of history. Birkin does not associate with the mass of
humanity. He rejects contemporary nostalgia for the primitive. Through the character of Birkin, Lawrence argues in favor
of the Heraclitean "dry soul," the single individual who escapes
the dark river of dissolution yet who is part of the inevitable
cycle of death and rebirth. Throughout the novel, Birkin asserts that if there is to be a new beginning, there must be
a collapse. Lawrence redefines destruction as an essentially
creative act.

Lawrence refashions the concept of the individual, its relation to the other, and its place in history. He perceives power
as resting within the person, and he grants the individual the
capacity to form history. Thus, he defines power as the ability
to make history. Power is the *Wille zur macht* (will to power).
In "Blessed Are the Powerful" (1925), he disapproves of the
vagueness of Nietzsche's terminology: "We have a confused
idea, that *will* and power are somehow identical. We think we
can have a will-to-power. A will-to-power seems to work out
as bullying."[15] The concept of power envisaged by Lawrence is
much more than the authority to rule granted Gerald by his
workers. Power is the capacity to create, to make of history
what one will, to redefine concepts, and refashion language:
"Power is *pouvoir:* to be able to. Might: the ability to make:
to bring about that which may-be."[16] For Lawrence, power is

creative energy that pushes the individual toward self-determination and the making of history. Against the background of what Lawrence terms "a modern weariness" (*LL* 2:102), Rupert Birkin attempts to break from the old world and enter a new one of his own fashioning. In *Women in Love*, Lawrence portrays a crisis, a society on the brink of a decisive apocalypse, the beginning of an epoch of individualism, the rejection of a mass society for singleness of being.

Self-realization is the subject of *Aaron's Rod* and *Kangaroo*. The protagonists of these novels are men who see themselves as saviors. Rawdon Lilly is "somewhat puzzled" by the world "but he had a certain belief in himself as a saviour" (*AR*, 73). Like Lilly, Richard Somers feels himself betrayed by those around him as they attempt to entice him into the net of their beliefs and demands. Both Lilly and Somers seek a "sheer, finished singleness" (*AR*, 128). Like Birkin, they struggle against the Christian doctrine of "the other cheek" and brotherly love. In *Aaron's Rod*, Jim Bricknell complains to Lilly, "'I'm losing life'" (*AR*, 77). Lilly's response is that "'it's nothing but love and self-sacrifice which makes you feel yourself losing life'" (*AR*, 80). Lilly rejects "'the ideal of love . . . the whole beehive of ideals . . . gone putrid, stinking'" (*AR*, 280–81). He renounces the "love-urge" in favor of the "power-urge" (*AR*, 297). Lilly's power is *pouvoir*, the ability to create, to shape the self. Lawrence's ideal leader is the man who possesses a power urge, the capacity to mold the self and lead the followers who have submitted "to the greater soul in a man" (*AR*, 299).

In *Kangaroo*, Richard Somers argues for a new aristocracy composed of masterpieces of self-definition. Somers asserts that man must live "according to his own idea of himself. . . . For the idea, or ideal of Love, Self-sacrifice, Humanity united in love, in brotherhood, in peace—all this is dead" (*K*, 263–64). The leader Somers foresees is a powerful figure who draws material for the self from the "non-human gods" (*K*, 341). He rejects Kangaroo's "cloying warmth" for the "cold, cold life, in the watery twilight" of self-sufficient individualism (*K*, 125). It is no surprise that Somers insists upon his wife's submission. The self-responsible man must stand alone, his power unadulterated by the presence of another.

Lawrence implements the image of the rainbow in *Kangaroo*. Ursula Brangwen is afforded her vision at the end of a novel in which past generations meet within the individual's struggle for selfhood. Somers, in turn, experiences the conjunction of the self with the universe:

> he looked up and saw the rainbow fume beyond the sea. But it was on a dark background like a coloured darkness. The rainbow was always a symbol to him—a good symbol: of this peace. A pledge of unbroken faith, between the universe and the innermost. (*K*, 155)

Despite his emphasis on the singleness of the individual, Lawrence never preaches entire isolation of the self. Free from the other, the self exists within a cyclical, dialectical relativism to the world. The past is simultaneously the present, and vice versa. The present contains the promise of the future.

The vision of hope that concludes *The Rainbow* is perceptible within the dying societies of *Women in Love, Aaron's Rod, Kangaroo,* and *Lady Chatterley's Lover*. In the first sentence of *Lady Chatterley*, Lawrence proclaims, "Ours is essentially a tragic age."[17] Yet the novel ends with the anticipation of renewal. It is because of the war that Connie Chatterley experiences a "resurrection of the body" (*LCL*, 85). The isolation of the individual is not the answer to a crumbling civilization. Instead, Lawrence creates a union between Mellors and Connie that results in life for both of them. In "the flux" of her "new awakening," Connie is able to see the society she wishes to escape, the world of postwar England (*LCL*, 136). She perceives "half-corpses . . . with a terrible insistent consciousness. . . . There was something uncanny and underground about it all. It was an underworld" (*LCL*, 153).

Such is the insane, emotionally and physically crippled world from which Connie attempts to re-create herself. In spite of Sir Malcolm Reid's anguished cry of "'My God, what a generation,'" Lawrence emphasizes that it is up to individuals like Connie to fashion a continuity of self and history (*LCL*, 282). The spark of life that Connie holds in the fragile chick must be protected and strengthened. Mellors writes to Connie that we must "trust in the little flame, and in the unnamed god that shields it from being blown out" (*LCL*, 301). Beneath the rubble of the collapsing world flickers a flame of hope, the beginnings of a cleansing conflagration.

In the crucial year of 1915, Lawrence divined the apocalyptic resurrection of the world:

> I believe an end is coming: the war, a plague, a fire, God knows what. But the end is taking place: the beginning of the end has set

in, and the process won't be slow. I am very much frightened, but hopeful—a grain of hope yet. (*LL* 2:426)

The rainbow Ursula sees at the conclusion of the Brangwen saga is an apocalyptic vision of past, present, and future in timeless unity. Although the warring society portrayed in *Women in Love* is the last remnant of a collapsing civilization, Lawrence sows seeds of hope for the future. Within their endless, futile conversations, Somers and Lilly set forth a scheme for the self's leadership of the mass, the reappearance of the dark god.

In *Lady Chatterley's Lover*, Lawrence describes the novel as essential to the inauguration of the self's revolution:

And here lies the vast importance of the novel, properly handled. It can inform and lead into new places the flow of our sympathetic consciousness, and it can lead our sympathy away in recoil from things gone dead. Therefore, the novel, properly handled, can reveal the most secret places in life: for it is in the *passional* secret places of life, above all, that the tide of sensitive awareness needs to ebb and flow, cleansing and freshening. (*LCL*, 101)

The novel as significant social force was urged by Lawrence during the First World War. He assured Bertrand Russell that the "bombs" of his novels would bring about a social revolution (*LL* 2:547). In his postwar novels, Lawrence portrays the revolution of the self in conjunction with the powers of the past. However, his battle was a paper one; the individuals who conquer reside only within his texts. Despite his developing enthusiasm over the leadership of the individual, he is frequently dissatisfied with his apocalyptic construct. The turning of history from the mass to the strong man often threatens to backtrack.

Although Lawrence consistently writes about his characters' progress toward a new day, the "Greater Day" to come,[18] he rarely provides an actual vision of this long-awaited rebirth, except for the Rip Van Winkle story of "An Autobiographical Fragment"[19] and "The Man Who Died" (1929). Like his theory of cyclical history, Lawrence's apocalyptic expectations began in the autumn of 1915. In his letters of this period, Lawrence describes the zeppelin raids upon London. He perceives the bombings as ushering in Armageddon. The "new world" he envisaged during the raids was the object of his fifteen-year quest subsequent to the war. In his characters' wanderings and disappointments, he sought to express what Lou Carrington in *St. Mawr* calls "the beginning of something else, and the end of something that's done with."[20]

Lawrence's fantasy of a wartime apocalypse combines the alpha and omega processes of death and rebirth. As much as he was appalled by the First World War, he saw in its wake the potential for a new order. However, early in 1924, he revised his opinion. The war did not prove as cataclysmic as he had hoped. He had doubts about the future. In *Apocalypse*, he sets forth the inherent duality of the self, the desire for self-glorification and self-destruction that manifests itself throughout the fictions. In his writings on Revelation, he urges the pagan concept of external time, seasonal change, the rhythm of birth, death, and resurrection.

He experienced a similar clash between death and resurrection within himself, a fight made evident in his late writings. In *The Plumed Serpent*, Lawrence wrestles with the paradox he set forth in *Fantasia of the Unconscious* between the individual and the "homogeneous" "bloodstream of mankind."[21] In *The Plumed Serpent*, he is careful to place the blame on Kate Leslie for the failure of her marriage to Cipriano. He discredits her for her inadequacy in the role of Malintzi. The character of Kate resembles a wooden doll with which Lawrence can act out the principal evil he perceives in modern European society—the stress placed upon the individual personality. At the conclusion of *The Plumed Serpent*, Lawrence shows Kate stubbornly enshrined within her isolated individuality. Yet we cannot blame her for wanting to escape the "hot, phallic passion" of Cipriano.[22] Lawrence condemns Cipriano's cloying phallicism as much as Kate's seclusion. Neither seems satisfactory. The blood-consciousness Lawrence argues as uniting individuals is paradoxically composed of single beings. The difficulties Lawrence faces in defining how an individual consciousness partakes in the homogeneity of a universal bloodstream are similar to those within his attempts to reconcile yet retain the tensions between past, present, and future. In *The Plumed Serpent*, each aspect of historical time is given separate prominence in the novel; indeed, the novel itself is a linear conception. Yet within Lawrence's "on-and-on-and-on" construct, Don Ramon preaches a religion of the past, reshaped in the present, which will mold the future (*A*, 96).

The problems of contradiction in Lawrence's construct of the self and history are evident in "The Man Who Died." He condemns the eschatological goal, the assertion of "individual self-realization" (A, 148). His Christ rejects "his striving self, which cares and asserts itself" and goes on to seek "being in touch" with the solitary priestess of Isis.[23] Originally, "The Man Who Died" ended at part 1, but in adding part 2 Lawrence emphasizes the necessity of individuals to seek self-realization together. For the reader, the difficulty lies in agreeing that a sense of oneness can be achieved through the type of sexual union he portrays between Christ and the priestess.

Lawrence's Christ makes the prescribed resurrection of the self. Yet he rises to live within the phenomenal world, the world of "the little, personal body."[24] The "greater day" is yet to come: "Risen from the dead, he had realized at last that the body, too, has its little life, and beyond that, the greater life."[25] "The greater day," the epoch beyond the present "common day," is the subject of Lawrence's "The Flying Fish" (1925). Lawrence's pun on Gethin Day's family name combines his vision of a new era with his hope for a strong leader, one who can "rise with the Son of Man, and ascend unto the Father" in order to "see the new day."[26] The parable carries with it its own disclaimers. Gethin Day has spent years in a fruitless voyage around the globe. He is permanently incapacitated by malaria and is forced to return to England on account of his sister's death. The family name has run out; there is "no Day in Daybrook."[27]

Gethin knows of the "hard, fierce finite sun of Mexico."[28] It has "made the ordinary day lose its reality to him."[29] The common day has "cracked like some great bubble."[30] His travels are a failure in the sense that what he has searched for resides at home. Daybrook, the ancestral home of the Days, is described in "the *Book of Days*." It is an ark, the safekeep of the guardians of the "Greater Day."[31] Daybrook rests between past, present, and future. It embodies the historical and personal center that Lawrence strives to describe again and again in his postwar fictions.

Lawrence's life was a journey toward self-discovery, a quest to find himself within the past of the lands in which he traveled. His encounter with Sardinia conjures a great memory. The aged, overworked landscape of Italy provides him with a physical map of the past. In his travel writings and novels, he argues that to enter a country is to reexperience human history. The countryside provides a means of entering human-kind's continuing, ever-connecting consciousness. However,

the instinctive knowledge of the past is not an entirely successful remedy for the mechanic mania of the present. There is a
sterility about the past, a sense of complacency, of being complete. The relatively unknown and uncultivated landscapes of
Sardinia, Australia, Mexico, and New Mexico held a fascination for Lawrence. In these unfurrowed lands there was, for
Lawrence, a looking forward, not just a rediscovery of what
was.

There are essential contradictions in Lawrence's search for
the self. Like his belief in a blood consciousness that connects
all races and cultures but that is dependent upon the individual for its vitality and force, his theory that we must look to
the past to understand better our present asserts the paradox
that we must search the unknown before we can comprehend
the known. During his life, he sought a country that at once
retained its primordial freshness while possessing an aura of
human antiquity. An outlaw denied access to established societies by his dislike of authority and authority's dislike of him,
Lawrence sought to discover the country of the self. His hopes
for a state of selfhood were disappointed. The search proved
contradictory and destructive. Sadly, the land of his body col-
lapsed with illness and nervous fatigue.

In *The Utopian Vision of D. H. Lawrence*, Eugene Goodheart
argues that Lawrence's historicity is "nothing more than the
freedom to discover in the past the possibilities of re-creating
the present."[32] Goodheart's discussion of the utopian theme in
Lawrence's writings emphasizes the *creation* of a new world.
However, throughout much of his work Lawrence underscores
the *destruction* of the self and the present to make way for the
future, and it is often a mythological, no longer existent past
toward which he turns. Such cataclysmic happenings are in
juxtaposition to his carefully crafted theory of historical and
personal unity. The dark sun behind the sun we see, the heart
beating within its shell of granite—these are images of a destructive energy that threatens to explode and shatter its context. Jascha Kessler has argued that Lawrence's novels never
attain completion. His characters are caught in a process of
"unindividualization"; they lack the context of a form of history "we know or can know."[33] It is well known that the final
scenes of Lawrence's novels lack resolution. In their inconclu-
siveness, they represent the futility of knowing that which is
their subject, for what is complete will eventually disintegrate.
His cycles of history, whether individual or universal, always

move toward an apocalyptic destruction that ushers in yet another self, another day, which in turn will be destroyed:

> I prefer to believe in what the Aztecs called Suns: that is, Worlds
> successively created and destroyed. . . .
> This pleases my fancy better than the long and weary twisting
> of the rope of Time and Evolution, hitched on to the revolving
> hook of a First Cause. I like to think of the whole show going bust,
> *bang!*—and nothing but bits of chaos flying about. Then out of the
> dark, new little twinklings reviving from nowhere, nohow.[34]

> > Now, I believe that you won't find it difficult to make
> > money by journalism. But I think you will find it extremely
> > difficult to say what you think—and make money. For in-
> > stance, about the war. If I were reviewing books now, I
> > would say this was a stupid and violent and hateful and
> > idiotic and trifling and ignoble and mean display. I would
> > say I am bored to death by war books. I detest the mascu-
> > line point of view. I am bored by his heroism, virtue, and
> > honour. I think the best these men can do is not to talk
> > about themselves anymore.[35] Virginia Woolf to the London
> > Society for Women's Service, 21 January 1931.

> > I am now & then haunted by some semi mystic very pro-
> > found life of a woman, which shall all be told on one occa-
> > sion; & time shall be utterly obliterated; future shall
> > somehow blossom out of the past. One incident—say the
> > fall of a flower—might contain it. My theory being that the
> > actual event practically does not exist—nor time either. But
> > I dont want to force this. (*D* 3:118)

Placed in juxtaposition, these two passages illustrate Virginia Woolf's ambivalent attitude toward the writing of
women's history. Appalled by the proliferation of texts on the
subject of the First World War, she wants to speak out against
"the masculine point of view." She urges masculine silence.
"The best these men can do," she says, "is not to talk about
themselves anymore." However, the muteness she prescribes
for men is the necessary state of women. She warns women
writers that writing women's truths and making money at the
same time are contradictory goals. In her own writing, Woolf
practices the expected restraints she disapproves of in
women's writing. The enthusiasm with which she speaks of
her vision of the unity of history must be toned down so her
concept can be understandable and acceptable. Her dream of
time's obliteration must not be "forced." The joyous concept
of time caught in the suspended fall of a flower, of events, such

as the Great War, denied cannot be spoken without impunity. The writing of a private history must be muted, camouflaged.

In an article entitled "The Double Helix," Margaret R. Higgonet and Patrice L.-R. Higgonet suggest that women's history follows the pattern of an ascending spiral. Women have been condemned to live within a construct of history that promises change but that, in reality, affords merely a repetition of that which has gone before.[36] Woolf's fictions manifest the double helix of female history. The unification of past and present underscores the constancy of female roles and the binary positions of male and female. The rewriting of history as recurrence illuminates the continuing struggle between the sexes and reaffirms the binary code of sexual difference. The women who attempt to create unity are in constant battle against misogynist, destructive men. Mrs. Ramsay's knitting is scoffed at by her husband. Clarissa Dalloway is interrupted at her sewing by Peter Walsh. In the midst of Clarissa's party, William Bradshaw, representative of masculine authority, speaks of Septimus's suicide. Septimus's death itself is an act that defies the harmony Clarissa struggles to create.

Woolf's writings center upon the problem of history. She was well aware of the difficulties of writing history, the predicament of presenting fact in narrative form. She noted the referential differences between fictional and historical narratives. She recognized that history is written from a point of view; it is a narrative that expresses the interests and ideologies of the writer.

For Woolf, history did not consist of great men performing significant acts. Instead, she was concerned with the secret, daily lives of women and men. In July 1925 she sketches out the "Lives of the Obscure—which is to tell the whole history of England in one obscure life after another" (D 3:37). The project remained with her for the rest of her life. In an entry for 21 August 1927, she argues that the continuity of history rests in the perpetual rituals of daily life. She sees herself as an explorer in an unknown land. She travels in her automobile throughout England, alighting in some small village "like a voyager who touches another planet with the tip of his toe" (D 3:153). The land of discovery is the present but it is also the past:

I am allowed to see the heart of the world uncovered for a moment. It strikes me that the hymn singing in the flats went on precisely so in Cromwell's time. (D 3:153)

Woolf set herself the task of documenting "all these infinitely obscure lives."[37] She anticipates with pleasure the chore of sorting through the accumulation of unrecorded life (*AROO*, 135). Her novels represent the history of the voiceless individual, the unheard "Anon" who speaks with a woman's voice (*AROO*, 74). Although Woolf's fictions treat the riddle of history in general, she specifically concentrates on the unspoken chronicles of women. Her goal is to make the voiceless speak, to articulate the unwritten verses and experiences of Shakespeare's sister, Woolf's representative silenced woman. The difficulties Woolf encounters in "rewriting history" are many (*AROO* 68). There is the problem of devising a language to express a feminine scheme of time. The very silence of her subject depresses her and makes her wary of words. In the end, her concern rests upon the ongoing struggles between men and women and the tyranny of speechlessness enforced by the male upon the other, the female. The conclusion of *Between the Acts* represents the paucity of language and its consequent inability to express the dynamics of human relationships. "Words escape" the playwright, Miss La Trobe, when she seeks to articulate her new play, a fantasy on "two figures, half concealed by a rock" (*BA*, 246). Paradoxically, she finds a mode of speech in the concept of "words without meaning—wonderful words," feminine words (*BA*, 248). Though we are told that the "first words" come into being, Woolf certainly never placed them on paper (*BA*, 248). *Between the Acts*, Woolf's last novel, ends with silence. The history of the cave dwellers, of Isa and Giles, remains unrecorded: "Then the curtain rose. They spoke" (*BA*, 256).

Much of Woolf's fiction relies upon a cyclical structure of time. Solar and seasonal recurrences play a large part in the progression of her narratives. *The Waves* charts the movement of the sun through the sky and its changing reflection upon the sea's fluctuating surface. In *The Years*, time's passage is indicated by the seasonal cycle. The development in the division of time from the hourly to the yearly in the interludes of the two novels reflects the change in her focus. *The Waves* is a study of the transformation of individuals in time. *The Years* examines changes, or the lack thereof, in domestic and national settings. In both novels the subject remains the same; Woolf illustrates the relation of personal to impersonal—how the individual fits into a construct of time.

Woolf's interest in the cyclical patterns of historical recurrence reflects that of her contemporaries, such as Yeats, whose concept of the "gyres" owes much to cabbalistic thought and the writings of Nietzsche, and Joyce, who was influenced by the works of Giambattista Vico. Woolf's own characters adopt this structuring of history. In *The Years*, Eleanor Pargiter wonders if history follows a gigantic, recurring pattern. Several of Woolf's critics have commented upon the cyclical patterns of historical recurrence in her fictions. Allen McLaurin asserts that her "keen sense of the repetitions of life has often found expression in a cyclical view of history."[38] He suggests that in her art Woolf seeks "a fully conscious acceptance of this rhythm of repeated creation and dissolution."[39] In contrast to McLaurin, Harvena Richter argues that although Woolf's concept of time is cyclical, the cycles are never identical. The repetition of "leitmotifs" in Woolf's fictions embodies her spiral structure of time: "these shifting images give a sense not only of time's passage but of its cyclical actions and occurrences—*the thing repeating but never quite the same*."[40] Although in the past, critics of Woolf and modernism in general have shifted away from discussions of myth and cyclical history, nevertheless, such an approach may tell us much about Woolf's view of war and its place in the structure of personal and public history. The bringing together of time's divisions, the unification of history are her antidotes to the cruelty and chaos of the postwar world. Yet the unity of time set forth in her fictions renders a dual function; it repieces the fragments of existence into a holistic vision of human history while at the same time repeating acts of violence and war. In bringing history together into what Bernard in *The Waves* calls "eternal renewal" (*W*, 325) Woolf makes war a Heraclitean experience, and its destructive power becomes simultaneous with acts of reconciliation. In its very timelessness the figure of Orlando represents how history comes together at a point. Though the clothes change to fit the man or woman, Orlando's personal identity remains. As Maria DiBattista has suggested, there are quite a few moments of comic reconciliation in Woolf's fiction, particularly *Orlando*.[41] Her sense of humor is given free rein. The playful image of a man-turned-woman who zestfully, if sometimes painfully, embraces life's experiences is central to the novel. Her joke is upon the stability of time, the self-seriousness of identity. Yet there is an underlying danger, an abyss beneath the gaiety of *Orlando*'s timeless Arcadia. By virtue of having lived for over three hundred years Orlando has experienced seemingly endless conflicts. Sounds of battle echo in her present from her past: "She listened for the sound of gun-firing out at sea. No—only the wind blew. There was no war to-day. Drake had gone; Nelson had gone" (O, 293). Although Drake and Nelson are dead, the sound of their cannons reverberates within the present. The fact that Orlando stops to listen and *expects* to hear the sound of explosions indicates that a history of the living past is not necessarily the history of peace.

The ever-changing, ever-metamorphosing Orlando represents stability in her person. Whatever her status, whatever her sex, she retains her essential identity. Her being in time encapsulates time itself; she is what she has lived through. In the continuity of her being, Orlando physically embodies a comforting unity of time, of past and present focused into a single personality. However, she is not immune to the disruptions of self and state. Her anguish over Sasha's betrayal finds sympathetic expression in the natural disaster of the flood that runs through Jacobean London. A similar juxtaposition of displaced affection and external agitation occurs in the last chapter. In the midst of the mechanical chaos following the First World War, Orlando stops and relives the emotional turmoil of three hundred years before:

> a whiff of scent . . . a figure—was it a boy's or was it a girl's . . . a girl, by God! furred, pearled, in Russian trousers; but faithless, faithless! (O, 272)

The disarrangement of the emotions, as in the London of earlier days, is reflected in the chaos of the outer world. Like the destructive flood of the seventeenth century, the present is swept away by mechanical contraptions, by the mechanization of time itself:

> the process of motoring fast out of London so much resembles the chopping up small of identity which precedes unconsciousness and perhaps death itself that it is an open question in what sense Orlando can be said to have existed at the present moment. (O, 276)

"'Nothing is any longer one thing,'" complains Orlando (O, 274). However, to what extent was anything ever "one" in the construct of *Orlando?* Although Woolf's narrative appears to urge a concept of history that predicates the simultaneity of time, like all narratives her novel unfolds in a linear manner. In *A Room of One's Own*, she readily acknowledges the difficulties of creating a vision of unity using the sequential structure of the sentence. As we will later see, for Woolf the problem of history is at bottom a problem of language.

Gillian Beer has astutely noted that Woolf's vision of a united past and present results in temporal stasis. She argues that Woolf recognized "the inertness of the human condition."[42] If we admit that Woolf regarded alterations in time and the human condition as illusory, then, Beer claims, history for Woolf was simply a game, "playful, a spume of language."[43] Beer's optimistic view of Woolf's approach to history is reassuring. Yet there is a negative aspect to Woolfian timelessness. In *Orlando*, the constancy of change is changelessness itself: "Change was incessant, and change perhaps would never cease" (*O*, 160). The absence of transformation within continued mutability suggests a stifling immobility of being. Despite the changes in age, position, and gender that Orlando undergoes, for over three hundred years she retains the same self. In spite of the years she has lived through and the changes she has experienced, she still suffers the identical emotional pain that has affected her for hundreds of years. She remembers the anguish caused by Sasha in the reign of James I well into the twentieth century. For better or worse "Time has passed over" Orlando (*O*, 274). Pleasant sensations and suffering possess a homogeneity that is concurrently rich and stagnant.

Plus ça change, plus c'est la même chose. The phrase illuminates the historical construct within Woolf's texts. In her fictions, women predominantly play the role of unifiers, creators who seemingly bring together disparate elements into momentary unity. The word *momentary* is significant for, in the end, Woolf's female characters are no more successful at constructing unity of word and person than are male counterparts. The binary at the heart of her vision of oneness is not between men, who fragment the world through acts of war, and women, who seek to resolve conflict, but rather between acts of cohesion and acts of dissolution.[44] The process of amalgamation described by Woolf is often represented by the act of knitting. The power Mrs. Ramsay displays through her knitting is terrible in its immensity. As she knits, Mrs. Ramsay strings out the fate of individuals and fashions their future:

> Smiling, for an admirable idea had flashed upon her this very second—William and Lily should marry—she took the heather

mixture stocking, with its criss-cross of steel needles at the mouth of it, and measured it against James's leg. (*TL*, 45)

Mrs. Ramsay knits a stocking for the lighthouse keeper's crippled son.[45] Her dinner brings together lonely, rejected human beings. The table unites Mr. Carmichael, the saturnine poet who takes opium; Lily Briscoe, a woman conscious of her age and unmarried status; William Bankes, a quiet bachelor; Charles Tansley, the nervous, insecure sycophant of Mr. Ramsay. These incompatible elements join together at Mrs. Ramsay's table. She creates form out of seating arrangements and *boeuf en daube*. She is forever knitting people and things together, producing order and purpose out of chaos:

> There it was, all round them. It partook, she felt, carefully helping Mr. Bankes to a specially tender piece, of eternity. . . . there is a coherence in things, a stability; something, she meant, is immune from change, and shines out . . . in the face of the flowing, the fleeting, the spectral, like a ruby. . . . Of such moments, she thought, the thing is made that remains for ever after. This would remain. (*TL*, 163)

Like Clarissa Dalloway, who dreads her own party, Mrs. Ramsay fears failure: "Nothing seemed to have merged. They all sat separate" (*TL*, 130). In the end, she appears to succeed; Minta and Paul become engaged, Lily Briscoe is pleasant to the awkward Tansley. For a moment, Mrs. Ramsay triumphs.

Although Clarissa Dalloway does not knit, she sews. Her sewing provides the same conjoining of elements as Mrs. Ramsay's knitting. The act of knitting forms a garment from separate, minute acts. In sewing, Clarissa mends a tear in her dress and unites that which has been divided. Like Mrs. Ramsay's dinner, Clarissa's party integrates contradictory figures; the Prime Minister and the pathetic Ellie Henderson are both her guests.

The creative acts of Mrs. Ramsay and Mrs. Dalloway serve to resolve division in the external world and assert the oneness of the self. In *To the Lighthouse*, Mrs. Ramsay functions as the focus of the novel. She is the center line, the significant form of Lily's painting; she represents the unity of vision that Lily has striven to attain throughout the novel. For her daughter, Prue, Mrs. Ramsay represents the Platonic ideal of being in itself: "That is the thing itself, she felt, as if there were only one person like that in the world; her mother" (*TL*, 179).

In *Mrs. Dalloway*, Clarissa is the core around which the rest of the novel's elements are arranged. Just as her heart is her most essential part, so Clarissa rests at the heart of the novel. She is being itself. Her very existence fashions unity, wholeness. Mrs. Ramsay and Clarissa Dalloway integrate their worlds through acts of creation (knitting and sewing) and their respective parties. Through the rituals of domestic life they create an integral center upon which human activity can focus. Throughout Woolf's novels, the female figure serves as a figure of unity; she is the artist who brings all things together.

However, confusion exists within the unified worlds of Woolf's fictions. Her female inventors may embody the essence of being for its own sake; yet they contain within themselves the seeds of destruction. Although Clarissa is an integrator, her physical frailty threatens to bring about the collapse of her body and the world she has constructed. She suffers from heart disease. Her illness is emblematic of the strain caused by her struggle against chaos and disorder. In her capacity to empathize, as seen in her identification with Septimus Warren Smith and the old woman at the window, Clarissa takes into herself the very thing against which she battles. Hollowness, the emptiness at the center, is what Clarissa fights against both in herself and in her life. Her heart is symbolic of the integrity she seeks to impose upon the world. However, her weak heart promises the advance of death. She combines life and death, unity and destruction. She is at once the nucleus of her world, the unifying line, as well as that which will shatter the core. From out of disorder, she fashions her party. Yet death approaches, enters, and becomes one of her guests. In experiencing life and death, creation and destruction simultaneously, Clarissa personifies Woolf's concept of contemporaneous history. The continual cycles of the collapse and rebirth of human history are reenacted within her. As Peter Walsh notes, she is at once "terror" and "ecstasy" (*MD*, 293).

In Woolf's fictions, the concept of the female as creator and destroyer is not limited to single figures such as Mrs. Ramsay or Clarissa Dalloway. In *Jacob's Room*, the feminine act of knitting represents domestic and historical stability:

> at sunset, when the ships in the Piraeus fire their guns . . . and the women roll up the black stockings which they are knitting in the shadow of the columns, call to their children, and troop off down the hill back to their houses. (*JR*, 241–42)

The unidentified Greek women are as timeless as the architecture beneath which they sit. Like the Parthenon, they, too, seem "likely to outlast the entire world" (JR, 243). However, their changelessness is sinister. In the midst of war, they remain unmoved:

> But the red light was on the columns of the Parthenon, and the Greek women who were knitting their stockings and sometimes crying to a child to come and have the insects picked from its head were as jolly as sand-martins in the heat . . . until the ships in the Piraeus fired their guns. (JR, 287)

The women's actions remain unvaried despite the outbreak of the First World War. Their immutable activities of knitting and child caring diminish the differences apparent between the two passages. In the first extract, the Parthenon represents the constancy of human history. It is "far from being decayed"; its beauty is "immortal" (JR, 242–43). In the second passage, Woolf emphasizes the tragic alteration in the world. The Parthenon no longer rests in "silent composure" (JR, 243). The reverberations of war are felt throughout Greece:

> The sound spread itself flat, and then went tunnelling its way with fitful explosions among the channels of the islands.
> Darkness drops like a knife over Greece. (JR, 287–88)

In the domesticity of their actions, the knitting women reveal a terrible strength. The eternal consistency of their daily life provides a stable base upon which chaos develops.

The "elderly grey nurse" in *Mrs. Dalloway* is another example of the dual nature of Woolf's female characters (MD, 85). Like Mrs. Ramsay and the Greek women in *Jacob's Room*, she is a knitter. As she measures off her yarn and plies her needles she watches "a baby asleep in its perambulator" and Peter Walsh napping on a park bench. "Moving" her hands "indefatigably" in the changing rhythms of her knitting, the nurse is a Fate who marks out the lives of the sleepers (MD, 86–87). As she knits "over" Walsh and the baby their web of dreams is contrived. Walsh's dream reveals the joyous perpetuity and catastrophic disappointments of human history:

> The solitary traveller is soon beyond the wood; and there, coming to the door with shaded eyes, possibly to look for his return, with hands raised, with white apron blowing, is an elderly woman who

seems . . . to seek, over the desert, a lost son . . . to be the figure of
the mother whose sons have been killed in the battles of the world.
So, as the solitary traveller advances down the village street where
the women stand knitting . . . the evening seems ominous; the figures still; as if some august fate, known to them, awaited without
fear, were about to sweep them into complete annihilation. (*MD*,
88–89)

The women the "solitary traveller" encounters represent both
birth and death. In spite of their recognition of approaching
disaster they continue with their homely labors. Their sons
"have been killed in the battles of the world" in which they do
not or cannot take part. Knitting and reproduction are two of
many ways Woolf portrays women as battling against their
"old antagonist, life," a battle that will surely be lost but that
they nevertheless must endure.

Despite Woolf's assertion in *Three Guineas* that "to fight has
always been the man's habit, not the woman's" (*TG*, 13), in her
writing she occasionally characterizes women as encouraging
conflict. Clarissa Dalloway is the wife of a politician. Lady
Bruton is "a strong martial woman" who conceives a eugenic
plan for populating Canada with "both sexes born of respectable parents" (*MD*, 164). Miss Kilman, too, has "lost her sense
of proportion" (*MD*, 164). Her bitterness against the loss of her
education and her brother's death in the First World War has
led her to hate. The nationalistic animosity that led to her
brother's death inspires Miss Kilman against Clarissa.

Perhaps the most disquieting image of women participating
in the destruction of a world they labor to sustain occurs at
the conclusion of *Jacob's Room*. Mrs. Flanders amalgamates
domestic constancy with military catastrophe:

far away, she heard the dull sound, as if nocturnal women were
beating great carpets. . . . were the chickens safe? Was that some-
one moving downstairs? . . . No. The nocturnal women were beating great carpets. (*JR*, 288)

Woolf uses the image of women beating carpets to suggest the
sound of distant shell fire. The conceit had previously appeared
in an article entitled "Heard on the Downs: The Genesis of
Myth" in the *Times* of 15 August 1916. In this short article,
Woolf discusses how the war has made its way into local rumor, ghost stories, and tales of addled eggs. The stories were
created by the denizens of the Sussex downs in response to the

shell fire that could be heard across the Channel and to the general stress created by the war. None of the myths she reports is as bizarre as her domestic fantasy. The guns in France sound

> like the beating of gigantic carpets by gigantic women, at a distance. You may almost see them holding the carpets in their strong arms by the four corners, tossing them into the air, and bringing them down with a thud while the dust rises in a cloud about their heads.[46]

The strange image exemplifies Woolf's combination of domestic permanence and the chaos of war. For Woolf, the order created by women in the home always threatens to disintegrate. Unity perpetually rests on the verge of collapse.

In *To the Lighthouse*, the tranquility Mrs. Ramsay toils to attain falls apart. Chaos descends upon the house in the Hebrides, breaking the fragile structure of human domesticity. The downfall of order culminates in the outbreak of war. The decomposition of the Ramsay household has its parallel in the collapse of world order. The steady stroke of the lighthouse's beam no longer serves as a unifying factor. The ominous presence of death and destruction that Mrs. Ramsay had camouflaged with love is disclosed. The shawl she uses to cover the boar's skull falls loose, revealing the memento mori beneath.

Mrs. Ramsay dies and Mr. Ramsay is forced to grasp at emptiness during the night. Prue dies in childbirth, her own effort at creation a failure. Andrew Ramsay is killed by an exploding shell in France. Woolf applies the chaos of war to a domestic setting so that the anarchy of a world at arms is also the collapse of family order, of wood and stone, glass and china. Muffled sounds, like the burst of distant shells, create minute vibrations throughout the house. Jacob Flanders's death is poignantly foreshadowed by his empty room. Woolf does not describe the moment of his death on the battlefield. She portrays the desolation caused by Jacob's demise in the gesture of his mother who holds out "a pair of Jacob's old shoes" to his best friend, Bonamy (*JR*, 290). The homely motion disguises the brutality of war. In Mrs. Flanders's simple gesture, Woolf brings war into the home. Although the image is in contrast to works by male writers who dwell upon the horrors of the battlefield, Woolf's depiction of war is no less affecting in its mundanity.

The "Time Passes" section of *To the Lighthouse* is the central line around which the novel is arranged. In *To the Lighthouse*, the war functions as an abyss, a gap in time into which all order collapses. The integrity Mrs. Ramsay creates founders. Beneath the tranquility of children making mud pies and fishing boats placed in readiness for the next day's outing is "something out of harmony" (*TL*, 207). The powers of change—daily and yearly cycles, bad weather and fine—hold "their court without interference" (*TL*, 208). The "gigantic chaos" of nature and war displays a terrifying indifference (*TL*, 208). The horror of time passing, death, and war is expressed in domiciliary terms. The destruction of war is signified through the emptiness of a coffee cup, the echoing vacuum of a family home. As Lily looks out of the window that had previously framed Mrs. Ramsay engaged with her knitting, she sees the frightening apparition of the widowed Mr. Ramsay exclaiming upon death and human isolation:

> Suddenly, Mr. Ramsay raised his head as he passed and looked straight at her . . . ("Alone" she heard him say, "Perished" she heard him say) and like everything else this strange morning the words became symbols. (*TL*, 227–28)

Like Lily's empty cup, Mr. Ramsay's words point to the disappearance of the prewar life. The abundance that distinguished Mrs. Ramsay and her home is no more.

The cleaning woman, Mrs. McNab, bitterly notes the changes brought about by the war. Household staff is no longer easy to find and prices have gone up. She nostalgically reflects on the years preceding the war. Servants were treated properly and were well fed. Numerous exotic guests were entertained. In contrast, the newcomer, Mrs. Bast, who helps Mrs. McNab clean the house, has no "ball of memories" to unwind (*TL*, 217). Yet she perceives a difference between the old, prewar days and the present: "Ah, said Mrs. Bast, they'd find it changed. . . . They'd find it changed" (*TL*, 217–18).

The war in Woolf's novels functions as a temporal abyss. There is no passing of time in "Time Passes." Only the gradual disintegration of the house's physical order marks the changes of the years. In *Mrs. Dalloway*, Septimus has a vision of the emptiness of unity, the chaos behind order. He sees a "gradual drawing together of everything to one centre before his eyes, as if some horror had come almost to the surface and was about to burst into flames" (*MD*, 24–25). A similar image occurs in *The Waves*. Rhoda observes "the brightness on the side of that jug like a crack in darkness with wonder and terror" (*W*, 243). Louis's hallucination of apocalyptic destruction moves from the single human creation to the disintegration of all human history and the chronicles of human time:

> "But listen," said Louis, "to the world moving through abysses of infinite space. It roars; the lighted strip of history is past and out; Kings and Queens; we are gone; our civilisation; the Nile; and all life. Our separate drops are dissolved; we are extinct, lost in the abysses of time, in the darkness." (*W*, 246)

Yet across the abyss of the war's destruction can be heard the refrain "'D'you remember? . . . D'you remember?'" (*TL*, 263). This simple song of recollection suggests that when one reexperiences the past in the present, guilt may be expiated, disorder overcome. The song asserts that life is worth the living. In remembering Mrs. Ramsay, Lily Briscoe is able to complete her painting. Her work places limits upon the unceasing flux of change and creates stability in the midst of turmoil like a lighthouse at sea. In recalling the prewar idyll of "The Window," Woolf's characters underscore the discrepancy between the harmony of the past and the disorder of the present. Ultimately, *To the Lighthouse* is an elegaic recollection of the prewar world.

The war in *To the Lighthouse* is neither a factor of change nor an indicator of permutation. The war simply brings the illusion of difference. After the deaths of so many of the Ramsay family and the cataclysmic leviathan dance of the war, life must be altered. After crossing the abyss of the war, the present cannot be the same. Yet the Ramsay home in "The Lighthouse" is depressingly similar to that in "The Window." Like Mrs. Ramsay, Lily works to bring forth an order that contains its own collapse. Mr. Ramsay demands female support. Sadly, his son, James, is no different. Cam has assumed the role of pacifier that her mother held before her.

The double helix of women's history is nowhere more apparent than in *The Years*. In this novel Woolf exemplifies her claim in *Three Guineas* that "It seems as if there were no progress in the human race but only repetition" (*TG*, 120). The repetitions in women's history are central to both *The Years* and *Three Guineas*. Although separate works, Woolf originally conceived them as a whole under the title of *The Pargiters* and worked on them simultaneously. The title of *The Years* suggests progression, as does the narrative's linear movement. The First World War appears to bridge the passing of the old days at Abercorn Terrace and the advent of the new generation of Pargiters. *The Years* is an externalized version of *The Waves*. Whereas *The Waves* charts the ebb and flow of growing consciousness, *The Years* depicts the surface changes in the political realm. The passing of kings and queens, the raids on London during 1917, the armistice of November 1918 are all remarked. However, the postwar world of *The Years*, like that in *To the Lighthouse*, is depressingly similar to the Edwardian past.

The years go round and round but bring with them little that is new. Following an evening meal consumed in her cousin's cellar during a bomb raid, Eleanor Pargiter contemplates the "new world" toasted in by Sara. Eleanor feels remade beyond time, immune to the changes brought about by time and its companion, death. Although Eleanor feels as if she has escaped to "another space of time" where there is no mutability, the sense of expansion and freedom she shares with Nicholas can barely be articulated:[47]

> "About the new world . . ." she said aloud. "D'you think we're going to improve?" she asked.
> "Yes, yes," he said, nodding his head. . . .
> "But how . . ." she began, ". . . how can we improve ourselves . . ."
> "It is only a question," he said—he stopped. He drew himself close to her—"of learning. The soul. . . ." Again he stopped. (*Y*, 319)

The war appears to remove social barriers. In the passage quoted above, Eleanor speaks with Nicholas, a Polish homosexual, hardly an introduction she could have attained in 1880. Yet the conversation occurs in dislocated sentences, a structure in which the pauses are more significant than the words, suggesting that the two are not entirely communicating.

Conversational stasis reflects social stasis. Sarah, Eleanor's cousin, points out that communication is illusory—nothing new is said. She regards conversations as predictable. They inevitably follow the same patterns: "'people always say the same thing'" (*Y*, 320). The new world of *The Years* enters with neither a bang nor a whimper. The tension of waiting for social change and improved communication between individuals is comparable to waiting for the ever-approaching bomb to fall:

> The silence was profound. Nothing happened. . . . Another gun boomed. . . .
> There was a profound silence. Nothing happened. (Y, 313)

The changes effected by the war are minimal. Eleanor believes "That things have changed for the better. . . . What I mean is, we've changed in ourselves. . . . We're happier—we're freer'" (Y, 416). The inconclusive nature of Eleanor's assertion points to the improbability of her argument. Patrick questions the assumption that things have changed. He disagrees with Eleanor and Kitty that the quality of women's lives has improved: "'Now these ladies have got the vote,' he said, turning to North, 'are they any better off'" (Y, 433). Although his remark may sound as if he is against the women's movement, what Patrick's statement reflects is Woolf's own distrust of organized politics:

> "what do these fellows want to be shooting each other for? I don't join any societies; I don't sign any of these"—he pointed to the placard—"what d'you call 'em? manifestoes." (Y, 434)

North condemns Patrick for being "old" and for saying "the same thing all over again" (Y, 434). The characters in the last chapter of *The Years* repeat the conversations they had participated in many years before. Nicholas reiterates his opinion of "the psychology of great men" (Y, 339), a topic he had expounded in 1917. Sarah mimics the unchanging nature of Nicholas and Eleanor's conversation. North remarks that even Eleanor's physical appearance appears unchanged, despite the passing years. Conversely, Eleanor finds North just the same: "She still saw traces of the brown-eyed cricketing boy in the massive man, who was so burnt, and a little grey too over the ears" (Y, 330).

Woolf treats the stasis of human history with pessimism. Rose Pargiter's enthusiasm and fervent energy, her commitment to the cause of suffragism and her "war work" have been acknowledged with a mere "decoration," a "red ribbon" (Y, 387). The immutability of human existence, its ceaseless cycles of reproduction and birth weigh upon North. In seeking to alleviate the sameness of the human condition he prescribes yet another war. All change results in changelessness:

> The men shot, and the women . . . the women broke off into innumerable babies. And those babies had other babies; and the other babies had—adenoids. . . . Could nothing be done about it? he asked himself. Nothing short of revolution, he thought. The idea of dynamite, exploding dumps of heavy earth, shooting earth up in a tree-shaped cloud, came to his mind, from the War. But that's all poppy-cock, he thought; war's poppy-cock, poppy-cock. (Y, 405–6)

North's prescription for changing the eternal sameness of things is another war. As a soldier, he returns to that which he knows best. Woolf suggests that what may be the unknown quickly becomes, if it is not already, the all too familiar.

The Greek root for *nostalgia* combines "the return home" with the "pain" of remembrance. Linguistic acts in Woolf's fictions emphasize the unchanging nature of human history. In attempting to visualize the Berkelyean theories of Mr. Ramsay, Lily Briscoe must incorporate that which is familiar: "she always saw, when she thought of Mr. Ramsay's work, a scrubbed kitchen table" (TL, 40). Absence must be filled with the known. In envisaging Mr. Ramsay's philosophical theories, Lily is condemned to repeat the domesticity of feminine language. She is locked into the linguistic patterns of her sex.

In her introduction to *Life as We Have Known It, by Co-operative Working Women* (1931), Woolf suggests that the women of England's lower class employ the same force against which they struggle. She compares "swords" to hands, "rifles" to speeches.[48] She implies that in seeking to escape domination these women use the machinery of a violence they aim to overcome. Even the position of women as peacekeepers and men as warmongers underscores the essential polarity that is the root of all battle.

Woolf suggests that in their attempts to tell of their struggles for equal pay and equal rights the women write with the language "of those obscure writers before the birth of Shakespeare" who found "few words and those awkwardly."[49] Forced to use a borrowed language, the women of England's co-operative movement speak haltingly with "half articulate speech."[50] She describes a conference on "a hot June morning in Newcastle in the year 1913"[51] as dominated by "an inarticulate uproar."[52] The oxymoronic phrase points to the inadequacy of language in depicting human history, a subject she explores in her fictions.

Throughout her work, Woolf portrays the difficulty of breaking the silence of women's history as residing within the very nature of language itself. In "Woman's Sentence, Man's Sentencing," Sandra Gilbert asserts that Woolf's writings evince an "alienation from language."[53] Gilbert's comment sheds an interesting light on Woolf's repetitive style. The act of verbal repetition in Woolf's novels results in disjunction. North's obsession with the word *adenoidal* ultimately renders it meaningless. Although the repetition of phrases in Woolf's novels should underscore the concept of simultaneity in her writing as opposed to traditional linear narrative, it is important to look closely at what is being repeated. In *Jacob's Room*, phrases and whole sentences recur. However, these elements frequently describe death and destruction. As in *The Voyage Out*, Woolf uses the image of the moth or butterfly to represent the self's futile search for union with the other. Jacob's collecting of a butterfly results in death: "The tree had fallen the night he caught it. There had been a volley of pistol-shots suddenly in the depths of the wood" (*JR*, 34). Within the Flanders's kitchen lurks a death's-head moth. In section 3, the sound of a pistol shot once again signifies a death in the forest. The repetition within these passages points to the continuity amid change provided by memory. Yet memory recalls the inevitable fact of death; the stability afforded is one of certain destruction. The recollection of images from the past provides a dismal constancy.

The troublesome nature of linguistic acts is epitomized by the airplane in *Mrs. Dalloway*. The immediate message conveyed to the crowd surrounding Buckingham Palace is one of fear. Although the war is over, it still exists in memory. Clarissa jumps with nervous apprehension at the backfiring of a car, which sounds like "a pistol shot in the street outside" (*MD*, 22). Hearing the sound of an airplane's engine, the crowd before the palace looks up instinctively, the bomb raids of 1917 in their minds. The airplane's message is an ominous one suggesting death and destruction. The smoke letters it creates are indecipherable. Significantly, they disappear before the eyes of London's citizens and prove unreadable. The only message that remains is one of trepidation.

Septimus Warren Smith is not concerned with whether the airplane spells out an advertisement for "Glaxo" or "Kreemo" or "toffee" (*MD*, 33). He recognizes the letters as a bulletin from the dead in Thessaly, where words "split" their "husks" and lose their meaning (*MD*, 106). The beauty Septimus seeks exists in a kingdom without words. Like the "seedy-looking, nondescript man" in Saint Paul's, he looks for "something which has soared beyond seeking and questing and knocking of words together" (*MD*, 44). Although he tries to make it known, Septimus's communiqué that "no one kills from hatred . . . how there is no crime" miscarries (*MD*, 38–39). His papers reach no one. He burns his own words. Like the message written by the airplane, Septimus's efforts at communication drift away as smoke.

The disjointed fragments written by the airplane in the sky are comparable to the nonsensical song of the old woman at Regent's Park Tube Station. Both communicative acts signify nothing. Unlike the airplane, which at first suggests war and death and whose message is written in the impermanency of smoke, the woman's song tells the ancient story of female love. Her song is as ageless as the urge to unite and create. Though the person she sings of has "been dead these centuries," the "rude" mouth tells of the union of love (*MD*, 124). This act of love, this bringing together of that which is separate through syllables that have no meaning, is typical of the dual role language plays in Woolf's fictions. The syllabic form of the song questions the assumptions we make about the functions of language. Within the form of the song rests the tensions between order and disorder, creation and destruction that characterize Woolf's writings.

The image of the singing woman occurs in several of the novels. In *Jacob's Room*, an "old blind woman" sings not for money but out of "her gay wild heart—her sinful, tanned heart—for the child who fetches her is the fruit of sin" (*JR*, 107–8). There is something disreputable about all of Woolf's female singers. Mrs. McNab, in *To the Lighthouse*, sings a "dirge" in which there is twined some "incorrigible hope" (*TL*, 203). She is toothless; she leers, drinks, and gossips. Yet the "visions of joy" (*TL*, 203) in her life cause her to sing a song representing "persistency itself, trodden down but springing up again" (*TL*, 202). The image of the woman singing of love and death in incomprehensible syllables was an important one for Woolf. Apparently the figure came from an actual experience which she recorded in her diary entry for 8 June 1920:

> An old beggar woman, blind, sat against a stone wall in Kingsway holding a brown mongrel in her arms & sang aloud. There was a recklessness about her. . . . Defiant—almost gay, clasping her dog

for warmth. How many Junes has she sat there, in the heart of London? . . . Oh, damn it all, I say, why cant I know all that too? . . . It was gay, & yet terrible & fearfully vivid. . . . yet I can't say what "it" is. (*D* 2:47–8)

For Woolf, the singing woman represents the difficulties inherent in language. Lily Briscoe, in *To the Lighthouse*, questions the concept of linguistic meaning. She imagines Mr. Carmichael, the poet, as existing in a world where "'you' and 'I' and 'she' pass and vanish; nothing stays; all changes; but not words not paint" (*TL*, 276). Despite her affirmation of artistic creation, as she stands in front of her painting Lily questions the communicative act before life's desolation and disappointments:

What was it then? What did it mean? Could things thrust their hands up and grip one; could the blade cut; the fist grasp? Was there no safety? (*TL*, 277)

Lily envisages meaning as rent by violence. Communication falls before the animosity it seeks to conquer.

The rewriting of history Woolf prescribes in *A Room of One's Own* has little in common with Joan Scott's assertion that to write women's history we must break the silence that surrounds women's experiences in war.[54] Woolf argues that the silence of women's history is the silence within language itself. When the center of discourse no longer holds, the telling of history becomes problematic. In *Orlando*, the attempt to relate history as seen through the lives of individuals is shown to be ineffectual. Woolf refers to Sterne's linguistic joke in *Tristram Shandy* (1759–67) to depict the impossibility of expression and provides her own empty space to signify that which cannot be linguistically represented. In doing so, she uncovers the paradoxical nature of linguistic activity and discloses the silence that resides in all discourse. Although Sterne's joke is an old one, she uses it to represent the modern questioning of language and the emptiness of creative achievements in a world that misunderstands or destroys them.

However, in *The Waves* the disintegration of language is countered by the promulgation of new verbal forms. The book filled with Bernard's collected phrases drops to the floor and is swept away by the charwoman. All phrases are lost; a new means of expression must be sought: "I need a little language such as lovers use, words of one syllable. . . . I need a howl; a cry" (*W*, 323). The language Bernard desires is the language of

Woolf's singing women. As lovers, they speak a "little language" that recalls the image of the beloved. They use "words of one syllable" that are both celebration and elegy:

> ee eum fah um so
> foo swee too eem oo—
>
> (*MD*, 123)

These are the words Bernard seeks. He desires to recapture the language of children. His language is a joyous celebration of life, a cry of victory over death. "With an absence of all human meaning," these words articulate the inexpressible (*MD*, 123).

War and conflict occupy a central position in Woolf's fictions. The antagonism between meaning and nonmeaning, the struggle between unity and disorder, are polar concepts that comprise the essential struggles that inform her writings. Both Woolf and Lawrence subscribed to the concept of a cyclical or simultaneous history, one that provided for destruction as well as creation. In the writing of their histories, they portray the forces of disorder that threaten to dislocate the constructs of their narratives. In order to escape what they saw as the ongoing struggles between men and women, creation and destruction, language and silence, both authors turned to the supposedly ordered world of their fictions. Furthermore, during the events of the First and Second World Wars, Lawrence and Woolf took refuge in planned alternative cultures, respectively Rananim and the Society of Outsiders. Their fictions themselves could be, and often are, termed utopian; in the very act of writing they affirm the power of creation over surrounding linguistic and material chaos. Their novels precariously reaffirm the order and unity that modern warfare and the contemporary questioning of linguistic acts threaten to destroy. However, within their fictional works, the authors question the beneficence of history and the words that construct it. Like Elaine Scarry, they perceive war and history as at once a binary composed of warring dimensions and the coming together of these conflicting polarities into a unity that contains within itself a seething multiplicity.[55] Their fictions simultaneously affirm the positive nature of the written word and condemn the dubious acts of violence that it preserves. For Woolf and Lawrence, history and the language that constructs it are at once full of promise and desolation. On this razor edge of balance rests the significance of their art.

Conclusion

A COLLEAGUE ASKED ME THE TOPIC OF THE PROJECT ON WHICH I was currently at work. When I responded, "D. H. Lawrence and Virginia Woolf," he paused, then mused, "Ah ... strange bedfellows!" Indeed. His perplexity over this unusual combination is not unique. Many readers believe that given Woolf's dislike of patriarchal society and Lawrence's fascination with the dynamics of male leadership, they would have little in common. Yet the responses of these two writers toward the Great War complement and reveal one another. Although often different in degree or focus, their readings of the war and conflict—linguistic, domestic, or emotional—are similar in kind. Both authors saw the individual and society as caught within a cyclical, dialectical relativism in which the self, whether it be an individual or a nation, must always engage in a Hegelian struggle with the other. Between and within this tension rests the moment of definition, of being. Thus, through the tensions created by a comparative reading of their fictions, Woolf and Lawrence disclose and define one another.

Both writers adopted the stance of the other to society's self. From out of the ensuing struggle, they wrote the text of themselves and the alternative worlds they sought to inhabit. Paradoxically, it was only through their constant battles with the world around them that these writing, defining selves could construct their visions. The Society of Outsiders and Rananim exist in that balanced moment when the self found oneness and struggles were resolved. Of course, such a moment was fleeting, and Woolf and Lawrence ultimately found their utopias disappointing. Their new worlds can be found in their fictions, for it was in the very act of writing that the authors created a world of their own. In writing, they crafted moments when the essential struggle was forgotten and definition was attained. For them writing is an act of hope; it presupposes that the final work will withstand the vagaries of time and remain, however briefly, distinct from the world pressing upon it.

This discussion is but the beginning of a conversation that may continue between the contemporaries of these two writers, and their readers, as they engage in an ongoing dialogue about war, violence, and definitions of modernism. It is hoped that this essay may provide a starting point for such an interchange. The Great War was the event that changed Western consciousness's concept of itself; it restructured our sense of time, of what is past and what is modern. Through our reading of Lawrence, Woolf, and their contemporaries, we can come to better understand the nature and scope of conflict in their and our postwar worlds.

Notes

Introduction

1. Michel Foucault, *Power/Knowledge: Selected Interviews and Other Writings, 1972–1977*, ed. Colin Gordon, trans. Colin Gordon et al. (Brighton: Harvester, 1980), 114.

2. V. N. Voloshinov [Mikhail Bakhtin], *Marxism and the Philosophy of Language*, trans. Ladislav Matejka and I. R. Titunik (New York: Seminar, 1973), 86. In ascribing *Marxism and the Philosophy of Language* to Bakhtin I follow the example set by Katerina Clark and Michael Holquist, *Mikhail Bakhtin* (Cambridge: Harvard University Press, Belknap Press, 1984), 146–48, as well as Tzvetan Todorov, *Mikhail Bakhtin: The Dialogic Principle*, trans. Wlad Godzich (Manchester: Manchester University Press, 1984), 204.

3. Clark and Holquist, *Mikhail Bakhtin*, 204.

4. For example, "The Elizabethan Lumber Room" and "The Strange Elizabethans." Virginia Woolf, *Collected Essays*, ed. Leonard Woolf, 4 vols. (London: Hogarth, 1966–67), 1:46–53, 3:32–43 (hereafter cited as *CE*); all subsequent citations to Woolf's essays are to this edition, unless noted otherwise.

5. Virginia Woolf, *The Diary of Virginia Woolf*, ed. Anne Olivier Bell, 5 vols. (London: Hogarth, 1977–84), 5:151 (hereafter cited as *D*); all subsequent citations to Woolf's diary are to this edition.

6. Virginia Woolf, *The Letters of Virginia Woolf*, ed. Nigel Nicholson, 6 vols. (London: Hogarth, 1975–80), 3:454 (hereafter cited as *VWL*); all subsequent citations to Woolf's letters are to this edition.

7. D. H. Lawrence, *Apocalypse and the Writings on Revelation*, ed. Mara Kalnins (Cambridge: Cambridge University Press, 1980), 96–97 (hereafter cited as *A*); all subsequent citations to *Apocalpyse* are to this edition.

8. D. H. Lawrence, *The Letters of D. H. Lawrence*, ed. James T. Boulton et al., 8 vols. (Cambridge: Cambridge University Press, 1979–), 2:263 (hereafter cited as *LL*); all further citations to Lawrence's letters appear in the text.

9. George Steiner, *In Bluebeard's Castle: Some Notes towards the Re-Definition of Culture* (London: Faber, 1971), 13–27.

10. Ibid., 41.

11. D. H. Lawrence, *Aaron's Rod*, ed. Mara Kalnins (Cambridge: Cambridge University Press, 1988), 294 (hereafter cited as *AR*); all subsequent references to this work are to this edition.

12. Jean Bethke Elshtain, *Women and War* (Brighton: Harvester, 1987), x.

13. Virginia Woolf, *Orlando: A Biography* (Hogarth: London, 1928), 289 (hereafter cited as *O*); all subsequent citations are to this edition.

179

14. Virginia Woolf, *The Waves* (London: Hogarth, 1931), 164 (hereafter cited as *W*); all further references to are to this edition.

15. Virginia Woolf, *Night and Day* (London: Duckworth, 1919), 533 (hereafter cited as *ND*); all subsequent references are to this edition.

16. D. H. Lawrence, *The Rainbow*, ed. Mark Kinkead-Weekes (Cambridge: Cambridge University Press, 1989), 151 (hereafter cited as *R*); all subsequent references to *The Rainbow* are to this edition.

17. D. H. Lawrence, *Twilight in Italy*, ed. Paul Eggert (Cambridge: Cambridge University Press, 1994), 170 (hereafter cited as *TI*); all subsequent references are to this edition.

18. Hilary Simpson argues that "Lawrence develops in the twenties an explicit anti-feminism"; see *D. H. Lawrence and Feminism* (London: Croom Helm, 1982), 65. Judith Ruderman sets the date of Lawrence's turn against women as substantially earlier. In *D. H. Lawrence and the Devouring Mother*, Ruderman suggests that during the war years "Lawrence's reactions against women [rose] to a fever pitch"; *D. H. Lawrence and the Devouring Mother: The Search for a Patriarchal Ideal of Leadership* (Durham, N.C.: Duke University Press, 1984), 12. Simpson contends that his anti-female stance was due to the advances achieved by the suffragettes and female war workers (66–67). Ruderman, on the other hand, credits Lawrence's revolt against women to his desire to escape the overwhelming influence of his mother's memory and Frieda's presence before his sense of identity was "devoured" (14–19).

19. D. H. Lawrence, *Women in Love*, ed. David Farmer, Lindeth Vasey, and John Worthen (Cambridge: Cambridge University Press, 1987), 64–65 (hereafter cited as *WL*); all further references to *Women in Love* are to this edition.

20. D. H. Lawrence, *The Complete Poems of D. H. Lawrence*, eds. Vivian de Sola Pinto and Warren Roberts, 2 vols. (London: Heinemann, 1964), 1:269–70 (hereafter cited as *CP*); all further references to Lawrence's poems are to this edition.

21. D. H. Lawrence, "The Crown," in *Reflections on the Death of a Porcupine and Other Essays*, ed. Michael Herbert (Cambridge: Cambridge University Press, 1988), 291 (hereafter cited as *C*); all further references are to this edition. In quoting this essay I have made use of the 1915 variants of "The Crown" recorded in appendix 2 (469–79) of the Cambridge edition.

22. D. H. Lawrence, *The Fox, The Captain's Doll, The Ladybird*, ed. Dieter Mehl (Cambridge: Cambridge University Press, 1992), 82 (hereafter cited as *F*); all further references to "The Captain's Doll" are to this edition.

23. D. H. Lawrence, *The Prussian Officer and Other Stories*, ed. John Worthen (Cambridge: Cambridge University Press, 1983), 2–3 (hereafter referred to as *PO*); all further references to the stories collected in this work are to this edition.

24. D.H. Lawrence, *England, My England and Other Stories*, ed. Bruce Steele (Cambridge: Cambridge University Press, 1990), 33 (hereafter cited as *EME*); all subsequent references to the stories in this collection are to this edition.

25. D. H. Lawrence, "The Study of Thomas Hardy," in *The Study of Thomas Hardy and Other Essays*, ed. Bruce Steele (Cambridge: Cambridge University Press, 1985), 16 (hereafter cited as *STH*); all further references are to this edition.

26. Samuel Hynes, *A War Imagined: The First World War and English Culture* (New York: Atheneum, 1991), xi.

27. Claire M. Tylee, *The Great War and Women's Consciousnesses: Images of Militarism and Womanhood in Women's Writings, 1914–1964* (London: Macmillan, 1990), 13. Tylee fails to note these conflicts in the prewar fictions of Woolf and Lawrence. My point concerning Woolf's and Lawrence's prewar depictions of domestic violence is supported by Sandra M. Gilbert and Susan Gubar in *No Man's Land*, especially in chap. 1 of vol. 1, "The Battle of the Sexes: The Men's Case," where they discuss the power struggles as portrayed by Lawrence between men and women on the home front (see *No Man's Land: The Place of the Woman Writer in the 20th Century* New Haven: Yale University Press, 1988, 1:30–40). James Logenbach suggests further that "the Great War created not so much a turning point as an intensification of the war between men and women" (see "The Women and Men of 1914," in *Arms and the Woman: War, Gender and Literary Representation*, ed. Helen M. Cooper and Susan Merrill Squier [Chapel Hill: University of North Carolina Press, 1989], 114). Logenbach's argument is perceptive, but I would suggest that, seen as a domestic, everyday event, war is present in Woolf's and Lawrence's work long before the first guns were fired in August 1914.

28. Elaine Scarry, *The Body in Pain: The Making and Unmaking of the World* (Oxford: Oxford University Press, 1985), 21.

29. James Joyce, *Ulysses*, ed. Hans Walter Gabler, 3 vols. (New York: Garland, 1984), 1:69.

30. Virginia Woolf, *Three Guineas* (London: Hogarth, 1938), 194 (hereafter cited as *TG*); all subsequent references are to this edition.

31. Virginia Woolf, *To the Lighthouse* (London: Hogarth, 1927), 262 (hereafter cited as *TL*); all subsequent references are to this edition.

32. Lawrence, *Letters* 2:252 n. 3.

33. Richard Aldington, *D. H. Lawrence: An Indiscretion* (Seattle: University of Washington Press, 1927), 11.

34. Joyce, *Ulysses* 1:229.

35. Makiko Minow-Pinkney, *Virginia Woolf and the Problem of the Subject* (Brighton: Harvester, 1987), 25.

Chapter 1. Our Sad Eventful History: Woolf, Lawrence, and the Great War

1. Clive Bell, "Art and War," 1914; reprint in *Pot-Boilers* (London: Chatto and Windus, 1918), 241.

2. Quentin Bell, *Bloomsbury* (London: Weidenfeld and Nicolson, 1968), 14–15. My usage of the term "Bloomsbury" refers to Quentin Bell's "pattern" of the Bloomsbury group as it was in 1913. Bell sees the group at that time as consisting of E. M. Forster, David Garnett, Desmond and Molly McCarthy, Sydney Waterlow, Roger Fry, Vanessa Bell, Duncan Grant, Clive Bell, Virginia Woolf, Saxon Sydney Turner, Leonard Woolf, Lytton Strachey, Adrian Stephen, Maynard Keynes, Gerald Shove, James Strachey, Marjorie Strachey, H. T. J. Norton, and Francis Birrell.

3. Martin Ceadel, *Pacifism in Britain, 1914–1945: The Defining of a Faith* (Oxford: Oxford University Press, Clarendon Press, 1980), 3.

4. Ibid., 44.

5. Hynes, *A War Imagined*, 85.

6. David Garnett, *The Flowers of the Forest* (London: Chatto and Windus, 1955), 123.

7. S. P. Rosenbaum, *The Bloomsbury Group: A Collection of Memoirs, Commentary, and Criticism* (Toronto: University of Toronto Press, 1975), 41.

8. Michael Holroyd, *Lytton Strachey: A Critical Biography*, 2 vols. (London: Heinemann, 1968), 2:118.

9. Duncan Wilson, *Leonard Woolf: A Political Biography* (London: Hogarth, 1978), 93.

10. Bertrand Russell, *Justice in War-Time* (London: Open Court Publishing, 1916), 44.

11. Jo Vellacott, *Bertrand Russell and the Pacifists in the First World War* (Brighton: Harvester, 1980), 23.

12. D. H. Lawrence, "The Reality of Peace," in *Reflections on the Death of a Porcupine and Other Essays*, 43.

13. Holroyd, *Lytton Strachey* 2:174.

14. E. Sylvia Pankhurst, *The Home Front: A Mirror to Life in England during the World War* (London: Hutchinson, 1932), 99.

15. Ibid., 100.

16. Ibid., 36.

17. Ibid., 368.

18. C. E. Playne, *Society at War, 1914–1916* (London: Allen and Unwin, 1931), 266.

19. Mrs. C. S. Peel, *How We Lived Then, 1914–1918* (London: Bodley Head, 1929), 39.

20. Berenice A. Carroll, "'To Crush Him in Our Own Country': The Political Thought of Virginia Woolf," *Feminist Studies* 4 (1978): 117.

21. Stephen Greenblatt, "Invisible Bullets: Renaissance Authority and Its Subversion," *Glyph* 8 (1981): 40–61.

22. Paul Delany, *D. H. Lawrence's Nightmare: The Writer and His Circle in the Years of the Great War* (Hassocks, Sussex: Harvester, 1979), 250.

23. Eric Reed, *No Man's Land: Combat and Identity in World War I* (Cambridge: Cambridge University Press, 1979), 194.

24. Ibid., 195.

25. Ibid.

26. Ibid., 76.

Chapter 2. The Battle between Them: Sexual Conflict in the Early Fictions

1. Woolf, *To the Lighthouse;* 196–97 (hereafter cited as *TL*).

2. Gayatri Chakravorty Spivak, *In Other Worlds: Essays in Cultural Politics* (New York: Methuen, 1987), 15.

3. See Lee R. Edwards, "War and Roses: The Politics of *Mrs. Dalloway*," in *The Authority of Experience: Essays in Feminist Criticism*, ed. Arlyn Diamond and Lee R. Edwards (Amherst: University of Massachusetts Press, 1977), 162–63; Sallie Sears, "Theater of War: Virginia Woolf's *Between the Acts*," in *Virginia Woolf: A Feminist Slant*, ed. Jane Marcus (Lincoln: University of Nebraska Press, 1983), 229.

4. Virginia Woolf, *The Voyage Out* (London: Duckworth, 1915), 1 (hereafter cited as *VO*); all further references are to this edition.

5. Virginia Woolf, *Jacob's Room* (London: Hogarth, 1922), 35–36 (hereafter cited as *JR*); all further references are to this edition.

6. James Naremore, *The World without a Self: Virginia Woolf and the Novel* (New Haven: Yale University Press, 1973), 49.

7. Like the brutish and hostile goblin men in Christina Rossetti's "Goblin Market" (1862), the grotesques in this scene exhibit obvious sexual connotations. Rachel's pursuer resembles Rossetti's nightmarish characters with their feral attributes. See Christina Rossetti, "Goblin Market," in *The Complete Poems of Christina Rossetti*, ed. R. W. Crump, 2 vols. (Baton Rouge: Louisiana State University Press, 1979), 1:13.

8. Avrom Fleishman, *Virginia Woolf: A Critical Reading* (Baltimore: Johns Hopkins University Press, 1975), 8.

9. Ibid.

10. Michael Howard, *The Cause of Wars and Other Essays*, 2d ed. (London: Temple Smith, 1983), 8.

11. D. H. Lawrence, *The White Peacock*, ed. Andrew Robertson (Cambridge: Cambridge University Press, 1983), 1 (hereafter cited as *WP*); all subsequent references are to this edition.

12. D. H. Lawrence, *The Trespasser*, ed. Elizabeth Mansfield (Cambridge: Cambridge University Press, 1981), 73 (hereafter cited as *T*); all further references are to this edition.

13. D. H. Lawrence, *Sons and Lovers*, ed. Helen Baron and Carl Baron (Cambridge: Cambridge University Press, 1992), 296 (hereafter cited as *SL*); all further references are to this edition.

14. Prosper Merimée, "Le manuscrit du Professeur Wittembach," *Revue des deux mondes* 83 (1869): 290.

15. D. H. Lawrence, "New Eve and Old Adam," in *Love among the Haystacks and Other Stories*, ed. John Worthen (Cambridge: Cambridge University Press, 1987), 161 (hereafter cited as *LAH*); all further references to the stories in this collection are to this edition.

16. Robert Browning, "Porphyria's Lover," in *Robert Browning: The Poems*, ed. John Pettigrew, 2 vols. (New Haven: Yale University Press, 1981), 2:380–81.

Chapter 3. The Prisonhouse of Language: Writings of the War Years

1. Paul Fussell, *The Great War and Modern Memory* (New York: Oxford University Press, 1975), 139.

2. Ibid., 170.

3. Ibid., 174. See Bernard Bergonzi, *Heroes' Twilight: A Study of the Literature of the Great War*, 2d ed. (London: Macmillan, 1980), 41: "The literary records of the Great War can be seen as a series of attempts to evolve a response that would have some degree of adequacy to the unparalleled situation in which the writers were involved."

4. Delany, *Lawrence's Nightmare*, 101–2.

5. Fussell, *Great War and Modern Memory*, 182.

6. Delany, *Lawrence's Nightmare*, 102.

7. Keith Cushman, *D. H. Lawrence at Work: The Emergence of the Prussian Officer Stories* (Hassocks, Sussex: Harvester, 1978), 183.

8. Ibid.

9. Cornelia Nixon, *Lawrence's Leadership Politics and the Turn against Women* (Berkeley: University of California Press, 1986), 55–56.

10. In the end Lawrence got his dedication, but only in English. In a footnote to the above letter, George Zytaruk suggests that "this dedication to Frieda's sister may have exacerbated the anger of officialdom to the novel" (*LL* 2:349 n. 3).

11. Holroyd, *Lytton Strachey* 2:159.

12. James Douglas, review of *The Rainbow*, by D. H. Lawrence, *The Star*, 22 October 1915, 4, quoted in R. P. Draper, ed., *D. H. Lawrence: The Critical Heritage* (London: Routledge and Kegan Paul, 1970), 94–95.

13. Clement Shorter, "A Literary Letter," review of *The Rainbow*, by D. H. Lawrence, *Sphere*, 23 October 1915, 104, reprinted in Draper, *Critical Heritage*, 96–97.

14. "*The Rainbow:* Destruction of a Novel Ordered," report in *The Times*, 15 November 1915, 3, reprinted in Draper, *Critical Heritage*, 103.

15. J. C. Squire, "Books in General," review of *The Rainbow*, by D. H. Lawrence, *New Statesman*, 20 November 1915, 161, reprinted in Draper, *Critical Heritage*, 106.

16. Sir Edward Cook, *The Press in War-Time* (London: Macmillan, 1920), 5.

17. Ibid., 4.

18. Delany, *Lawrence's Nightmare*, 101.

19. Ibid., 251.

20. Henry Houston, *The Real Horatio Bottomley* (London: Hurst and Blackett, 1923), 151.

21. Ibid., 157.

22. Alan Hyman, *The Rise and Fall of Horatio Bottomley: The Biography of a Swindler* (London: Cassell, 1972), 169.

23. Ibid., 90–91. The bureau's original object "was to investigate any organization or individual suspected of acting nefariously. It was ironical that a man with Bottomley's shady reputation should set up an unofficial detective agency. . . . As a result of the Exposure Bureau *John Bull* received an enormous readers' postbag, and hordes of undesirables began turning up at the office, most of them cranks or crooks or petty blackmailers."

24. Ibid., 145.

25. *John Bull*, 14 August 1914, 4.

26. Hyman, *Horatio Bottomley*, 150.

27. Horatio Bottomley, quoted in Hyman, *Horatio Bottomley*, 150.

28. Horatio Bottomley, *Great Thoughts of Horatio Bottomley*, ed. H. B. Elliott (London: Holden and Hardingham, 1917), 10. This handy pocket edition came out before the end of the war and contains a selection of Bottomley's bons mots gathered from speeches and *John Bull*.

29. Horatio Bottomley, quoted in Hyman, *Horatio Bottomley*, 164.

30. A. J. P. Taylor, *The First World War: An Illustrated History* (London: Hamish Hamilton, 1963), 119.

31. Virginia Woolf, *Between the Acts* (London: Hogarth, 1941), 119 (hereafter cited as *BA*); all further references are to this edition.

32. D. H. Lawrence, "Him with His Tail in His Mouth," in *Reflections on the Death of a Porcupine*, 309–10.

33. Reed, *No Man's Land*, 47.

34. Hilary Simpson has suggested that there is a direct causal relationship between Lawrence's dislike of the women who participated in the war effort and the antifeminism displayed in his leadership novels; see Simpson, *Lawrence and Feminism*, 66, 105.

35. Gilbert and Gubar, *No Man's Land* 1:228.

36. Hynes, *War Imagined*, 8.

37. *EME*, 74. The reference is to a song made popular by Basil Hallam. According to Robert Giddings, in *The War Poets* (London: Bloomsbury, 1988), "Nut" or "Knuts" were the "prototypical public school twits who made good at the Front" (43). Thus in twitting Miss Stokes, Albert pokes fun at all ruling classes. In designating Stokes as a "nut," he places her in the position of traditional authority, thereby rejecting her gender and simultaneously mocking her "masculinity."

38. Simpson, *Lawrence and Feminism*, 70.

39. F. Schauwecker, *Im Todersrachen: Die Deutsche Seele im Weltkrieg* (Halle: Verlag Salle, 1921) 52, quoted in and translated by Reed, *No Man's Land*, 203.

40. Robert Graves, *Good-bye to All That*, rev. ed. (Harmondsworth: Penguin, 1960), 188.

41. Robert Graves, "The Great Years of Their Lives," interview by Leslie Smith, *Listener* 86 (15 July 1971): 74.

42. John Brophy and Eric Partridge, *The Long Trail: Soldiers' Songs and Slang, 1914–1918* (London: Sphere, 1969), 18.

43. D. H. Lawrence, *Fantasia of the Unconscious and Psychoanalysis and the Unconscious*, Phoenix ed. (London: Heinemann, 1961), 171.

44. H. M. Daleski, *The Forked Flame: A Study of D. H. Lawrence* (London: Faber, 1965), 128.

45. D. H. Lawrence, foreword, *Women in Love*, 485.

46. Jean-Jacques Lecercle, *The Violence of Language* (London: Routledge, 1990), 236.

47. Lawrence, foreword, *Women in Love*, 486.

48. Daleski, *Forked Flame*, 127.

49. Any discussion of the connection between self and other must take as its starting point Hegel's *Phenomenology of Spirit* (1807). Although it is difficult to prove to what extent Lawrence read Hegel, Jennifer Michaels-Tonks argues that by the end of 1908 he was familiar with works by the German philosopher. See *D. H. Lawrence: The Polarity of North and South—Germany and Italy in His Prose Works* (Bonn: Bouvier Verlag Herbert Grundmann, 1976), 31–32. In "Art and the Individual" (1908), Lawrence displays a familiarity with Hegel's aesthetic concepts. Whatever his actual knowledge of Hegel's theory of the dialectic, *Phenomenology of Spirit* provides terms useful in elucidating conflicts essential to the structure of *Women in Love*. Throughout the novel, dialogue serves to illustrate what Hegel perceived as the conflict between two consciousnesses eager to achieve self-identity:

> the relation of the two self-conscious individuals is such that they prove themselves and each other through a life-and-death struggle. They must engage in this struggle, for they must raise their certainty of being *for themselves* to truth, both in the case of the other and in their own case.

See G. W. F. Hegel, *Phenomenology of Spirit*, trans. A. V. Miller (Oxford: Oxford University Press, Clarendon Press, 1977), 113–14.

50. Hegel, *Phenomenology*, 111.

51. Steele, introduction to *Study of Thomas Hardy*, xix.

52. Hegel, *Phenomenology*, 76,

53. Daleski, *Forked Flame*, 13–14; Stephen J. Miko, *Toward "Women in Love": The Emergence of a Lawrentian Aesthetic* (New Haven: Yale University Press, 1971), 69.

54. Graham Holderness, *Women in Love* (Milton Keynes: Open University Press, 1986), 128.

55. Bell, *Virginia Woolf* 2:69.

56. Andrew McNeillie, introduction to *The Essays of Virginia Woolf* (London: Hogarth, 1987), 2:xiii.

57. Katherine Mansfield, *Katherine Mansfield's Letters to John Middleton Murry, 1913–1922*, ed. John Middleton Murry (London: Constable, 1951), 380.

58. Katherine Mansfield, "A Ship Comes into the Harbour," review of *Night and Day*, by Virginia Woolf, in *Novels and Novelists*, ed. J. Middleton Murry (London: Constable, 1930), 111.

59. Mikhail Bakhtin, "Discourse in the Novel," in *The Dialogic Imagination: Four Essays by M. M. Bakhtin*, ed. Michael Holquist, trans. Caryl Emerson and Michael Holquist (Austin: University of Texas Press, 1981), 272.

60. Clark and Holquist, *Mikhail Bakhtin*, 162.

61. Voloshinov [Bakhtin], *Marxism*, 86.

62. Clark and Holquist, *Mikhail Bakhtin*, 14.

63. Ibid., 15.

64. Voloshinov [Bakhtin], *Marxism*, 86.

65. Georg Lukacs, *The Historical Novel*, trans. Hannah Mitchell and Stanley Mitchell (London: Merlin, 1962), 41.

Chapter 4. The Senseless Boxing of Schoolboys: The Sport and Comradeship of War

1. Roger Caillois, *Man, Play, and Games*, trans. Meyer Barash (London: Thames and Hudson, 1962), 6.

2. Scarry, *Body in Pain*, 83.

3. Ibid., 85.

4. Lady Mary Wortley Montagu, *The Letters and Works of Lady Mary Wortley Montagu*, ed. Lord Wharncliffe, 3 vols. (London: Richard Bentley, 1837), 3:141. Woolf once planned to write an article on Lady Mary Wortley Montagu. In a letter of July 1908 to her friend Violet Dickinson, Woolf remarked that "I have . . . entered into a long correspondence with [Sir George] Prothero [editor of the *Quarterly Review*, 1899–1922], and we decided that I am probably to write about Ly. May [*sic*] Montagu" (*VWL*, 1:337). B. J. Kirkpatrick, in her *Bibliography of Virginia Woolf*, 3d ed. (Oxford: Oxford University Press, Clarendon Press,1980), 180, is unable to trace this proposed publication, nor is Andrew McNeillie able to provide a further reference in his edition of *The Essays of Virginia Woolf.*

5. Caillois, *Man, Play, and Games*, 7.

6. Virginia Woolf, *Roger Fry: A Biography* (London: Hogarth, 1940), 33 (hereafter cited as *RF*); all further references are to this edition.

7. Peter Stansky and William Abrahams, *Journey to the Frontier: Julian Bell and John Cornford, Their Lives and the 1930s* (London: Constable, 1966), 21–22.

8. Julian Bell, *Julian Bell: Essays, Poems, and Letters*, ed. Quentin Bell (London: Hogarth, 1938), 13.

9. Ibid.

10. Ibid.

11. Julian Bell, "Vienna," in *Work for the Winter and Other Poems* (London: Hogarth, 1936), 19.

12. Julian Bell, *Julian Bell*, 189–90.

13. Ibid., 190.

14. Q. Bell, *Virginia Woolf* 2:258–59.

15. Julian Bell, ed., *We Did Not Fight, 1914–1918: Experiences of War Resisters* (London: Cobden-Sanderson, 1935), xix.

16. H. G. Wells, *Little War: A Game for Boys from Twelve Years of Age to One Hundred and Fifty and for That More Intelligent Sort of Girls Who Like Boys' Games and Books* (London: Frank Palmer, 1913), 9–10.

17. Ibid., 7.

18. Ibid., 18.

19. Ibid., 20–23.

20. Ibid., 24.

21. Ibid., 30–31.

22. Ibid., 98.

23. Ibid., 100.

24. Ibid., 24.

25. H. G. Wells, *The War That Will End War* (London: Frank and Cecil Palmer, 1914), 11.

26. H. G. Wells, *Mr Britling Sees It Through* (London: Cassell, 1916), 99.

27. Wells, *Little Wars*, 63–64.

28. Wells, *Mr Britling*, 76, 32.

29. Ibid., 77.

30. Ibid., 84.

31. Sigmund Freud, *Beyond the Pleasure Principle*, trans. James Strachey (London: Hogarth, 1961), 29.

32. Ibid., 14.

33. Minow-Pinkney, *Virginia Woolf and the Problem of the Subject*, 28.

34. "Voloshinov" [Bakhtin], *Marxism*, 85.

35. Ibid., 102.

36. Ibid., 86, 89.

37. Siegfried Sassoon, *Collected Poems, 1908–1956* (London: Faber, 1961), 75.

38. Voloshinov [Bakhtin], *Marxism*, 86.

39. Virginia Woolf, *Mrs. Dalloway* (London: Hogarth, 1925), 131 (hereafter cited as *MD*); all further references are to this edition.

40. Freud, *Pleasure Principle*, 6.

41. Hilary Simpson sees his writings of the 1920s as a reaction to the employment of women in industry and formerly male-occupied positions (*Lawrence and Feminism*, 65). Cornelia Nixon asserts that "Lawrence's turn toward leadership politics" provides "a refuge from powerful women and

allows him to express the homoeroticism he found unacceptable in himself"
(*Lawrence's Leadership Politics*, 9). Nixon emphasizes that during the Great
War he experienced "a private, unadmitted crisis," presumably a homosexual encounter (ibid., 231). However, the evidence is highly problematic. She
bases her argument upon his supposed flirtations with homosexuality, his
dislike of heterosexuality, as portrayed in his fictions, and his inexplicable
vehemence towards the conspicuous homosexuality of J. M. Keynes, whom
Lawrence met in Cambridge in March 1915. Nixon's thesis centers around
the debatable statement that "on the subject of homosexuality Lawrence
protested too much" (ibid., 14).

42. D. H. Lawrence, *Kangaroo*, ed. Bruce Steele (Cambridge: Cambridge
University Press, 1994), 223 (hereafter cited as *K*); all further references are
to this edition.

43. D. H. Lawrence, "The Fox," in *The Fox, The Captain's Doll, The Ladybird*, ed. Dieter Mehl (Cambridge: Cambridge University Press, 1992), 14
(hereafter cited as *F*); all further references are to this edition.

44. D. H. Lawrence, "The Ladybird," in *The Fox, The Captain's Doll, The
Ladybird*, 165 (hereafter cited as *F*); all subsequent references are to this
edition.

Chapter 5. The Silver Globe of Time: War and History in the Postwar Fictions

1. D. H. Lawrence, *Movements in European History*, ed. Philip Crumpton
(Cambridge: Cambridge University Press, 1989), 9 (hereafter cited as *MEH*);
all further references are to this edition.

2. Evelyn Hinz, "History as Education and Art: D. H. Lawrence's *Movements in European History*," *Modern British Literature* 2 (1977): 146.

3. See L. D. Clark, *Dark Night of the Body: D. H. Lawrence's "The Plumed
Serpent"* (Austin: University of Texas Press, 1964); William York Tindall,
D. H. Lawrence and Susan His Cow (New York: Columbia University Press,
1939); John B. Vickery, *The Literary Impact of "The Golden Bough"* (Princeton:
Princeton University Press, 1973).

4. Oswald Spengler, *The Decline of the West*, 2 vols., trans. Charles F.
Atkinson (London: Allen and Unwin, 1926–28), 1:xiii.

5. Rose Marie Burwell, "A Catalogue of D. H. Lawrence's Reading from
Early Childhood," *D. H. Lawrence Review* 3 (1970): 242. Burwell records
that in 1916 Lawrence read John Burnet's *Early Greek Philosophers*, which
includes an extensive discussion of Heraclitus's theories.

6. Lawrence, *Fantasia of the Unconsious*, 41.

7. Ibid., 34.

8. Hinz, "History as Education and Art," 148.

9. Jascha Kessler, "D. H. Lawrence's Primitivism," *Texas Studies in Literature and Language* 5 (1963): 467–88.

10. D. H. Lawrence, "A Propos of *Lady Chatterley's Lover*" in *Lady Chatterley's Lover*, ed. Michael Squires (Cambridge: Cambridge University Press,
1993), 331.

11. D. H. Lawrence, *Sea and Sardinia*, Phoenix ed. (London: Heinemann,
1956), 34. All further references are to this edition.

12. Greenblatt, "Invisible Bullets," 39.

13. Lawrence, "Prologue," in *Women in Love,* 495–96.

14. Donald Eastman, "Myth and Fate in the Characters of *Women in Love,*" *D. H. Lawrence Review* 9 (1976): 178.

15. D. H. Lawrence, "Blessed Are the Powerful," in *Reflections on the Death of a Porcupine,* 321.

16. Ibid., 324.

17. D. H. Lawrence, *Lady Chatterley's Lover,* ed. Michael Squires (Cambridge: Cambridge University Press, 1993), 5 (hereafter cited as *LCL*); all further references are to this edition.

18. D. H. Lawrence, "The Flying Fish," in *St. Mawr and Other Stories,* ed. Brian Finney (Cambridge: Cambridge University Press, 1983), 209. All further references to this work are to this edition.

19. D.H. Lawrence, "An Autobiographical Fragment," in *Phoenix,* ed. Edward D. McDonald (London: Heinemann, 1936), 817–36.

20. Lawrence, *St. Mawr,* 154.

21. Lawrence, *Fantasia,* 172.

22. D. H. Lawrence, *The Plumed Serpent,* ed. L. D. Clark (Cambridge: Cambridge University Press, 1987), 443.

23. D. H. Lawrence, "The Man Who Died," in *The Complete Short Novels,* ed. Keith Sagar (Harmondsworth: Penguin, 1982), 571, 597. All further references are to this edition.

24. Ibid., 568.

25. Ibid.

26. D. H. Lawrence, "Resurrection," in *Reflections,* 234.

27. Lawrence, "Flying Fish," 207.

28. Ibid., 209.

29. Ibid.

30. Ibid.

31. Ibid., 208.

32. Eugene Goodheart, *The Utopian Vision of D. H. Lawrence* (Chicago: University of Chicago Press, 1963), 7.

33. Kessler, "Lawrence's Primitivism," 487–88.

34. D. H. Lawrence, *Mornings in Mexico,* Phoenix ed. (London: Heinemann, 1956), 4.

35. Virginia Woolf, manuscript notes dated 21 January 1931 for a speech given before the London/National Society for Women's Service, appendix to *The Pargiters: The Novel-Essay Portion of "The Years,"* ed. Michael Leaska (London: Hogarth, 1978), 164.

36. Margaret R. Higgonet and Patrice L.-R. Higonnet, "The Double Helix," in *Behind the Lines: Gender and the Two World Wars,* ed. Margaret R. Higonnet et al. (New Haven: Yale University Press, 1987), 34.

37. Virginia Woolf, *A Room of One's Own* (London: Hogarth, 1929), 134 (hereafter cited as *AROO*); all further references are to this edition.

38. Allen McLaurin, *Virginia Woolf: The Echoes Enslaved* (Cambridge: Cambridge University Press, 1973), 158.

39. Ibid., 148.

40. Harvena Richter, *Virginia Woolf: The Inward Voyage* (Princeton: Princeton University Press, 1970), 170.

41. Maria DiBattista, *Virginia Woolf's Major Novels: The Fables of Anon* (New Haven: Yale University Press, 1980), 55.

42. Gillian Beer, "Virginia Woolf and Pre-History," *Virginia Woolf: A Centenary Perspective*, ed. Eric Warner (London: Macmillan, 1984), 102.

43. Ibid.

44. Discussions of Woolf's novels that are similar to my own, if different in emphasis, may be found in Pamela L. Caughie, *Virginia Woolf and Postmodernism: Literature in Quest and Question of Itself* (Urbana: University of Illinois Press, 1991); Bette Lynn London, *The Appropriated Voice* (Ann Arbor: University of Michigan Press, 1990), and Minow-Pinkney, *Virginia Woolf and the Problem of the Subject*.

45. Maria DiBattista has observed the important role knitting assumes in *To the Lighthouse:* "[Mrs. Ramsay's] serene act of knitting, the sign of her creative urge to unite the separate strands of life into a seamless unity, is simultaneously a sign of her terrible power." (*Fables of Anon*, 78).

46. For a complete discussion of this article and others that Woolf wrote during the war see Karen L. Levenback, "Virginia Woolf's 'War in the Village' and 'The War from the Street': An Illusion of Immunity" in Hussey, *Virginia Woolf and War*, 40–57.

47. Virginia Woolf, *The Years* (London: Hogarth, 1937) 315; (hereafter cited as *Y*); all further references are to this edition.

48. Virginia Woolf, introduction to *Life as We Have Known It, by Cooperative Working Women*, ed. Margaret Llewelyn Davies (London: Hogarth, 1931), xviii–xix.

49. Ibid., xxxvii.

50. Ibid., xxxix.

51. Ibid., xvi.

52. Ibid., xix.

53. Sandra M. Gilbert, "Woman's Sentence, Man's Sentencing: Linguistic Fantasies in Woolf and Joyce," in *Virginia Woolf and Bloomsbury: A Centenary Collection*, ed. Jane Marcus (London: Macmillan, 1987), 218.

54. Joan W. Scott, "Rewriting History," in Higgonet et al., *Behind the Lines*, 29.

55. Scarry, *Body in Pain*, 87.

Bibliography

Aldington, Richard. *D. H. Lawrence: An Indiscretion*. Seattle: University of Washington Press, 1927.

Bakhtin, Mikhail. "Discourse in the Novel." In *The Dialogic Imagination: Four Essays by M. M. Bakhtin*, edited by Michael Holquist, translated by Caryl Emerson and Michael Holquist. Austin: University of Texas Press, 1981.

Beer, Gillian. "Virginia Woolf and Pre-History." In *Virginia Woolf: A Centenary Perspective*, edited by Eric Warner, 99–123. London: Macmillan, 1984.

Bell, Clive. "Art and War." In *Pot-Boilers*. London: Chatto and Windus, 1918.

Bell, Julian. *Julian Bell: Essays, Poems, and Letters*. Edited by Quentin Bell. London: Hogarth, 1938.

——. *Work for Winter and Other Poems*. London: Hogarth, 1936.

——, ed. *We Did Not Fight, 1914–1918: Experiences of War Resisters*. London: Cobden-Sanderson, 1935.

Bell, Quentin. *Bloomsbury*. London: Weidenfeld and Nicolson, 1968.

——. *Virginia Woolf: A Biography*. 2 vols. London: Hogarth, 1972.

Bergonzi, Bernard. *Heroes' Twilight: A Study of the Literature of the Great War*. 2d ed. London: Macmillan, 1980.

Bottomley, Horatio. *Great Thoughts of Horatio Bottomley*. Edited by H. B. Elliott. London: Holden and Hardingham, 1917.

Brophy, John, and Eric Partridge. *The Long Trail: Soldiers' Songs and Slang, 1914–1918*. London: Sphere, 1969.

Browning, Robert. "Porphyria's Lover." In *Robert Browning: The Poems*, edited by John Pettigrew, 2 vols., New Haven: Yale University Press, 1981. 2: 380–81.

Burwell, Rose Marie. "A Catalogue of D. H. Lawrence's Reading from Early Childhood." *D. H. Lawrence Review* 3 (1970): 193–324.

Caillois, Roger. *Man, Play, and Games*. Translated by Meyer Barash. London: Thames and Hudson, 1962.

Carroll, Berenice A. "'To Crush Him in Our Own Country': The Political Thought of Virginia Woolf." *Feminist Studies* 4 (1978): 99–131.

Caughie, Pamela L. *Virginia Woolf and Postmodernism: Literature in Quest and Question of Itself*. Urbana: University of Illinois Press, 1991.

Ceadel, Martin. *Pacifism in Britain, 1914–1945: The Defining of a Faith*. Oxford: Oxford University Press, Clarendon Press, 1980.

Clark, Katerina, and Michael Holquist. *Mikhail Bakhtin*. Cambridge: Harvard University Press, Belknap Press, 1984.

Clark, L. D. *Dark Night of the Body: D. H. Lawrence's "The Plumed Serpent."* Austin: University of Texas Press, 1964.

Cook, Sir Edward. *The Press in War-Time.* London: Macmillan, 1920.

Cushman, Keith. *D. H. Lawrence at Work: The Emergence of the Prussian Officer Stories.* Charlottesville: University Press of Virginia, 1978.

Daleski, H. M. *The Forked Flame: A Study of D. H. Lawrence.* London: Faber, 1965.

Delany, Paul. *D. H. Lawrence's Nightmare: The Writer and His Circle in the Years of the Great War.* Hassocks, Sussex: Harvester, 1979.

DiBattista, Maria. *Virginia Woolf's Major Novels: The Fables of Anon.* New Haven: Yale University Press, 1980.

Douglas, James. Review of *The Rainbow* by D. H. Lawrence. *The Star,* 22 October 1915, 4. Reprint, Draper, *Lawrence,* 93–95.

Draper, R. P., ed. *D. H. Lawrence: The Critical Heritage.* London: Routledge and Kegan Paul, 1970.

Eastman, Donald. "Myth and Fate in the Characters of *Women in Love.*" *D. H. Lawrence Review* 9 (1976): 177–93.

Edwards, Lee R. "War and Roses: The Politics of *Mrs. Dalloway.*" In *The Authority of Experience: Essays in Feminist Criticism,* edited by Arlyn Diamond and Lee R. Edwards, 160–77. Amherst: University of Massachusetts Press, 1977.

Elshtain, Jean Bethke. *Women and War.* Brighton: Harvester, 1987.

Fleishman, Avrom. *Virginia Woolf: A Critical Reading.* Baltimore: Johns Hopkins University Press, 1975.

Foucault, Michel. *Power/Knowledge: Selected Interviews and Other Writings, 1972–1977.* Edited by Colin Gordon, translated by Colin Gordon et al. Brighton: Harvester, 1980.

Freud, Sigmund. *Beyond the Pleasure Principle.* Translated by James Strachey. London: Hogarth, 1961.

Fussell, Paul. *The Great War and Modern Memory.* New York: Oxford University Press, 1975.

Garnett, David. *The Flowers of the Forest.* London: Chatto and Windus, 1955.

Giddings, Robert. *The War Poets.* London: Bloomsbury, 1988.

Gilbert, Sandra. "Woman's Sentence, Man's Sentencing: Linguistic Fantasies in Woolf and Joyce." In *Virginia Woolf and Bloomsbury: A Centenary Collection,* edited by Jane Marcus, 208–224. London: Macmillan, 1987.

Gilbert, Sandra, and Susan Gubar. *No Man's Land: The Place of the Woman Writer in the Twentieth Century.* Vol. 1. New Haven: Yale University Press, 1988.

Goodheart, Eugene. *The Utopian Vision of D. H. Lawrence.* Chicago: University of Chicago Press, 1963.

Graves, Robert. *Good-bye to All That.* Rev. ed. Harmondsworth: Penguin, 1960.

———. "The Great Years of Their Lives." Interview by Leslie Smith. *Listener* 86 (15 July 1971): 73–75.

Greenblatt, Stephen. "Invisible Bullets: Renaissance Authority and Its Subversion." *Glyph* 8 (1981): 40–61.

Hegel, G. W. F. *Phenomenology of Spirit.* Translated by A.V. Miller. Oxford: Oxford University Press, Clarendon Press, 1977.

Higgonet, Margaret et al., eds. *Behind the Lines: Gender and the Two World Wars.* New Haven: Yale University Press, 1987.

Higgonet, Margaret, and Patrice L.-R Higgonet. "The Double Helix." In Higgonet et al. *Behind the Lines,* 31–47.

Hinz, Evelyn J. "History as Education and Art: D. H. Lawrence's *Movements in European History." Modern British Literature* 2 (1977): 139–52.

Holderness, Graham. *Women in Love.* Milton Keynes: Open University Press, 1986.

Holroyd, Michael. *Lytton Strachey: A Critical Biography.* 2 vols. London: Heinemann, 1968.

Houston, Henry. *The Real Horatio Bottomley.* London: Hurst and Blackett, 1923.

Howard, Michael. *The Cause of Wars and Other Essays.* 2d ed. London: Temple Smith, 1983.

Hyman, Alan. *The Rise and Fall of Horatio Bottomley: The Biography of a Swindler.* London: Cassell, 1972.

Hynes, Samuel. *A War Imagined: The First World War and English Culture.* New York: Atheneum, 1991.

John Bull, 15 August 1914.

Joyce, James. *Ulysses.* Edited Hans Walter Gabler. 3 vols. New York: Garland, 1984.

Kessler, Jascha. "D. H. Lawrence's Primitivism." *Texas Studies in Literature and Language* 5 (1963): 467–88.

Kirkpatrick, B.J. *Bibliography of Virginia Woolf.* 3d ed. Oxford: Oxford University Press, Clarendon Press, 1980.

Lawrence, D. H. *Aaron's Rod.* Edited by Mara Kalnins. Cambridge: Cambridge University Press, 1988.

———. *Apocalypse and the Writings on Revelation.* Edited by Mara Kalnins. Cambridge: Cambridge University Press, 1980.

———. *The Complete Poems of D. H. Lawrence.* Edited by Vivian de Sola Pinto and Warren Roberts. 2 vols. London: Heinemann, 1964.

———. *England, My England and Other Stories.* Edited by Bruce Steele. Cambridge: Cambridge University Press, 1990.

———. *Fantasia of the Unconscious and Psychoanalysis and the Unconscious.* Phoenix ed. London: Heinemann, 1961.

———. *The Fox, The Captain's Doll, The Ladybird.* Edited by Dieter Mehl. Cambridge: Cambridge University Press, 1992.

———. *Kangaroo.* Edited by Bruce Steele. Cambridge: Cambridge University Press, 1994.

———. *Lady Chatterley's Lover; "A Propos of 'Lady Chatterley's Lover'".* Edited by Michael Squires. Cambridge: Cambridge University Press, 1993.

———. *The Letters of D. H. Lawrence.* Edited by James T. Boulton et al. 8 vols. Cambridge: Cambridge University Press, 1979–.

———. *Love among the Haystacks and Other Stories.* Edited by John Worthen. Cambridge: Cambridge University Press, 1987.

------. "The Man Who Died." In *The Complete Short Novels*, edited by Keith Sagar. Harmondsworth: Penguin, 1982.

------. *Mornings in Mexico*. London: Heinemann, 1956.

------. *Movements in European History*. Edited by Philip Crumpton. Cambridge: Cambridge University Press, 1989.

------. *Phoenix*. Edited by Edward D. McDonald. London: Heinemann, 1963.

------. *The Plumed Serpent*. Edited by L.D. Clark. Cambridge: Cambridge University Press, 1987.

------. *The Prussian Officer and Other Stories*. Edited by John Worthen. Cambridge: Cambridge University Press, 1983.

------. *The Rainbow*. Edited by Mark Kinkead-Weekes. Cambridge: Cambridge University Press, 1989.

------. *Reflections on the Death of a Porcupine and Other Essays*. Edited by Michael Herbert. Cambridge: Cambridge University Press, 1988.

------. *St. Mawr and Other Stories*. Edited by Brian Finney. Cambridge: Cambridge University Press, 1983.

------. *Sea and Sardinia*. London: Heinemann, 1956.

------. *Sons and Lovers*. Edited by Helen Baron and Carl Baron. Cambridge: Cambridge University Press, 1992.

------. *Studies in Classic American Literature*. London: Heinemann, 1964.

------. *The Study of Thomas Hardy and Other Essays*. Edited by Bruce Steele. Cambridge: Cambridge University Press, 1985.

------. *The Trespasser*. Edited by Elizabeth Mansfield. Cambridge: Cambridge University Press, 1981.

------. *Twilight in Italy*. Edited by Paul Eggert. Cambridge: Cambridge University Press, 1994.

------. *The White Peacock*. Edited by Andrew Robertson. Cambridge: Cambridge University Press, 1983.

------. *Women in Love*. Edited by David Farmer, Lindeth Vasey, and John Worthen. Cambridge: Cambridge University Press, 1987.

Lecercle, Jean-Jacques. *The Violence of Language*. London: Routledge, 1990.

Levenback, Karen L. "Virginia Woolf's 'War in the Village' and 'The War in the Street': An Illusion of Immunity." In *Virginia Woolf and War: Fiction, Reality, and Myth*, edited by Mark Hussey, 40–47. Syracuse: Syracuse University Press, 1991.

Logenbach, James. "The Women and Men of 1914." In *Arms and the Woman: War, Gender, and Literary Representation*, edited by Helen Cooper, 97–123. Chapel Hill: University of North Carolina Press, 1989.

London, Bette Lynn. *The Appropriated Voice*. Ann Arbor: University of Michigan Press, 1990.

Lukacs, George. *The Historical Novel*. Translated by Hannah Mitchell and Stanley Mitchell. London: Merlin, 1962.

McLaurin, Allen. *Virgina Woolf: The Echoes Enslaved*. Cambridge: Cambridge University Press, 1973.

McNeillie, Andrew. Introduction to *The Essays of Virginia Woolf*. Vol. 2. London: Hogarth, 1987.

Mansfield, Katherine. *Katherine Mansfield's Letters to John Middleton Murry, 1913–1922*. Edited by John Middleton Murry. London: Constable, 1951.

———. "A Ship Comes into the Harbour." Review of *Night and Day*, by Virginia Woolf. In *Novels and Novelists*, edited by J. Middleton Murry, 107–11. London: Constable, 1930.

Merimée, Prosper. "Le manuscrit du Professeur Wittembach." *Revue des deux mondes* 83 (1869): 257–90.

Michaels-Tonks, Jennifer. *D. H. Lawrence: The Polarity of North and South: Germany and Italy in His Prose Works*. Bonn: Bouvier Verlag Herbert Grundmann, 1976.

Miko, Stephen J. *Toward "Women in Love": The Emergence of a Lawrentian Aesthetic*. New Haven: Yale University Press, 1971.

Minow-Pinkney, Makiko. *Virginia Woolf and the Problem of the Subject*. Brighton: Harvester, 1987.

Montagu, Lady Mary Wortley. *The Letters and Works of Lady Mary Wortley Montagu*. Edited by Lord Wharncliffe. 3 vols. London: Richard Bentley, 1837.

Naremore, James. *The World without a Self: Virginia Woolf and the Novel*. New Haven: Yale University Press, 1973.

Nixon, Cornelia. *Lawrence's Leadership Politics and the Turn Against Women*. Berkeley: University of California Press, 1986.

Pankhurst, E. Sylvia. *The Home Front: A Mirror to Life in England during the World War*. London: Hutchinson, 1932.

Peel, Mrs. C. S., *How We Lived Then, 1914–1918*. London: Bodley Head, 1929.

Playne, C. E. *Society at War, 1914–1916*. London: Allen and Unwin, 1931.

"*The Rainbow:* Destruction of a Novel Ordered." *The Times* (London), 14 November 1915; 3. Reprint, Draper *Lawrence*, 102–3.

Reed, Eric. *No Man's Land: Combat and Identity in World War I*. Cambridge: Cambridge University Press, 1979.

Richter, Harvena. *Virginia Woolf: The Inward Voyage*. Princeton: Princeton University Press, 1970.

Rosenbaum, S. P. *The Bloomsbury Group: A Collection of Memoirs, Commentary, and Criticism*. Toronto: University of Toronto Press, 1975.

Rossetti, Christina. "Goblin Market." In *The Complete Poems of Christina Rossetti*, edited by R. W. Crump. 2 vols, 1:11–26. Baton Rouge: Louisiana State University Press, 1979.

Ruderman, Judith. *D. H. Lawrence and the Devouring Mother: The Search for a Patriarchal Ideal of Leadership*. Durham, N.C.: Duke University Press, 1984.

Russell, Bertrand. *Justice in War-Time*. London: Open Court Publishing, 1916.

Sassoon, Siegfried. *Collected Poems, 1908–1956*. London: Faber, 1961.

Scarry, Elaine. *The Body in Pain: The Making and Unmaking of the World*. Oxford: Oxford University Press, 1985.

Scott, Joan W. "Rewriting History." In Higgonet et al., *Behind the Lines*, 21–30.

Sears, Sallie. "Theater of War: Virginia Woolf's *Between the Acts*." In *Virginia Woolf: A Feminist Slant*, edited by Jane Marcus, 212–35. Lincoln: University of Nebraska Press, 1983.

Shorter, Clement. "A Literary Letter." Review of *The Rainbow*, by D. H. Lawrence. *Sphere*, 23 October 1915, 104. Reprint, Draper, *Lawrence*, 96–97.

Simpson, Hilary. *D. H. Lawrence and Feminism*. London: Croom Helm, 1982.

Spengler, Oswald. *The Decline of the West*. Translated by Charles F. Atkinson. 2 vols. London: Allen and Unwin, 1926–28.

Spivak, Gayatri Chakravorty. *In Other Worlds: Essays in Cultural Politics*. London: Methuen, 1987.

Squire, J. C. "Books in General." Review of *The Rainbow*, by D. H. Lawrence. *New Statesman*, 20 November 1915, 161. Reprint, Draper, *Lawrence*, 104–7.

Stansky, Peter, and William Abrahams. *Journey to the Frontier: Julian Bell and John Cornford, Their Lives and the 1930s* London: Constable, 1966.

Steele, Bruce. Introduction to *The Study of Thomas Hardy and Other Essays*. Cambridge: Cambridge University Press, 1985.

Steiner, George. *In Bluebeard's Castle: Some Notes towards the Re-Definition of Culture*. London: Faber, 1971.

Taylor, A. J. P. *The First World War: An Illustrated History*. London: Hamish Hamilton, 1963.

Tindall, William York. *D. H. Lawrence and Susan His Cow*. New York: Columbia University Press, 1939.

Todorov, Tzvetan. *Mikhail Bakhtin: The Dialogic Principle*. Translated by Wlad Godzich. Manchester: Manchester University Press, 1984.

Tylee, Claire M. *The Great War and Women's Consciousnesses: Images of Militarism and Womanhood in Women's Writings, 1914–1965*. London: Macmillan, 1990.

Vellacott, Jo. *Bertrand Russell and the Pacifists in the First World War*. Brighton: Harvester, 1980.

Vickery, John B. *The Literary Impact of "The Golden Bough."* Princeton: Princeton University Press, 1973.

Voloshinov, V. N. [Mikhail Bakhtin]. *Marxism and the Philosophy of Language*. Translated by Ladislav Matejka and I. R. Titunik. New York: Seminar, 1973.

Wells, H. G. *Little Wars: A Game for Boys from Twelve Years of Age to One Hundred and Fifty and for That More Intelligent Sort of Girls Who Like Boys' Games and Books*. London: Frank Palmer, 1913.

———. *Mr. Britling Sees It Through*. London: Cassell, 1916.

———. *The War That Will End War*. London: Frank and Cecil Palmer, 1914.

Wilson, Duncan. *Leonard Woolf: A Political Biography*. London: Hogarth, 1978.

Woolf, Virginia. *Between the Acts*. London: Hogarth, 1941.

———. *Collected Essays*. Edited by Leonard Woolf. 4 vols. London: Hogarth, 1966–67.

———. *The Diary of Virginia Woolf*. Edited by Anne Olivier Bell. 5 vols. London: Hogarth, 1977–84.

———. *The Essays of Virginia Woolf*. Edited by Andrew McNeillie. 4 vols. London: Hogarth, 1986–.

———. Introduction to *Life as We Have Known It, by Co-operative Working Women*. Edited by Margaret Llewelyn Davies. London: Hogarth, 1931.

————. *Jacob's Room*. London: Hogarth, 1922.

————. *The Letters of Virginia Woolf*. Edited by Nigel Nicholson. 6 vols. London: Hogarth, 1975–80.

————. *Mrs. Dalloway*. London: Hogarth, 1925.

————. *Night and Day*. London: Duckworth, 1919.

————. *Orlando: A Biography*. London: Hogarth, 1928.

————. *The Pargiters: The Novel-Essay Portion of "The Years."* Edited by Michael Leaska. London: Hogarth, 1978.

————. *Roger Fry: A Biography*. London: Hogarth, 1940.

————. *A Room of One's Own*. London: Hogarth, 1929.

————. *Three Guineas*. London: Hogarth, 1938.

————. *To the Lighthouse*. London: Hogarth, 1927.

————. *The Voyage Out*. London: Duckworth, 1915.

————. *The Waves*. London: Hogarth, 1931.

————. *The Years*. London: Hogarth, 1937.

Index

198